1998

The Cox-owned Companies

Cox Communications, Inc.

publicly-traded; NYSE (COX)
- cable television
- local & long-distance telephone service
- digital television
- high-speed Internet access

INVESTMENTS IN:
- programming networks
- PCS wireless telecommunications

Cox Broadcasting, Inc.
- television stations
- majority owner of Cox Radio, Inc. (NYSE: CXR)
- TV advertising sales representation
- TV programming production
- research

Cox Newspapers, Inc.
- daily newspapers
- weeklies & shoppers
- direct mail advertising
- book publishing
- advertising publications

INVESTMENTS IN:
- magazine publishing
- classified consumer publications

Manheim Auctions, Inc.
- automobile auctions (traditional and Internet)
- government auctions
- financing for independent dealers
- vehicle valuation subscription service
- full-service sports marketing firm

Cox Enterprises, Inc. is a pioneer in online news, information and entertainment via the Internet, through Cox Interactive Media.

JOURNEY THROUGH OUR YEARS

The Story of Cox Enterprises, Inc.

CHARLES E. GLOVER

LONGSTREET
ATLANTA, GEORGIA

Published by
LONGSTREET
A subsidiary of Cox Newspapers,
A subsidiary of Cox Enterprises, Inc.
2140 Newmarket Parkway
Suite 122
Marietta, GA 30067

Printed in the United States of America
1st printing 1998
Library of Congress Catalog Card Number: 98-89267
ISBN 1-56352-570-4

Book and cover design by Jill Dible

Photo Credits: Thanks to the photographers and designers whose work has preserved history, enabling us to have a glimpse of many of the events and people associated with our company. Many of those artists are unknown. Visuals were compiled, primarily, from corporate, divisional and local businesses files, as well as personal collections of retirees and employees. Special appreciation to these contributors: Sol Smith, who designed and produced *Dayton Ink*, the story of 100 years of the *Dayton Daily News* under Cox ownership; Mary Civille, *The Atlanta Journal* and *Constitution*; Tami Rivnick, WSB-TV, Atlanta; Ken Walters, *The Palm Beach Post*; Howard Kleinberg; Chuck Glover; Steve Niswonger, WHIO(TV), Dayton; Scot Post, WFTV(TV), Orlando; Joe Murray, *Lufkin Daily News*, and Pulitzer-prize winning editorial cartoonists Mike Luckovich (*The Atlanta Constitution*), Mike Peters (*Dayton Daily News*), Ben Sargent (*The Austin American-Statesman*), and Don Wright (*The Palm Beach Post*).

Table of Contents

Acknowledgments

Complex histories such as this tend to involve many talented and eager hands. One person alone cannot accomplish everything that needs to be done. We owe a special thanks to Lynda Stewart, director of communications for Cox Enterprises, for providing me with research information promptly and pleasantly, although I must have driven her to distraction with my incessant telephone calls.

I am beholden to my editor, Arnold Rosenfeld, an old friend and colleague, for his patience, encouragement and guidance.

Our majority owners, Anne Cox Chambers and Barbara Cox Anthony, were particularly forthright and giving of their time in recalling memories of their father, former Ohio Governor James M. Cox, founder of the company.

We would be remiss if we did not give thanks to Angela Strougal, executive secretary in the Newspaper division, who transcribed the interview tapes. She often worked late into the night and on weekends to keep the information flowing.

In all, there were some 53 interviews, far too many to acknowledge here. We were struck by the number of people, both retired and active, who told us how much they enjoyed working for the Cox organization.

It is fitting to recognize those interviewed who had a close association with either Governor Cox, James M. Cox Jr., or both. They are:

Ernie Adams, Marcus Bartlett, Elmo Ellis, Jim Fain, Carl Gross, Henry Harris, Cliff Kirtland, Florence Mahoney, Stan Mouse, Bob Sherman, Miriam Snyder and Jack Tarver.

Charles E. Glover
Atlanta, Georgia
September 15, 1998

"Human nature may not change, but human intelligence can and does increase. It is clear now that with the new destructiveness of war nations must conform to the demands of decency and humanity or perish at each other's throats. This is the supreme question before the human race today. Upon it all other issues hinge."

— James M. Cox
in his autobiography
"Journey Through My Years," 1946

What Jimmy Wrought

Jimmy Cox's company is 100 years old.

That milestone was reached on August 15, 1998, a century after Cox, who was only 28, bought the Dayton Evening News Publishing Company for $26,000.

As Cox Enterprises faces a new millennium, its owners and managers view the company's future in the next 100 years with excitement, enthusiasm and confidence.

Young James M. Cox, who would go on to be a congressman, a governor three times and a nominee for president of the United States, changed the name of the paper to the *Dayton Daily News* and published his first edition on August 22, 1898.

It was a time when horses far outnumbered the newfangled horseless carriages. There were hot air balloons, but no airplanes, and most of America was rural and without electricity.

For the first 36 years of its existence, the company's only business was publishing newspapers. With Governor Cox, as he preferred to be known, insisting on hard-nosed, accurate reporting, and keeping his eye on the bottom line, the newspapers prospered.

With newspaper profits, he built his first radio station in 1934. Cox also was a pioneer in television, putting WSB-TV, Atlanta, the company's and the South's first television station, on the air in 1948. In the same year, Cox introduced FM radio to the South.

Although more papers were acquired across the country, both in the East and the West, and newspaper earnings continued to be significant, the Cox organization was about to undergo a distinct change. The seeds for this were sown in the 1960s when Cox expanded its broadcasting operations through growth and great acquisitions, and ventured into cable television, one of the first broadcasters to do that, and wholesale auto auctions, a fast-growth, service-oriented business.

What began as getting Cox's feet wet in cable and auto auctions turned into a flood. Growth of these two businesses in the past two decades can only be described as explosive. Cox has more cable subscribers than newspaper subscribers, and in 1997 it began selling telephone service in Orange County, California. Manheim Auctions' gross revenues for 1997 topped $1 billion.

James M. Cox bought *The Dayton Evening News* because "I could not get out of my head the idea of owning a newspaper."

The company's chairmen, all family members: Governor James M. Cox (1898 – 1957), James M. Cox Jr. (1957 – 1974), Garner Anthony (1974 – 1987) and James C. Kennedy (1988 – present).

September 1, 1985, was one of the most notable dates in the history of the company, for on that day publicly held Cox Communications, Inc. merged into Cox Enterprises, Inc., making the company entirely private and creating one of the ten largest media corporations in the nation.

As diversification continued in the late 1980s and early 1990s, Cox focused on the mass distribution of coupons by direct mail, and did something about it, buying Val-Pak and turning it into the largest direct mail publishing operation in the world. In 1997, Val-Pak distributed 11 billion coupons.

A direct mailer of national cooperative advertising, Carol Wright Companies, now known as Cox Direct, became a part of the company in March 1996. Cox also holds a 50 percent stake in the Trader Publishing Company, whose weekly single-interest magazines sell about anything that rolls or floats, from tough, over-the-road trucks to stately yachts.

Cox Enterprises has a significant position in the brave new world of the Internet, creating Cox Interactive Media in July 1996 to provide local, interactive services to its customers better and faster than its competitors. At the end of 1997, Web sites had been established in 14 cities where Cox does business. By the end of 1998, Cox Interactive Media expects to have city Web sites operating in 34 markets.

Nothing has grown more rapidly than radio since federal restrictions on how many stations a single operator could own were lifted. By mid-1998, publicly traded Cox Radio had 58 stations and counting.

On April 15, 1912, the tragic tale of the great ocean liner Titanic with the loss of 1,517 lives filled the pages of Jimmy Cox's papers in Dayton and Springfield, Ohio. Almost 86 years later, Digital Domain, a company partly owned by Cox Enterprises, won the Oscar for special effects in the 1998 Academy Award-winning film "Titanic," which captured 11 Oscars overall.

With more than 53,000 full- and part-time employees, Cox Enterprises has become a company of many cultures, but the Cox style of always looking to the future for better ways to serve its customers remains unchanged.

Cox is also a company of stability. In its first 100 years, it has had only had four chairmen: Governor James M. Cox, James M. Cox Jr., Garner Anthony and James C. Kennedy.

It has been a great century. Cox looks forward to the next one.

JOURNEY THROUGH OUR YEARS

The Story of Cox Enterprises, Inc.

From a single newspaper, Cox Enterprises, Inc. has become one of the largest media companies in the nation, the world's largest operator of automobile auctions and provider of the most local content sites on the Internet. More than 53,000 employees serve Cox customers through businesses that include these shown above and on the opposite page: broadband communications (cable, Cox Digital, and *Cox@Home*), newspaper publishing, TV and radio broadcasting and automobile auctions.

PART ONE

The Founding Years — 1898–1957

Jimmy

On the spring morning of March 31, 1870, Eliza Andrews Cox delivered her seventh and last child in a farmhouse in Jacksonburg, Ohio. The child was a boy, and Eliza and her husband, Gilbert, named him James.

The American Civil War, which ended in 1865, was still a fresh memory. Custer's Last Stand at the Little Big Horn was six years in the future.

Describing that period of American life, a writer of the time said:

"The buffalo herds still roamed the Western plains; there was still the Overland stagecoach with its four- and six-horse teams. The Arapahoes, Cheyennes and Sioux were on the warpath; the Younger brothers, Dalton boys and the Jesse James gang were engaged in their nefarious raids; and last but not least among these primitive methods and hardships to be endured was the devastating pest, the grasshopper, devouring everything."

Although the young Cox would be known formally as James Middleton Cox, his long-time private secretary, Charles Morris, said the old family Bible used the name James Monroe Cox. The Middleton seems to have had its origin in a bit of journalistic levity, Morris said, probably referring to Middletown, the city in which he got his early training as a newspaper reporter.

When James M. Cox was born on March 31, 1870, buffalo roamed the Western plains, the stagecoach rumbled through the settlement and Jesse James was "wanted."

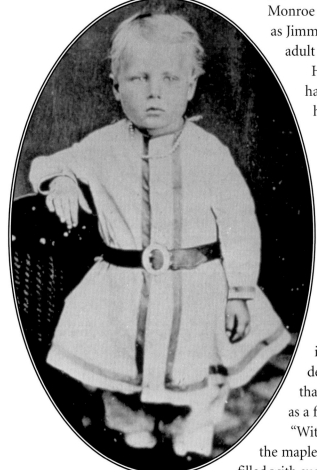

Monroe or Middleton? It didn't matter. He soon became known as Jimmy, a name that many would call him for much of his adult life. As for Cox, he never wrote or spoke of the matter.

He started school when he was five, and began lending a hand with the work of the family farm at an early age. In his 1946 autobiography, "Journey Through My Years," he recalled: "It was hard work in season and out. In summertime we were in the fields at sunrise; we came in for dinner at eleven o'clock, had supper at four o'clock and then followed the plow or sickle until sundown.

"On some occasions in the corn-husking season we went to the fields by morning moonlight. When the moon went down, there was not enough light to work by and we ran up and down the fence corners to keep warm until the labor of the field could start.

"There was not a playing card in the house and definitely no liquor. The saloon in the village I never looked into. We were taught to believe that it was a den of the devil, and it remained so abhorrent in my consciousness that when I became governor (of Ohio) I had it condemned as a fire menace and torn down by the state marshal.

"With the first thaw of spring, when the sap was running in the maple trees, came a joyful season. The gathering of buckets filled with sugar water, the boiling process running through the night

as well as day, and then the taffy pulls —
those were the times!"

It was said of him that during summer
noon hours, when other boys went swimming
or squirrel hunting, young Jimmy would walk
several miles to town to get a copy of the
Cincinnati *Commercial Gazette*, which he
would read from the front page to the last.

By the time he was 15, he had a "passion-
ate interest" in newspapers, noting, "It
became plain that there was no future for me
in farming. In the middle of the forenoon,
while I was following the plow, I would often
see one of the neighborhood schoolteachers
starting to work, and about four in the afternoon, while I still had long hours of toil
ahead of me, I would see the teacher coming
home. This spectacle might have given spur
to my ambition to make a brief pedagogic
career a stepping-stone to something better."

In 1886, Cox moved to Middletown, eight
miles east of Jacksonburg, to complete his
high school education. He lived at the home
of his sister, Anne, and her husband, John Q.
Baker, headmaster at the country academy
Cox attended, and owner and publisher of the
Middletown *Weekly Signal*.

Baker tutored his young brother-in-law
for the Ohio teachers examination, which Cox took one Saturday at the Butler County
seat of Hamilton. "To my surprise, I received a two-year certificate to teach," he said.

After teaching at West Middletown and the village of Rockdale, he was sent to "the
best country school in the county." He also supervised the Middletown night school
during the winter months, where one of his students was an elderly ex-slave.

And on top of all of this, he spent Saturdays delivering the entire circulation of the
Weekly Signal. When Baker took his newspaper daily, Cox abandoned the classroom to
pursue his passion for newspapering.

He explained: "My teaching experience was never more than an incidental pastime
because, to use an old expression, printer's ink had moved into my blood. I was the
only reporter on the paper. This was a very valuable experience. It enabled me to know
the leading men of the town."

One of those leading men was Paul Sorg, a wealthy tobacco manufacturer and
member of the Butler County school board. Sorg would quickly play a major role in
the life of Jimmy Cox.

The *Daily Signal's* only reporter also was the local correspondent for the big-city
Cincinnati Enquirer, and soon grabbed that newspaper's attention with a clean

**Cox, as a teen-
ager, taught
school and, on
Saturdays, deliv-
ered the
Middletown
Weekly Signal.**

"scoop." There was a train wreck at Heno, a small village near Middletown, and at least two people were killed and others injured.

To control the Middletown telegraph wire to Cincinnati until he could transmit his story about the accident, Cox tore a page from the *Daily Signal*, gave it to the telegrapher and said, "Send this until I get back."

He ran all the way to Heno, gathered his facts, came dashing back and sent his account of the wreck to the *Enquirer* over the telegraph line he had enterprisingly appropriated. It was a celebrated "beat" for the *Enquirer*, and it landed Cox a job on the paper. He was now in his element and would remain so for the rest of his life. Cox was assigned to the railroad beat and worked with the telegraph editors in the evening, which he called magnificent training to get in touch with the world. His future seemed assured when an exclusive story he had written appeared as the lead article on Page One. But there was trouble ahead.

The anger of a Cincinnati railroad baron came down hard on Jimmy Cox after he had written a story about a stock manipulation by Samuel M. Felton, president of the Queen and Crescent Railroad. Furious, Felton got in touch with John R. McLean, owner of the *Enquirer*, then living in Washington, and pleaded to have Cox fired.

"McLean," Cox said, "was under some obligations to Felton. He had often used the railroad executive's private car, and subsequently Felton designed one for McLean's private use. There was a wire from McLean's Washington office to the *Enquirer* at Cincinnati, and the order came that I was to be 'let out.'

"There was a remonstrance from the *Enquirer* newsrooms, but it was finally arranged that I was to be relieved of my railroad assignment and put on other work. Out of this incident came a turn in my whole career. I could not help being impressed by the thoughtless injustice imposed upon me, and when an offer came to go to Washington, I accepted. I doubt whether I would have left the *Enquirer* except for that order from McLean."

On June 28, 1998, the Middletown, Ohio, Journal *printed an article about Governor Cox's early life in his native Butler County. Town historian George Crout wrote:*

"His reputation as a teacher spread and the Middletown Board of Education offered him the principalship of a new night school, meeting on the second floor of the City Building downtown.

"Mrs. Ira Kern of Mount Pleasant Retirement Village in Monroe recalled in an interview a few years ago that her mother, Nina Baird Long, was Cox's assistant at the night school. She said many of the young men enrolled there were from the Irish settlement of Little Dublin.

"She recalled one incident when Cox's students became angry over a test he had given. They planned to beat him up after class one evening. Overhearing their plot, Sarah Mitchell, another student who was a middle-aged ex-slave, decided otherwise.

"She had enrolled in the same class to work toward a high school diploma. On the appointed evening she waited for Cox to leave his room, walked in front of him down the steps at the City Building, proclaiming, 'Nobody's going to lay a hand on my teacher.'

"They didn't, and she saw he made it safely home. Cox never forgot Sarah Mitchell."

Sacred Soil

In April 1894, George W. Houk, representative of the 3rd Congressional District of Ohio, died suddenly in Washington.

A special election was ordered and Paul Sorg of Middletown defeated his Republican opponent, much to the delight of the embattled Democrat in the White House, President Grover Cleveland.

When Sorg told a judge of the Common Pleas Court of Hamilton and Butler Counties that he was looking for a newspaperman to be his private secretary, the judge said, "I have the man for you. He comes from your town and you must know him. He is young Cox, now working on the *Cincinnati Enquirer.*"

Sorg made the offer and Cox accepted, later writing, "I left the *Cincinnati Enquirer* with reluctance because I loved the newspaper business. Yet the thrill that came to me when I first saw the Capitol and the White House at Washington must have been the same which comes to every youngster when he first steps on what to him has been sacred soil."

Fascinated by the nation's leaders of the era, Cox studied and admired the skills of successful politicians, lessons from which he would draw during his own political career.

Hoke Smith, President Cleveland's secretary of the interior and later a Georgia governor and senator, was one of these men. "I saw Hoke Smith frequently," Cox said,

Ohio Congressman Paul Sorg lured reporter Cox (L) to Washington from the *Cincinnati Enquirer.*

"and little could he know, nor could I, that *The Atlanta Journal,* owned by him, and even then a powerful newspaper with a marked liberal tradition, would some day become the property of the impecunious young congressional secretary in front of him."

The approaching election of 1894 appeared to be a difficult one for Sorg. The economic outlook was bad and getting worse. President Cleveland had fallen from favor with the voters.

Sorg had won the special election with a plurality of 1,800 votes. Ohio's lieutenant governor, a man with a fine Civil War record, was nominated by the Republicans. The residents of the National Soldiers' Home at Dayton had voted almost as a block for the GOP candidates in the special election.

Cox was determined to switch those Republican votes to Sorg. He organized an office force that dealt exclusively with the handling of veterans' pension matters. He also helped other former servicemen to transfer to the Dayton institution.

Cox's efforts paid off. His special treatment of veterans brought many former Republican votes to Sorg, who won by the narrow margin of 202 votes.

Sorg did not seek another term in 1896, and Cox returned to his home in Ohio's Miami Valley. "I departed from the city with some regret," he later wrote, "though I retained my passion for the newspaper business. I had in fact learned more from my Washington years than I supposed.

"Not merely had I learned how Congress works and become acquainted with the practical side of politics, I had also begun to appraise some of the forces underneath the politics of the day. Young as I was, I could see that the country was full of discontent, that a demand for correction of social and economic abuses was rising, and that great changes would have to be made.

"My sympathy was with these impulses. I had a young man's interest in new ideas and new movements. Ohio in 1896 and for long afterwards was ranked among the conservative Republican states. I was a dissenter in that environment.

"I was a Democrat and something more; my experience as a farm boy and my work with Mr. Sorg in Washington had made me a Democrat aligned with the progressive tendencies of the time."

Cox soon would find a new and larger platform from which to preach his progressive gospel, and also fulfill a longtime dream. He would buy a newspaper.

Publisher at 28

The *Evening News* was one of four newspapers in Dayton, Ohio, when Cox bought it in 1898 for $26,000. Much of the money was borrowed. After Sorg loaned him $6,000, he put up some funds of his own and sold stock in amounts as low as $50 a share.

The paper had been bumping along over the rocks of near-bankruptcy for years. The bumps continued, and for several years the young publisher was only a few steps ahead of a sheriff's sale.

No single Dayton paper was dominant. The *Cincinnati Post* had more circulation in the city than all the Dayton papers combined.

Cox chose the *Evening News* because it had the Associated Press wire service. He picked Dayton over Toledo, he said, because it was the "very heart of the Miami Valley, with no richer farming country on earth, and was alive with industry."

He ran a signed announcement in the *Evening News*, stating: "The *Dayton Evening News* will not formally issue under new management until Monday, August 22, by reason of the addition of new equipment, which an increase in the size of the paper involves. From and after that time, it will be the endeavor of the new management to give the City of Dayton an aggressive newspaper."

The *Dayton Journal* noted the arrival of a new publisher with this sour note:

"The *Evening News* has been sold and will hereafter be a Democratic paper. Democratic papers have never paid in Dayton and never will. Four of them have failed."

Cox ignored the barb, gave his paper a new name and launched his first issue of the *Dayton Daily News* on August 22, 1898, saying later, "I was 28 years old — too young to be running a newspaper."

He was told that he was buying a circulation of 7,500, but he could only find 2,600 subscribers. The narrow four-story newspaper building housed an eight-page press that 20 years before was said to be 100 years ahead of its time, but its time already was rapidly running out.

The young publisher changed "Evening" to "Daily" before the first Cox newspaper made its debut on August 22, 1898.

Cox had his new newspaper building designed like a bank to retaliate when he was turned down for a loan in 1908.

"When I took charge," Cox wrote, "we had a staff of four reporters, to which I added a woman society editor. We all worked like beavers and with fraternal cooperation. I read all the copy, looked after make-up, answered the business correspondence and kept an eye on details, writing my editorials after dinner at night. Competition was keen and we were kept busy hustling. But we all loved the work, and I in particular found it fascinating."

None of the Dayton newspapers had legitimate advertising rate cards in those days, which caused retailers to wonder if they were getting a paper's best rate. Woe to the newspaper that told an advertiser he was getting the lowest rate, only to have him learn that a competitor was getting a better deal.

"Many trade announcements were printed without change from season to season," Cox said. "I found watermelons advertised in the Christmas holidays and ice skates on the Fourth of July.

"The bookkeeper was once asked how much business we would have to carry to break even. His figures seemed to confuse him, but he finally said that if we had no news and every column was filled with advertising we would lose $500 a week. There might have been some value in unbridled youth after all. A wise man might well have then quit."

Cox published an advertising rate card, and put in a rule that no advertisement would be run continuously without a copy change. There would be no deviation from card rates, no under-the-table deals.

"The advertisers were not long in discovering that we were dealing in good faith with all alike," he said.

The young publisher also was a salesman. The Rike-Kumler department store had been running a half column of advertising in the *Daily News* three days a week. Cox proposed that the store run a half page every weekday for 90 days.

If the ads produced results, Rike-Kumler would pay card rates. If not, they would pay nothing. This bold move worked, and Rike-Kumler went on to become one of the largest retail advertisers in the country. Cox later enjoyed taking some of the credit for the store's success. Store officials, of course, teased back, saying they had provided the money for his own growth.

And the *Daily News* was growing, mostly at the expense of its competitors. Cox replaced the limited service Associated Press pony wire with a double wire, which delivered national, international and sports news to the paper. He also started running a "New York letter" from a fellow Ohioan, the renowned O. O. McIntyre.

All of this permitted Cox to give more news to his readers than the other papers in town. When he bought the *Evening News*, a good part of the paper was filled with standard filler material, which was shipped in daily. Much of it consisted of romantic stories. It contained no "hard" news.

When Cox ordered all such material out of the paper, the composing room foreman complained that without boilerplate it would be impossible to get out the paper.

To emphasize the meaning of the order, Cox had the newly arrived plates thrown out the back window. "We had only three typesetting machines," he said, "and from that day on, the paper was set every day. We paid bonuses for high production from our Linotype operators, and within the course of two years we broke the world's record in line production three times."

Pictures from crude chalk plates began appearing in the paper, and a market page was added, which ran the stock tables and grain and livestock reports. Cox also imported an experienced ad writer who prepared ads based on merchandise he saw displayed in the stores.

Some merchants looked with doubt upon the new idea, he reported, but customers increased and the idea was accepted as a better way of doing business. "All of this was inspiring, but we were conscious of our duties which ran beyond the business office, and the paper gave editorial attention to affairs long neglected by the community," he said.

Cox was a fighter, who believed deeply that it was a newspaper's duty to retain or acquire that which was good for the community and oppose or get rid of that which was bad. From the beginning he called the *Daily News* the "People's Paper."

He vigorously attacked the plans of an interurban railroad to build grade crossings through new residential sections of the city "that had not yet been defaced" by crossings at grade.

A man named A. E. Appleyard owned the railroad company. After Cox called him a

Wayward bank customers walked inside Cox's bank-like building, much to his delight.

The newspaper's open lobby further reflected a bank's interior.

"financial adventurer" and worse in print, Appleyard filed a criminal libel suit against the *Daily News*. Since Appleyard had given the local court bond to have the property taken over by the Montgomery County sheriff, the sheriff and several deputies arrived at the paper about noon one day and locked the front door.

Under Ohio law, Cox could post his own bond and put the paper back in business, but he needed money to do that. "Quick action was necessary," he said. "There was no time to make contact with a bonding company."

He immediately telephoned a prominent Democratic businessman in town, who hurried from his place of business and paid for Cox's bond. Meanwhile, the two other afternoon newspapers were on the streets with extra editions, trumpeting the closing of the *Daily News*.

"The county fair was on," Cox said, "and the papers were grabbed up in excitement. Within a half hour the *News* was on sale all over the city and at the fairgrounds with the front page emblazoned with the story of the closing that had not closed."

The suit was dismissed. Appleyard lost his railroad and passed out of the picture. "The experience naturally did the paper a great deal of good," Cox said. "We installed a three-deck press and typesetting machines, and red ink disappeared from our ledger."

By 1903, Cox had bought up with personal notes all of the outstanding stock of the Dayton News Company. The paper had become an unquestioned business success.

With annual profits amounting to his purchase price of the paper — $26,000 — the successful young publisher turned his attention to expansion. An opportunity came in 1905 when the *Dayton Press*, which at one time had the largest circulation in town, folded.

Cox bought the equipment of the fallen newspaper and looked about for a place to use it. He chose Springfield, 25 miles northeast of Dayton. The town had four newspapers, two in the morning and two in the afternoon.

Cox bought the morning *Press-Republic*, changed its name to the *News*, made it an afternoon paper and switched its politics from Republican to Democrat. Within a few years, the other two afternoon newspapers went out of business.

While Jimmy Cox and his associates were hustling to make a success of his newspapers, two Dayton brothers — Orville and Wilbur Wright — were in their own quiet way adding a lofty dimension to the knowledge of mankind.

The Wright brothers were building a flying machine in their Dayton bicycle shop. On December 17, 1903, with Orville at the controls, the first successful powered flight by man in a heavier-than-air craft took place at Kill Devil Hill, N.C.

The *New York Daily Tribune* ran a one-paragraph story on the historic event, noting, "The machine had no balloon attachment, but got its force from propellers worked by a small engine."

The *Dayton Daily News* carried not a line, and would not for some time. Cox later freely admitted that he and his newspaper staff had missed the greatest news story to come out of Dayton.

He explained: "It is difficult nowadays to understand the incredulity that possessed the public mind. Reports would come to our office that the ship had been in the air over the Huffman prairie just east of the city, but our news staff would not believe the stories. Nor did they ever take the pains to go out and see.

"In after years Daniel E. Kumler, our very efficient managing editor, admitted that the staff was just stupid in not establishing the fact of the flights. I frankly confess my own share of culpability.

"It is not much comfort to think that other newspapers were equally negligent, and that the general public refused to credit the flights even when evidence had become overwhelming. We began to wake up when we heard of correspondents arriving in Dayton from abroad, chiefly from France and England, to investigate."

Cox, Orville and his sister, Katherine, would later become fast friends.

With Dayton growing and the *Daily News* thriving, Cox decided he needed a new and larger building, but no one wanted to lend money to something as fly-by-night as a newspaper.

"When a loan was sought at a local bank," he wrote in his autobiography, "the fine, kindly, conservative banker said, 'Why, I didn't think you were making your salt. Newspapers have never been known to earn money. Of course we can't accommodate you.'"

A defiant Cox told the banker that he had such faith in the future of the newspaper business that he wouldn't trade it for the bank, and found his financing elsewhere. He made sure the new building would be an imposing one, with the solid look of a bank.

Designed in Greek Revival style, like so many banks of that era, the new home of the *Daily News* did not have a sign on it. Much to the publisher's delight, many people wandered into the building, mistaking it for a bank or post office. There was a gala opening and some 10,000 people came by to visit.

Meanwhile, daily circulation had grown from a measly 2,600 in 1898 to 35,000.

In the midst of all of this, Jimmy Cox turned his attention to politics and public service.

Congressman from Ohio

With the Republicans divided over a candidate for the 3rd Congressional District of Ohio, leaders of the Democrat Party in 1908 pleaded with Jimmy Cox to run for the seat.

Reluctantly accepting the assignment, he won the election handily and found himself back on the sacred soil of Washington.

His first meeting with President William Howard Taft touched off a national news story. "My son, Jim, then six years old, went along," Cox related. "Taft made quite a fuss over the youngster and the next morning the lad broke out with measles.

"The question was widely discussed in the press of whether the president was immune. Some editors facetiously asked whether the president had been deliberately exposed to a Democratic infection."

As a member of the important House Appropriations Committee, Cox gained attention by presenting statistics which showed that more money was being spent to feed the monkeys in the Washington zoo and federal prisoners at Leavenworth than was being spent for the 7,000 veterans at the Dayton Soldiers' Home.

Arguing for the Civil War veterans who had "saved the Union," he quickly won increased appropriations for the Soldiers' Home. In the congressional election of 1910, he carried every precinct of that former Republican bastion and easily won re-election.

By now, the journalist-politician had his eyes on higher office, one that would take him back to Ohio. He became a statewide figure because of his early and enthusiastic support for a constitutional convention to overhaul an antiquated state government.

The convention was convened and its work was completed on June 6, 1912. Even though the proposed amendments had to be approved at a special election in September, Cox quickly adopted them as the platform from which he would seek the governorship of Ohio.

Campaigner Cox drafted his newsboys to march in his parades as a drum corps, the Cox Juniors.

The state Democratic convention assembled in Toledo to nominate its candidate for governor. "The counties were called in alphabetical order," Cox recalled, "and when the last was reached, the convention broke into a demonstration — for my name was the only one presented. Everybody felt that the gathering was naming the future governor."

In a fiery acceptance speech, he declared, "I stand for a progressive charter, believing that the intelligence, the genius, the ambition and the higher destiny of man should not be retarded by a plan of government long since ill-fitted to our needs. If our race is to develop a real genius for government, each generation must play its part in construction. This is not an age for laggards."

"That," he said, "was the tempo of our whole campaign. No apologies were made for the new constitution. We insisted that it cut the fetters and open the gate for the adoption of a program of constructive liberalism."

Cox's hard-driving campaign paid off. Thirty-four amendments to the state constitution were approved by Ohio voters at the special September election, and in November Jimmy Cox was swept into the governor's office with 439,323 votes, beating his nearest competitor by more than 166,000 ballots.

He also led the ticket, receiving more votes than the president-elect, Woodrow Wilson. When he returned to Washington in December for the final sessions of the 62nd Congress, he received a loud and sustained ovation from both sides of the chamber.

It was said that Speaker Champ Clark broke two gavels in attempting to end the enthusiastic demonstration.

The Great Ohio Flood

The one-time farm boy and country schoolteacher was sworn in as governor of Ohio January 13, 1913, in the rotunda of the historic old stone Capitol, a date "which might have shocked a superstitious mind," he said. However, if there was an omen, it could have been that it was raining steadily when the governor-elect left Dayton the night before.

Governor Cox attacked his new job with vigor, laboring to complete the mandate of the state constitutional convention. Believing deeply in social justice, he pushed for a workman's compensation law, a uniform school system, new roads and prison reform.

But after barely two months in office, his work was interrupted by what he called "the great Ohio catastrophe, which formed one of the most dramatic chapters of my life."

Late in March 1913, a heavy rainfall poured on southern Ohio. In five days more than 11 inches fell over the region. Riverbanks quickly overflowed, sending a deluge of water across the land.

The worst flooding was at Dayton, where the Great Miami, Little Miami, Mad and Stillwater rivers come together. The ground floor of the *Daily News* building was under 12 feet of water. Newsprint rolls, weighing more than a ton, floated from the basement into the accounting room.

"It seemed as if the windows of heaven had been opened," the *Daily News* reported. "There was lightning and mad rain."

In a 24-hour period the Great Miami rose from three to 29 feet. Statewide, the known death toll exceeded 430, but the exact number undoubtedly was higher. An estimated 20,000 homes were destroyed and property damage exceeded $300 million. Three days into the flood, fires raged across downtown Dayton.

The new governor's first mission was to save lives. From his command post in Columbus he declared martial law, called out the National Guard and took possession of the telegraph and the railroads. In Dayton, the National Cash Register Company's woodworking shop built lifeboats as fast as it could make them. The woodworkers also made coffins.

"Once the waters had run out," Cox wrote, "the desolate scenes told how complete the disaster was. On the streets of Dayton the carcasses of one thousand horses were found."

One soggy victim said that martial law was so strict that if you bent over to pluck a dollar bill from the mud, you risked being arrested or shot.

Determined to get the *Dayton Daily News* back on the street, Cox literally published the paper there. Columbus newspaper publisher Robert E. Wolfe shipped a second-hand press to Dayton. Powered by a threshing machine and set up on the pavement, it soon started churning out newspapers. The *Dayton Daily News* was back in business.

On December 20, 1913, President Woodrow Wilson notified the governor that the American Red Cross, by unanimous vote, had awarded him its gold medal of merit for his relief work in the great Ohio flood.

The New York *World* praised him as "the greatest provider of food and clothing the state has ever known, the principal health officer, the sanest counselor, the severest disciplinarian, the hardest worker, the most helpful prophet, the kindest philanthropist and the best reporter . . . who gets his story in the first edition."

Remembering the promises they made in the attic, Dayton's citizens soon voted to approve a $40 million flood prevention program that has kept their city dry ever since. All this was put in motion when Governor Cox signed the Ohio conservancy or flood protection law in February 1914.

The *Daily News* was published on the street when the 1913 flood dumped 12 feet of water in the building's ground floor.

Success and Defeat

With the great Ohio flood behind him, the governor swiftly moved to turn his liberal programs into law. He pursued social reform with gusto, winning legislative approval for every one of the 56 progressive measures he wanted enacted.

A new workman's compensation law, old-age pensions, mothers' pensions, home rule for municipalities, and public school and prison reforms were part of the historic package.

Especially proud of the workman's compensation legislation, Cox wrote in his autobiography:

"The finest tribute ever paid to this law was a dramatic incident which attracted attention all over the country. The state line between Ohio and Pennsylvania ran through a manufacturing plant. A workman one day was badly injured. He was paralyzed from the hips down, but his mind was clear and he had strength in the muscles of his arms.

"His machine was in Pennsylvania. He reached out, took hold of a lathe, and pulled himself across the state line from Pennsylvania into Ohio. The case came to me and I ordered an award be made to him."

Standing for re-election in 1914, the governor faced a tide of growing opposition. Conservative Democrats were unhappy with his progressive programs; the Republicans were calling him a political boss, asking that Ohio be returned to its people; insurance companies were attacking the workman's compensation law.

Despite a vigorous campaign, Cox lost the election to Frank Willis, a popular rural politician. Now, for the first time in six years, he could devote full time to his newspapers, "taking up again the pleasant tasks of journalism," as he put it.

In his political absences, the governor placed responsibility for the *Daily News* on the shoulders of "conscientious, hard-working and public-spirited Richard B. Meade," his chief financial offi-cer, who would work for Cox for more than 40 years.

Meade's daughter, Miriam, remembers going to the *Daily News* on election nights,

where Cox was a grand host. "I was very bashful, but he would go out of his way to be kind to me," she recalled. "He loved children."

She remembers her father saying at Thanksgiving, "Thank God, and thank Governor Cox."

Many years later, Miriam's husband and Meade's son-in-law, Robert C. Snyder, would become executive vice president and general manager of Dayton Newspapers, Inc.

Left in charge of the news and editorial department was Daniel E. Kumler, whom Cox called one of the "most golden characters I ever knew, who combined the qualities of sound judgment, devotion to the best journalistic ethics and great industry and loyalty."

Once back in his Dayton office, Cox sounded like an editor of the 1990s when he said, "It seemed to me that the press was not dealing adequately with the background of the news. Spot news, so-called, was being well covered, but conditions out of which came the drama of human activities had scant attention."

KETTERING
HOME OF
JAMES M. COX,
GOVERNOR OF OHIO,
1913-15, 1917-21
AND OF
CHARLES F. KETTERING
INVENTOR

He told Kent Cooper of the Associated Press and John N. Wheeler of the North American Newspaper Alliance that, if newspapers failed to move in that direction, weekly magazines would.

Thinking in terms of today's arts and entertainment coverage, the Dayton publisher in 1915 tried in vain to have Cooper put on the Associated Press wires every morning a fresh and comprehensive glimpse of New York City.

He asked for a report that would cover weather, new plays and films, critical comment and editorial excerpts from New York papers on matters of moment and interesting bits gleaned from special cable correspondence.

"Mr. Cooper even had me write two or three samples," Cox said. "This I did, but he gave the unsatisfactory, although complimentary, response that if I would come to New York and do it, he would initiate the service."

On a more serious note, Cox also spoke out for worldwide press responsibility, declaring:

"The public opinion of the world cannot be intelligent or controlling unless it is formed from a truthful presentation of what is going on. Europe has suffered great confusion and worse by dishonest and untruthful propaganda. Out of it came venal newspapers which, under the process of subsidy and corruption, found a lazy way of making a living."

Meanwhile, Cox, keeping a close eye on the Columbus State House, noted that the new administration did not dare touch the major features of his progressive legislation. The politician in the 45-year-old publisher again was coming to the forefront.

Vindication

"Fighting Jimmy," as many of his supporters called him, reclaimed the Ohio governor's chair in 1916. Not only did he lead the Democratic ticket, but his overwhelming victory delivered the state to President Wilson, who won a second term.

Every Wilson vote was crucial. Charles Evans Hughes, the Republican candidate, went to bed election night believing he had been elected, but late returns from the West kept Wilson in the White House.

Filled with the excitement of a newsman who had just scored a major beat on the competition, Cox proudly reported that the *Dayton Daily News* was the first newspaper in the country to claim Wilson's election in a special edition.

"Judge William A. Budroe of our city, in my private office, had been carefully compiling the figures that had come in, particularly in strategic states," he wrote. "About three o'clock in the morning, he exclaimed, Wilson is elected!' Before daylight our paper was on the streets heralding for the first time the news which cheered the Wilson followers."

Governor Cox told the newly elected Ohio legislature there was no need for major legislation, saying, "The laws that came from the new constitution four years ago have stood the test of time, and they have successfully run the gauntlet of sustained, insidious and artful opposition."

"Trailsend," built near Dayton during World War I, was Gov. Cox's primary home for the rest of his life.

Cox was back in office for less than three months when Wilson, whose 1916 campaign banners had read "He kept us out of war," asked Congress for a declaration of war against Germany.

Ohio was expected to provide more than 500,000 of her sons. The state's National Guard was mobilized as the 37th Infantry Division. Governor Cox went to the East Coast to see them off to France. He made sure Ohio was a leader in industrial production, rail transportation, Red Cross donations and military recruitment.

In the severe winter of 1917–18, a fuel shortage brought great suffering to Ohioans. After Governor Cox's appeals for relief went unanswered, he had railway coal shipments rolling across the state seized and turned over to local communities.

He justified his action by explaining that the coal was headed for the Northwest, where it could not conceivably be used until probably the first of May, yet tens of thousands were without the means of resisting the most severe winter in a generation.

Cox said, "President Wilson approved what we had done, as it was apparent to everyone that we were attempting to further the war effort rather than impede it."

This action added yet another footnote to the legend of "Fighting Jimmy."

It was in this period that Governor Cox built a new home near Dayton, which he called Trailsend. Overlooking the Great Miami Valley, it was built on what was thought to be a former Indian camping ground where several trails terminated. It would be his primary home for the rest of his life. Some thought it looked a bit like the White House.

Nominated by Ohio Democrats for a third term in 1918, he made no political speeches, confining himself to the war effort. Running against his old nemesis, Frank B. Willis, he again was victorious, becoming Ohio's first three-time Democratic governor. Overall, it was a bad year for the Democrats, who lost heavily in the congressional elections. Cox was the only Democrat elected on the state ticket. Across the land the Republicans were in ascendancy.

A few days after the election, on November 11, 1918, the Allies signed an armistice with Germany. The "war to end all wars" was over. Cox later wrote, "The third term would not have been possible except for the war. In the utmost sincerity, I can state that, instead of seeking it, I would, in other circumstances, have rejected it. I asked for re-election in 1916 purely as a matter of vindication."

His followers were fond of saying:

In his first term a flood
In his second term a war
In his third term reconstruction

Victorious American doughboys came home from France and were welcomed with cheers, bands and parades from a grateful nation. But they soon found they could not buy a drink in their homeland. Prohibition became law on January 16, 1920, and bootlegging became a major American industry.

Governor Cox deplored this, saying, "Prohibition had deprived the state treasury of all the revenues which had come from licensing saloons."

He pushed the Ohio legislature to pass a law forbidding the teaching of the German language in the state's grade schools, declaring, "For generations, the theory of the German superman has been implanted in youthful minds, germinated and developed finally into a conviction so concrete as to exclude any devotion whatsoever to the ideals of America." The law passed, but soon was set aside by the United States Supreme Court.

Because his gubernatorial victory in 1918 appeared as an oasis in an otherwise Democratic desert, he was being viewed by national party leaders as possible presidential timber in the upcoming elections of 1920.

Boxing promoter Tex Rickard apparently felt that "Fighting Jimmy" would get the nomination. In the spring of 1919 he visited Cox's New York hotel room, telling the governor:

"I think you are going to be the nominee. I always have been interested in your liberal and progressive tendencies and I want to help by putting $25,000 in escrow to be used in case you are nominated."

"No, Tex," Cox replied, "that isn't what you are interested in. You want to pull off that big prize fight (heavyweight champion Jess Willard vs. Jack Dempsey) in Ohio, and you have found out that under existing law this is probably the only place where it can be legally held."

Writing about the incident years later, Cox recalled that Rickard, "in great confusion," left the room. "The next morning he came back full of apologies. I told him that his experience with public officials had probably given him a false impression, and that there were many more than he thought who respected the ethics."

A lifelong boxing fan, Cox advised Rickard that Ohio's attorney general would be consulted and if the match was considered legal, it would go forward, adding that not a penny would be spent anywhere to "grease the way," and no sheriff, constable or anyone was to be subsidized.

"Well," said Tex, "it will be a very funny fight. The whole thing is new to me, but I will go through with it as you say."

On July 4, 1919, under a blazing sun at Toledo, Dempsey destroyed Willard before thousands of sweltering, straw-hatted fight fans, launching Dempsey's storied championship reign.

"Dempsey always said after his triumph that I had made him champion and he was grateful," Cox said.

From time to time, Governor Cox would place a conference call to his editors to discuss the news events of the day. Invariably, he would ask a question about some obscure national or international story that ran in the back pages of the papers.

When there was dead silence on the line, he would say, "Why am I the only one who really reads our newspapers?" and hang up.

Carrying Wilson's Banner

When delegates to the Democratic National Convention gathered at San Francisco in 1920, James M. Cox was at best a dark horse in the contest for the party's presidential nomination.

Although lagging at first, his support grew with each tally. After eight days and 44 ballots, which saw the leading contenders fall by the wayside, the weary delegates settled on Cox as their nominee for president of the United States.

Since there was no radio, Cox received the dramatic news by telegraph at 4:50 a.m., July 6, at the *Dayton Daily News*, where he had followed the balloting.

By the time he returned to Trailsend, Edmond Moore, his floor manager at the convention, was on the telephone asking his preference for a vice presidential running mate.

"I told him I had given the matter some thought and that my choice would be Franklin D. Roosevelt of New York," Cox said.

"Moore inquired, 'Do you know him?'

"I did not," I said. "In fact, so far as I knew, I had never seen him, but I explained to Mr. Moore that he met the geographical requirement, that he was recognized as an Independent and that Roosevelt was a well-known name."

Moore consulted with Charles F. Murphy, head of the New York delegation, and told him the reasons for Cox's selection, adding that if it were offensive, the choice would come from Iowa.

According to Cox, Murphy told Moore: "I don't like Roosevelt. He is not well known in the country, but, Ed, this is the first time a Democratic nominee for the presidency has shown me some courtesy. That's why I would vote for the devil himself if Cox wanted me to. Tell him we will nominate Roosevelt on the first ballot."

"I don't know what emotions have come to other men under the impact of their nomination for the presidency," Cox said. "I very distinctly remember mine. Following the long contest in the convention, there was a letdown, of course, but I was completely benumbed by what had taken place.

1920 presidential candidate Gov. Cox and his running mate, Franklin D. Roosevelt, present themselves first to Daytonians on "Notification Day," August 7.

"With the coming of the next day and its flood of telegrams, and with the evidences around me of such a feverish excitement as had never before overtaken our section of the country, I came to realize that the banner of Woodrow Wilson had really been put in my hands. I resolved to carry on with such strength of mind and body as I possessed."

Several days after his nomination Cox met his 38-year-old running mate in Columbus, remarking, "I liked him from the outset. His mind was alert and he was keenly alive to the conditions that would bear on the campaign. Our relationship during the campaign could not have been pleasanter."

Governor Cox and young Roosevelt traveled to Washington together to visit President Wilson. It was a meeting that would set the course for the Cox-Roosevelt campaign. No less an authority than President Roosevelt himself would describe the event many years later.

Learning that Governor Cox was writing his auto-biography, the president told Claude Bowers, then ambassador to Chile, that he hoped the governor would tell the untold story of their Washington trip.

According to Bowers, Roosevelt then told the story himself, saying in his booming, aristocratic voice: "I accompanied the governor on the visit to Wilson. A large crowd greeted us at the station and we went directly to the White House. There we were asked to wait fifteen minutes, as they were taking the president to the portico facing the grounds.

"As we came in sight of the portico we saw the president in a wheelchair, his shoulder covered with a shawl which concealed his left arm, which was para-

Original 1920 campaign items are from Cox Enterprises' private collection.

lyzed, and the governor said to me, 'He is a very sick man.'

"The governor went up to the president and warmly greeted him. Wilson looked up and in a very low, weak voice said, 'Thank you for coming. I am very glad you came.' His utter weakness was startling, and I noticed tears in the eyes of Cox.

"A little later Cox said, 'Mr. President, we are going to be a million percent with you and your administration, and that means the League of Nations.' The president looked up again, and again in a voice scarcely audible, he said, 'I am very grateful,' and then repeated, 'I am very grateful.'

"As we passed out we came then to the Executive offices and, in this very room, Cox sat down at this table (and here Roosevelt struck the table) and asked Tumulty (Joseph P. Tumulty, Wilson's private secretary) for paper and a pencil, and there he wrote the statement that committed us to making the League the paramount issue of the campaign. It was one of the most impressive scenes I have ever witnessed."

Newspaper cartoonists had a field day with the decision. An enlarged copy of one cartoon still hangs in Governor Cox's old office at the *Dayton Daily News*. It shows him with a wrapped mummy labeled "The League as a Party Issue." The caption reads, "Jimmie, how could you?"

Another depicts him clinging to a donkey on a narrow cliffside trail, with the donkey burdened down with "Wilsonian Policies." Meanwhile, a bag labeled "Cox's policies" tumbles down the mountainside.

One of the satiric rhymes of that time went:

There once was a person named Cox,
Who wanted to wear Wilson's sox,
But his friends made a holler,
When they found Wilson's collar
Was wrapped in the very same box.

And another:

Jimmy was a candidate, full of pep and vim;
Jimmy went to Washington and Wilson talked to him;
When it reached the public ear that both were in accord,
Jimmy found that losing votes must be his sole reward.

of war by Congress as our Constitution provides. And first, within the League itself, the United States by its own vote may veto any proposal of war which it does not approve.

7. The League of Nations is the only practical working plan for World Peace. It means LIFE—life for the young sons of the mothers now living, and life for the sons of mothers who come after us.

Show where the women of America stand.
Your vote for COX and ROOSEVELT is
A vote for the LEAGUE of NATIONS and
A VOTE FOR PEACE

(Issued by Woman's Bureau, Democratic National Committee)

1   475

Some Democratic leaders were opposed to Cox's meeting with Wilson, calling it politically unwise. But the governor made it clear that he would see Wilson regardless of political consequences, later writing:

"He had made a gallant fight for the cause of peace and the League of Nations and had impaired his health and risked his very life by doing it. As the nominee of our party, the leadership in the campaign passed from him to me. There was some doubt at this time as to whether Mr. Wilson would live long. I would have reproached myself everlastingly if he had passed on without my going to him."

Two weeks before San Francisco, the Republicans met in Chicago and nominated Ohio Senator Warren G. Harding, publisher of the *Marion Star*, for president. Massachusetts Governor Calvin Coolidge was nominated for vice president.

George Harvey, editor of the *North American Review* and a power broker at the convention, later wrote, "There was no popular explosion for Harding. There was little spontaneity. He was nominated because there was nothing against him, and because the delegates wanted to go home."

Harding, a poker player, said, "We drew to a pair of deuces and filled."

There was one thing certain about the upcoming election. An Ohio newspaper publisher would become the 29th president of the United States. The candidates had two other things in common. They both chewed tobacco and smoked cigars.

A political custom of the time was "Notification Day," on which the presidential nominee would be officially told of his selection and then make an acceptance speech. Notification Day in Dayton was August 7, 1920. The town was festooned with flags, bunting and photographs of Cox and Roosevelt. A parade began in downtown Dayton and marched out South Main Street to the Montgomery County fairgrounds.

Short, compact Jimmy Cox and tall, angular Franklin Roosevelt led the procession, walking the entire parade route and waving their straw hats to the cheering throngs.

Some 100,000 gathered at the fairgrounds to hear Governor Cox accept his party's nomination and declare:

Cox's support of the League of Nations was a liability, but he kept his pledge to President Woodrow Wilson.

In his quest for the presidency, Gov. Cox traveled 22,000 miles by train, visiting 36 states.

"These are fateful times. Organized government has a definite duty all over the world. The house of civilization is to be put in order. The supreme issue of the century is before us and the nation that halts and delays is playing with fire. The finest impulses of humanity, rising above national lines, merely seek to make another horrible war impossible."

Not having much taste for widespread electioneering, Harding conducted what became known as the "Front Porch" campaign from his home in Marion. He called for a "return to normalcy," which became the catch phrase of his campaign.

Cox, on the other hand, campaigned extensively, visiting 36 states, traveling 22,000 miles and delivering 394 scheduled speeches. Alarmed, Republican leaders pulled Harding off the front porch and put him on the road.

No matter. Harding and the Republicans were running more against Wilson and his policies than they were against Cox. Harding biographer Francis Russell wrote:

"Irrationally, inevitably, Wilson and the Democrats were held to blame — for controls and high prices and strikes, for a world not kept safe for democracy, for the twistings of the Paris Peace Conference and the League of Nations, for ungrateful allies."

On Election Day, November 2, 1920, Harding won the presidency in a walk. Cox's own *Dayton Daily News* published an "extra" edition at 11 o'clock that night. The headline topping the story said, "Republican Landslide: Harding Wins."

Reporters who called found the governor smiling and smoking a cigar. He showed no emotion, an attitude he maintained throughout the evening, following a day spent quietly at his home. Friends who visited him during the evening said the candidate realized his defeat long before the appearance of his newspaper's extra.

The country's first commercially licensed radio station, KDKA-Pittsburgh, broadcast the results, a first for a presidential election.

Cox wired the president-elect: "In the spirit of America, I accept the decision of the majority, tender as the defeated candidate my congratulations, and pledge as a citizen my support to the executive authority in whatever emergency might arise."

On November 4, the *New York Times* editorialized:

"Governor Cox is as good-natured and philosophical after his defeat as he was ardent, energetic and resourceful in his campaign. Never was a political forlorn hope led more gallantly. There is nothing personal to Governor Cox in the result. He did all that could be done and more than most men could have done. He has won the thanks of the Democratic Party and the liking and respect of the country."

Reflecting on the election, Cox wrote in his autobiography, "As for me, my only unhappiness was in the conviction that Harding and those above him meant to wreck the League. Now, I can say without reservation that the sting of defeat did not touch me. To have been given the banner of world peace from the hands of the stricken Wilson and to have carried it unsullied was happiness enough for any man."

Cox resolved never again to seek or accept public office, saying, "I had this great advantage: I was still in public life. I had my newspapers."

Evidence of his continuing position of prominence on the world stage came in 1922, when he created international headlines while touring Europe with his son Jim. Despite his attempt to stop the teaching of German in Ohio grammar schools three years earlier, he now found himself on the side of the new German Republic.

After visits to Paris, Berlin and London, he became convinced that Germany's faltering democratic republic could not survive without a reduction of the war reparations it owed the Allied victors.

Knowing that England, France and Germany could make the first move, and concerned that a collapse of the German Republic would destroy all hope of European stability, Cox cabled President Harding, suggesting that Secretary of Commerce Herbert Hoover take America's seat on the Reparations Commission. Hoover was highly regarded by Europeans for his post-World War I role of supervising relief efforts to the continent's war-battered countries.

Governor Cox told Harding, "Hoover's decision as to what Germany can pay would be, beyond much question of doubt, accepted by France — and that means by all the parties interested. I believe that every chancellery in Europe would welcome his coming. The mere announcement of his selection would stabilize things."

To a *New York Times* correspondent, Governor Cox said, "The fate of the world is in the hands of America. Days wasted in procrastination now will bring years of self-reproach later."

The Harding administration issued a noncommittal answer, and did nothing. Cox would later write: "It has always been my opinion that if reparations had been leveled off, the Republic of Germany would have lived, and, if it had lived, there would have been no Hitler, and if there had been no Hitler, there would have been no war."

Harding died of a stroke less than three years after his election, and his scandal-ridden administration would go down as one of the worst in U.S. history.

Sunshine and Shadow

"The governor," as Cox preferred to be called, accepted Hoosier entrepreneur Carl Fisher's invitation to visit Miami in 1923, and "fell completely in love with the place."

Fisher was a man of many parts — builder of the Indianapolis Motor Speedway, developer of Miami Beach and one-time automobile and bicycle racer. Fisher came to know Cox in Dayton through his visits to international bicycle racing champion Earl Kiser's garage, which was next door to the *Daily News*.

Cox was so enthralled with Miami ("I was confident that it would grow into a great city.") that he quickly made up his mind to winter there. It was Fisher who suggested the governor buy the afternoon Miami *Metropolis*, the oldest newspaper in south Florida, to occupy his time.

He even arranged a meeting between Cox and *Metropolis* owner, Bobo Dean. Cox and Dean swiftly came to terms and the deal was made for cash, reported to be $1 million. The *Metropolis* made its debut on May 15, 1896, several months before Miami was incorporated as a city. Governor Cox changed its name to the *Miami Daily News*.

In a front-page statement announcing the purchase of the *Metropolis*, he said: "The *Metropolis* will uphold the principles of Jeffersonian Democracy and devote itself to the public interest. Any city, growing as Miami is, needs a vigilant press. The public interest must always be paramount. The function of a newspaper carries a grave responsibility. It is the agency of information and truth. Its news columns should give all

Gov. Cox was so enthralled with Miami that he bought a newspaper there.

sides of an issue of general concern, regardless of the convictions which the paper has. A journal without convictions is of little use to a community. Influence of public opinion should be sought in the fairest manner. Either misrepresentation or suppression of essential facts profanes the traditions of a great profession."

Before heading back to Dayton in the spring of 1923, Cox bought land on Miami Beach, where a home was built. Home in Dayton that summer and "in an expansive state of mind," he made another newspaper acquisition, buying the *Canton* (Ohio) *Daily News*.

Cox had not seen the likes of Canton. It was a tough steel town with more than its share of corruption. He would later write, "It is no reflection upon a fine community to say that on mature consideration, I was not very keen about our investment."

He built a new plant. "One of the most beautiful and best-arranged buildings I have ever seen," he said, and his hand-picked editor, Don R. Mellet, launched a crusade against the city's organized crime with an editorial on New Year's Day, 1926.

Mellet's attack on corruption caused the suspension of Canton's chief of police, and put heat on the prostitution, bootlegging and gambling rackets. So much heat that a crooked cop and his racketeering associates decided to murder the 36-year-old editor.

On the night of July 16, 1926, two gunmen opened fire on Mellet as he walked from his garage to his house. A neighbor couple, who just had come back from a dance with Mellet and his wife, ran from the house to find the editor mortally wounded.

Cox pledged to continue his dead editor's crusade, and offered a $27,000 reward for information leading to the arrest of Mellet's murderers. Several days after the assassination, a tip led to the arrest and eventual imprisonment of the killers.

It was proven that the fatal shot was fired by the Canton Police Department's chief of detectives. Given life sentences, he and the other gunman died in prison.

For its battle against organized crime, the *Canton Daily News* won the 1927 Pulitzer Prize for community service. It was the first of many Pulitzers that would be awarded to Cox newspapers.

With the nation tumbling into the depths of the Great Depression, there was no way Canton could support two independent newspapers. Cox sold the *Canton Daily News* to Brush-Moore newspapers, publishers of the *Canton Repository*, in July 1930, for what he said was a handsome offer.

Two years earlier, the governor had made a deal with another Northern Ohio publisher, buying the *Springfield Morning Sun* from Charles Knight, owner of the *Akron Beacon Journal*, and father to future newspaper giant Jack Knight.

A new building to house both the *Morning Sun* and the *Springfield Daily News* was dedicated in 1929. A special 242-page edition was published, showcasing everything from comics and features to news and sports coverage. Former President Calvin Coolidge flipped a switch at his home in Northampton, Massachusetts, to start the new presses.

One of the most stylish and elegant newspaper homes ever built rose on Miami's Biscayne Boulevard in the mid-1920s. The 279-foot *Miami Daily News* tower was the city's first skyscraper and a Miami landmark for years.

It was inspired by the 15th century Giralda Tower in Seville, Spain, and imported Spanish tile was used in its construction. With powerful lights atop the tower's dome, the building was registered as a federal lighthouse, said to be visible on a clear night 50 miles out to sea.

A proud Governor Cox in 1925 dedicated his magnificent new 15-story structure to the growing Miami community, which he fondly called "Dream City." Less than a year later, a monster hurricane swept over South Florida, creating disastrous tidal waves and laying waste to the city.

The newspaper's stylish and elegant new 1920s home, Miami's first skyscraper, served as a federal lighthouse.

The *Miami Daily News* put such double-barreled pressure on mobster Al Capone (bottom) that Dan Mahoney Sr. (top), who ran the paper, got a call asking if he'd like to be fitted for a coffin.

The *Miami Daily News* tower weathered the storm, and the newspaper printed a one-page edition, cranked out by hand, and continued to publish under emergency conditions until power was restored.

Cox soon sent Daniel J. Mahoney, his former son-in-law, to Miami to run his newspaper and support the city's recovery from what South Floridians called "the big blow." Mahoney had been married to Helen Cox, the governor's daughter, who died in her mid-twenties of an infection. Even though he later remarried, to the governor he was always "my son-in-law."

Big and colorful, Mahoney had been a soldier of fortune, having served as a scout for Gen. John J. Pershing in his campaign against Mexico's Pancho Villa, and, later, as an Army lieutenant in France during the World War WWI. To his friends, he was "big Irish," a man charming and courtly with women and remarkably profane with those he viewed as scoundrels.

One such figure was Chicago mobster Al Capone, who was attracted to Miami for its winter sunshine as well as the easy money to be made in illegal gambling. The *Miami Daily News* exposed the presence of Capone and his gang and at once declared him a public enemy.

Cox and Mahoney attacked the scar-faced hoodlum in a series of front-page editorials. One that appeared on April 21, 1930, declared: "Al Capone, with all his aliases, has arrived at Miami Beach. Except for a temporary restraining order, which came from the United States Court, he would have been met at the state line, under orders from the governor of the state and transported north.

"There is no surprise in Capone's defying the spiritual sense of the people of Florida. He laughs at the law, he gives it no respect; through the organized forms of criminal operation he has with one exception escaped, up until this day, anything beyond arrest or detention upon suspicion."

When Mahoney started getting telephone calls, asking him if he would like to be measured for a coffin, he responded defiantly: "I would like to meet at any hour at any place the man who thinks he is big enough to put me in it."

Cox said that Capone and his criminal entourage were recurrent visitors to Miami, but the community seemed unaware of it. He reported that, under assumed names, the mobsters were playing golf on a municipal course on Miami Beach several times a week.

On one occasion, Cox said, the golfing gangsters spotted a car speeding down a street next to the golf course. When the car came to a stop, the foursome jumped into a bunker and pulled sawed-off shotguns from their golf bags.

"This was the tip-off," he said. "The best elements of the town joined in the movement to get rid of the pestilence."

The unrelenting pressure from the *Miami Daily News* to run Capone out of town led to the one-time brothel bouncer and his unsavory associates attempting to buy the newspaper.

The governor recalled, "One day a well-dressed gentleman walked into my office and laid down a certified check for $500,000, stating that he represented clients who wanted to present this as the first payment on the purchase of the *Daily News* for $5 million cash.

"The property was not worth that amount at the time, and there was not the slightest doubt in my mind that the Capone interests were behind the offer. This later proved to be the fact."

Cox shamed the emissary for representing someone like Capone and told him that no amount of money would be tempting, that it would not be a matter of disposing of a newspaper, but of selling out a community that was in sore need of protection.

Legend has it that the governor also said, "If you want to buy the *Daily News*, you can get it on any street corner for a nickel." Capone was convicted in Chicago of federal income tax evasion in the early 1930s, and began his sentence at the Atlanta federal penitentiary. In 1934, he was transferred to "the rock," otherwise known as Alcatraz, in San Francisco Bay. Five years later, he was released as a helpless man, his health wrecked by untreated syphilis. He returned to his Florida estate on Miami's Star Island, where he died of a massive brain hemorrhage in January 1947.

Mahoney's widow, Florence, said the governor once told her, "I have no special talent, I'm just passionately curious." He called her "Doc," because she had taken pre-med courses in college. He was fascinated with medicine and health, she said, and when the subject would come up, he would ask, "What do you think about this, Doc?"

Florence, who was born on April 20, 1900, has a small needlepoint pillow in the sitting room of her Georgetown home. On the pillow are these words: "Age is a number. Mine is unlisted."

The *Miami Daily News* elegant newsroom-wireroom of the late 20s.

In his 1946 autobiography, Cox wrote, "The best-built machine needs constant attention if it is to work and wear well, though one should not become obsessed with the subject of health. That is the road to hypochondria."

"I just loved the governor," Florence said. "He was so kind. I spent many quiet evenings with my husband, the governor and his wife, Margaretta, who was a lovely person. We talked about many things, but the governor would never talk about politics in front of the ladies.

"He used to take me fishing with him in Miami. He would fish and I would read a book. He was a serious fisherman and didn't want to talk much. He just wanted someone along. He loved the quiet."

Remembering Daddy

Barbara Cox Anthony, the governor's youngest child, remembers, "When I was very little, everybody in the house was in awe of him and I was very aware of that. But, personally, I was never awed by him.

"My mother could have killed me, because I was always telling people who he was. One time, before she had a license, my sister, Anne, was out driving when she banged into somebody.

"I was there with my mother when the other people were told that the car was registered in the name of James M. Cox. In a speak-up kind of voice, I said, 'That's Governor James M. Cox.' I know my mother could have whipped me.

"Daddy could be a strong disciplinarian, but he spoiled me. He was 53 when I was born, so I was the baby of the family. Oh, but when he got mad, I was really scared of him. He didn't get mad too often, but when he did, 'Ooooh!' When I stepped over the line, he was not amused, and called me impertinent.

"I would go to Daddy's room and we would talk for hours. I remember his saying, 'Come on, Hon, go with me.'

I asked, 'Where are we going?'

" 'I'm going to get the golf balls,' he said. We would go down to the Kettering's place and I'd have to chase those damned balls. But that was all right. You know, he would tell you what to do, and you didn't argue."

Daughter Anne Cox Chambers of Atlanta said that as a child she also was sometimes scared of her father. "The word that comes to mind when I think of him is formidable," she said.

Anne and Barbara loved going to the Old Home Farm with their father. Barbara said if she had her way, she would have lived there. When the family was in Dayton, they would travel there every weekend. Her mother didn't like it, Barbara said, because she complained that all she ever did there was wash dishes.

Anne recalled: "We used to drive from Dayton to the farm in an open touring car. People in the little towns along the way would sit on their front porches and call out, 'Hi, Jimmy,' as we passed.

"Daddy really didn't like to be in Dayton during the winter, so one year he said we were going to spend Christmas in Miami. Barbie and I were both really upset. We couldn't imagine Christmas there, but then we saw the boat parade.

"I don't know how many boats went by our house with their beautiful lights and decorations. It was very impressive. So after that we became accustomed to Christmas in Florida.

"During Prohibition we had a nanny in Miami who was, oh, so terrified that she was living in a house where liquor was present. There was a circular driveway in front of our house, where we would ride our bicycles.

"Suddenly, one day, motorcycle policemen roared up the driveway. Our nanny thought they were coming to take Daddy to jail because of the liquor. But it really was a police escort for Al Smith who was coming to call. He had just been defeated in the 1928 presidential election."

Barbara was a teen-ager when President Roosevelt stayed at Trailsend during one of his third-term campaign trips in 1940.

"The day before the President arrived," she said, "I was entering our driveway when the Secret Service stopped me. They searched the entire length of the driveway. They looked under the beds. They looked in the closets. They looked everywhere.

"The evening of the day he came, I sat with Daddy and the president and listened. It was wonderful. Daddy always asked everybody questions, you know, and President Roosevelt was the first person I ever heard who could answer all of them.

"I remember the blinds being drawn; I guess so no one could shoot him through

Gov. Cox and his daughters Anne (L), age 5, and Barbara, 2.

Barbara Cox Anthony, Chairman, Dayton Newspapers; Director, Cox Enterprises, Inc.

the windows. When his helpers started to put him in his wheelchair for dinner, the president said, 'Just save some time and pick me up.'

"So they just picked him up and carried him. Of course, that was something he never did in public. He was a very, very attractive man, who could charm anyone, and he liked his bourbon strong.

"I rode in the car with President Roosevelt when he was driven to the railroad station to make a speech from the rear platform of his train. My mother whispered, 'What if you get shot at?' It would be worth it, I told her."

Asked if her father showed any bitterness over his defeat for the presidency, Barbara replied, "No, not really. He would get mad at people, you know, and say, 'Damn fools; I'll never count on them again.'"

Anne said, "My brother, Jim, used to talk about the 1920 campaign for president and the train ride across the country, but Daddy never talked about politics. The one thing he did talk about was how he had preached that if the United States did not join the League of Nations it could not survive. He really was so far ahead of his time in his thinking.

"Because of my father, people would say after I was grown, 'But, of course, you would be a Democrat.' There was never any conversation with Daddy about party affiliation. I don't know how I chose to be a Democrat. My brother Jim, of course, was very conservative."

Barbara recalled going to the newspaper (the *Dayton Daily News*) with her father when she was little. "I'd sit next to him at his desk and scribble," she said. "I called that 'doing my work.'

"Actually, I think they hated to see me coming. Si Burick had waited for what seemed like all his life to get a new typewriter. I was older then, and I went into his office with my mother and said, 'Oh, look at the new typewriter. I want it.'

"Si was terrified, but I didn't get it. However, I think he thought I might."

Barbara and her big brother, Jim, were close, but he enjoyed teasing her as she was growing up. "Oh, he was terrible," she said with a laugh. "I didn't like him at all. One year I wanted a football for Christmas, and, after I got it, he kicked it over the house and way down in the woods."

Anne was not spared from being teased by her brother. "Anne and Catherine or 'Cass' were two of my aunts," she said. "Anne was thought of as the sweet one and Cass as the mean one. Jim used to say that I was named after the wrong aunt. He would always call me Aunt Cass. That was after I was grown, of course.

"I remember going to Aunt Cass' funeral with my mother and father. When the car pulled up in front of the church, Daddy wouldn't get out. He was listening to a baseball game on the radio.

"'We have to go in,' Mother told him.

"'Cass isn't going anywhere,' he said. 'There are two outs in the bottom of the ninth and the bases are loaded.' So we had to wait until the game was over."

"I loved Dan Mahoney Sr.," Barbara said. "He was like a big brother to Jim and very protective of him. Daddy and Jim enjoyed kidding Dan because he would tell you the obvious," she said. "There was a story in our family that when Anne was three years old she heard Dan say something about the Federal Reserve System.

"When she asked, 'What's that,' Dan sat down and began to explain it to her. At three, she couldn't have cared less. Afterwards, if a complicated subject came up, Daddy or Jim would say, 'Well, Dan, why you don't sit down and tell us about that?'

"I also knew that Daddy was planning to buy *The Atlanta Journal* and the Atlanta *Georgian* about a year before it happened. I was 14 or 15, and had flown to Atlanta from Tucson, where I attended boarding school. I had been sick with pneumonia, so Jim agreed to meet me in Atlanta and fly with me to Miami.

Anne Cox Chambers, Chairman, Atlanta Newspapers; Director, Cox Enterprises, Inc.

"We were walking around in the Atlanta airport terminal when Jim said, 'I want to take a look at these Atlanta newspapers.'

"'Oh, that's because Daddy's buying them,' I said brightly.

"'What did you say?' he asked. He was absolutely horrified. It was supposed to be the biggest secret in the world. He demanded to know how I knew. I had plopped down in one of our living room chairs in Dayton while they were talking about Atlanta. They couldn't see me, and had no idea I was there.

"I just stayed and listened to the whole thing. When I told Jim what had happened, he gave me hell and made me promise I wouldn't talk about it again."

After the acquisition of the *Journal* was announced, Anne made her first trip to Atlanta to see the world premiere of "Gone With the Wind." "I was in school in New York," she said. "My mother called me and said, 'Get on the train. This is going to be a spectacle that you'll never see again.' It was quite dazzling. It was during that visit that I met my first husband. We were married six months later.

"My two daughters used to visit their grandfather in Dayton every summer. They, of course, loved and adored him. My daughter Kathy and I were in a car one day and we saw this woman, all bent over and shuffling along. Kathy asked, 'What's the matter with that woman?'

"And I said, 'She's just old.'

"'What do you mean "old"', Kathy said.

"'Well, she's old,' I answered, 'like Grandpa.'

"Well, she was furious. 'He's not old,' she said.

"While the girls were visiting Dayton one year, Daddy took them to one of those Fourth of July games, where there were contests in running, jumping and so on.

"He called me that night and he was angry. 'They didn't win a single ribbon,' he said. 'They didn't know how to do anything.'

"So the next summer, he said, 'Send them a week early. We're going to train.'

"The girls told me later that he had a stopwatch and he would time them running, jumping and going through barrels. And so he called me that year and very proudly said, 'We have three blue ribbons and two red ones.' He was so competitive.

"All of my life, even in his last years when he was old, just knowing he was there was like the Rock of Gibraltar for me. I always had the feeling that no matter what went wrong, he could fix it."

Ralph Smith, "Smitty," the governor's pilot, would not fly if the weather was threatening. To Smitty, that could mean there was a single cloud in the sky, some joked.

"Daddy always believed what Smitty said," Barbara recalled. "If he said we can't go, we didn't go. I was stuck in Oklahoma City one time because Smitty said there were storms along the flight path to Dayton.

As children, Anne and Barbara loved going to the Old Home Farm, but their mother complained that all she ever did there was wash dishes.

"I had my son, Jimmy, with me. He was only five months old and the trip was taking forever. And I said, 'Damn it, I'm going to take an airliner.'

"'No you're not,' Daddy said, 'not with my grandson.' So we stayed in an Oklahoma City hotel and I had to wash Jimmy's diapers in the bathtub."

She recalled that in 1933, when she was 10, and her sister Anne was 13, they accompanied their father to London for the World Monetary and Economic Conference.

"Upon arrival in England," Barbara said, "the American delegation lined up to have photographs taken, and I just ran up and got in the picture. Daddy never seemed embarrassed that I was so pushy all my life, but my mother was upset. Anyway, I was in the picture, standing there grinning."

Barbara confirmed that it was Jim Jr. who got the governor interested in radio. "Jim was totally responsible," she said. "Daddy went along with radio, but he was very suspicious about television.

"Both Daddy and Jim could be tight. They were very cautious and afraid of debt. I had to talk Jim into buying television station KTVU, San Francisco-Oakland (1963), and the Palm Beach newspapers (1969).

"Jim would say, 'Are you crazy?' or 'Leonard Reinsch is crazy. Look at all the things he wants to buy.' At first, he was horrified when Leonard recommended buying the auto auctions.

"My father was a worrier. He worried about things that he couldn't do anything about. When family members were traveling, he would say things like, 'I wonder where the travelers are now? Why haven't they called?'

"Fortunately, I inherited my mother's outlook on life, which was happy and sunny.

"Freddie Robbins, our English butler, was my best friend when I was growing up at Trailsend. I was seven or eight when he came to us, and he was only eighteen. I loved him dearly and we did everything together. He taught me how to play ping-pong. He used to play baseball with me. I wasn't allowed to have Coca-Cola, because I was sort of addicted to it, so he would sneak it to me.

"After Freddie got married and had a son, he asked Daddy if he could work at the newspaper because he didn't want young Freddie having to say his father was a butler.

"Daddy told him he would have to take a cut in pay, and Freddie said that would be all right. I remember he took a second job at Sears & Roebuck after he went to the newspaper."

Robbins worked in the *Daily News* reference library, wrote obituaries, served on the editorial copy desk, became news editor and retired in 1973 as industrial editor of the paper.

Gov. Cox's butler, Freddie Robbins Sr., asked his employer to let him work at the *Dayton Daily News* so his young son wouldn't have to say his father was a butler.

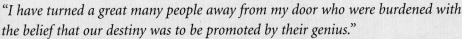

"I have turned a great many people away from my door who were burdened with the belief that our destiny was to be promoted by their genius."

—GOVERNOR JAMES M. COX

The Governor's Renowned Caddy

It was Governor Cox who gave James "Scotty" Reston, perhaps America's most respected journalist of his time, his first newspaper job.

Reston's family moved from Scotland to Dayton, Ohio, when he was a youngster. He wrote in his memoir, "Deadline," "We could have been going to any one of the eighteen Daytons in the United States, but our destination was the one in Ohio. When we arrived, the place was in a joyful uproar.

"The reason, as I learned later, was that the owner of the local paper, James Middleton Cox, was running for president of the United States. I don't know who arranges these lucky accidents, but they are the story of my life. For this was my introduction to politics, and Cox, the publisher of the *Dayton Daily News*, was later responsible for getting me into the newspaper business."

Reston first met the governor on a golf course, explaining, "After the 1920 election, apparently under the illusion that golf might be a consolation for defeat, Governor Cox played every weekend at the Dayton Country Club and usually the old Scotch pro, Nipper Campbell, played favorites and let me caddy for him.

"The governor was a good politician and a wobbly golfer. His backswing was better than his follow-through, and he conceded himself putts that were longer than the rules allowed. He encouraged me to learn the game, gave me a couple of old clubs and a free lesson from the assistant pro, and I began hacking around on the pitch-and-putt spread behind the caddy house."

As a senior, Reston won the state high school golf championship and several other titles, noting, "It was success in these tournaments that got me into my first newspaper office," he said. "I made friends with the sportswriters during these events, particularly with Si Burick, the sports editor of the *Dayton Daily News*, a thoughtful and friendly teacher.

"In the wintertime after school, I would hang around his desk, and when the basketball scores came in by phone from the local schools, Si would let me take them down and write 'shorts' that to my surprise and delight actually appeared in the paper exactly as written."

Reston was attending the University of Illinois when the stock market crashed in 1929. By the time he was a

Gov. Cox let teen-ager "Scotty" Reston (below) caddy for him in the '20s and, later, gave him his first newspaper job.

junior, the bank on which his $25 tuition check was written closed. Told he could not stay at the university, he hitchhiked to Dayton.

"I went at once to the *Daily News* building, without going home with the bad news," he said, "and explained this disaster to Governor Cox. He immediately wrote out a check for $100 as a loan, wished me good luck, and to my delight said to come back after graduation and maybe there would be a job for me on the *News* or at his other paper in Springfield."

Cox kept his promise and sent Reston to Edgar Morris, publisher of the Springfield *Daily News*, who gave him a job in the sports department at $10 a week.

When the sports editor retired, he wrote, "I was appointed in his place, given a two-dollar-a-week bonus and called to the publisher's office. Mr. Morris said it was an honor for one so young to be made one of the principal editors of the paper, and he added that, in keeping with this exalted position, he thought I should wear a hat when I came to work in the morning.

"I learned to write headlines, an artful challenge in discipline and compression. We all knew the horror of the careless editor on one of the midwestern dailies, who wrote a headline, MAN FALLS OFF BRIDGE, BREAKS BOTH LEGS, and left out the 'G' in bridge.

"In short, I discovered that you learned this business the way you learned how to play baseball, not by meditating about it, but by practicing it and by ducking at the right time."

Reston left Springfield in 1933 to become sports publicity director at Ohio State University. He went to work for the Associated Press in 1934, and joined the London staff of the *New York Times* on September 1, 1939, the day Adolf Hitler's German legions invaded Poland and started World War II.

Reston won two Pulitzer Prizes at the *Times*, and retired in 1987 as executive editor of the paper. In addition to receiving 28 college and university honorary degrees, he was awarded the Presidential Medal of Freedom in 1986. He died on December 6, 1995, at the age of 86.

"A wobbly golfer" is how Reston described Gov. Cox (R), shown with Al Smith, governor of New York and the 1928 Democratic presidential candidate.

Back into the Arena

Gov. Cox (R) campaigned for former running mate Franklin D. Roosevelt in 1932, accompanied by Dayton's famed aviator Orville Wright (C).

Governor Cox kept his promise never again to run for public office, but that did not keep him out of the political arena. In July 1924, he traveled to New York to break a hopelessly deadlocked Democratic National Convention that had been in session for two weeks.

He made sure the compromise candidate, John W. Davis of West Virginia, who won the nomination on the 103rd ballot, would support America's entry into the League of Nations. The governor said of him, "If the Almighty ever created a finer man than John W. Davis, I never knew of him. He possessed every quality of statesmanship."

Cox campaigned for Davis, delivering speeches in Ohio, Indiana, Kentucky and Tennessee, but none of this mattered. Calvin Coolidge won the election handily.

In 1928, the Democrats nominated New Yorker Al Smith for president, and the

Republicans chose Californian Herbert Hoover. A Democrat to the core, the governor "proudly" supported Smith, who lost the election.

"The major opposition to Al Smith was based on religious bigotry," Cox commented. "It was the most unworthy exhibition in our history. For the first time, a Catholic had been nominated for the presidency and was rejected, not because he was lacking in character or ability, but because he grew up in the church of his mother."

A Democrat to the core, Gov. Cox supported Al Smith for president in 1928.

Urged to run for the United States Senate in 1930, Cox said, "I would be the unhappiest man in the world were I to wake up and find myself either governor, senator or president."

After Franklin Delano Roosevelt was nominated for president in 1932, the governor made a nationwide radio speech on behalf of his old running mate and supported his candidacy in his newspapers.

Cox and Roosevelt stayed relatively close through correspondence after their unsuccessful campaign in 1920. Roosevelt was stricken with polio a year later. In a letter to the governor, dated September 10, 1921, Eleanor Roosevelt wrote:

"My husband was so much pleased by your kind telegram. It is a strange thing to have infantile paralysis at his age, but luckily it had been a mild attack and the doctors say he has every chance for a complete recovery and at the worst will only be lame."

In a "Dear Jim" letter of December 8, 1922, Roosevelt said, "The combination of warm weather, fresh air and swimming has done me a world of good; in fact, in some respects, I am in far better physical shape than ever before in my life, and I have developed a chest and pair of shoulders on me which would have made Jack Dempsey envious."

Governor Cox declined to be part of the new Roosevelt administration, turning down offers to be ambassador to Germany and chairman of the Federal Reserve Board. However, four months after Roosevelt's inauguration, he did agree to the president's request that he serve as a delegate to the World Monetary and Economic Conference to be held in London in the late spring of 1933.

Secretary of State Cordell Hull was selected as chairman and president and Cox as vice president and vice chairman. The governor, accompanied by his wife, Margaretta, and his two daughters, Anne and Barbara, sailed for England on Memorial Day, 1933.

Only days into the conference, President Roosevelt, concerned about the rising value of the dollar back home, backed away from a tentative plan to stabilize the world's currencies. After that, Cox said, "There was no heart in the conference," which ended without resolution.

"I knew Franklin D. Roosevelt long and well," he would later write. "We were not always of one mind in applying our philosophy of government, but that never disturbed our pleasant relationship."

Tough Times

Bob Sherman, who went to work in the classified advertising department of the *Dayton Daily News* as a teen-ager in 1928, said it took Governor Cox some time to decide whether he liked you or not.

Sherman said that once Cox made up his mind about that, everyone knew where they stood. "Most people thought he was difficult to work for," Sherman said, "and, in a way, he was, but he really was very mellow. He had real affection for his people."

"After he decided that I wasn't going to run off with the cash register, he put me to work in the cashier's cage. After the governor made up his mind that he liked me, he called me into his office and asked, 'Where did you go to school?'

"'Here in Dayton, at the Emmanuel School,' I said. 'It's a Catholic school.'

"'I don't have much to do with Catholic people,' he answered, quickly adding, 'but most of them are honest.'

"'That's not necessarily true, governor,' I said. 'If you look across the spectrum of people, they will all come out about the same.'

"'Well, I guess that's about right,' he said."

Sherman said one of the funny things he remembers is that when the governor was given the monthly financial figures, he would burn them in his fireplace. "He would burn everything," Sherman said. "But it didn't matter. We had seven or eight more copies."

One of the places the governor loved the most was the Old Home Farm, which was about 30 miles from Dayton. He lovingly restored the old farmhouse in which he was born. It was built by his grandfather between 1817 and 1820.

There was a fireplace in every room and a giant one in the combination sitting and dining room. Cox spent many weekends there, discussing scientific farming with Ralph Schramm, who managed the 885-acre property for 50 years. The place always was stocked with fresh bedding and linens for the governor and his guests.

Bob Sherman began at the *Dayton Daily News* at age 18 and retired 50 years later as executive vice president and a director of Cox Enterprises.

One Depression summer, *Dayton Daily News* sports editor Si Burick went to the farm and helped paint a barn. Fresh vegetables from the farm were often placed outside the newspaper's switchboard room, where they were sold to employees at cut-rate prices.

"I used to go there with him a lot," Sherman said. "He really enjoyed being there." The governor sometimes would bend over, pick up an acorn and push it into the soil, perhaps thinking of the old adage, "Big oaks from little acorns grow."

The newspapers went through a very bad time in the Depression, Sherman said.

"Just between you and me," he chuckled, "I wouldn't be surprised if there wasn't some check kiting between the papers in those days."

"In Dayton, we weren't laid off, but we had to take a 10 percent pay cut," Sherman remembered. "In four or five years we got 10 percent back. However, we did not get back all we had lost, because 10 percent taken from $30 is more than 10 percent restored on $27."

Because of the scarcity of cash, employees were occasionally paid in "scrip," which was accepted by merchants. Printed in various denominations, scrip was redeemable at the issuing bank.

After the 1929 stock market crash, Cox ordered his newspapers to keep the news of the economic collapse off the front page, telling the Associated Press he made the decision with the best interests of the community at heart, since stock buying was "an incidental thing" in the life of the country.

"It (The Crash) is nearly if not quite over," he said, "and yet all of our newspapers are filling the public mind with the idea of a disaster. This can easily develop a psychological condition hurtful to the general interest.

"The great masses of our people who are not involved can pursue, uninterrupted, their part in commerce. Otherwise, the impression will grow that we are on the verge of a serious industrial depression. My thought as publisher was to help our public forget the panic."

Of course, not even Cox could wish away the dark clouds of depression that descended on the country and the world, and stayed there for most of the 1930s.

During the Depression, fresh vegetables from the Governor's Old Home Farm were sold to employees at cut-rate prices.

On the Air

After graduating from Yale in 1928, Jim Cox Jr. went to work as a cub reporter for the *Dayton Daily News*. He really wasn't a junior because he and his father did not share the same middle name.

His was McMahon, the last name of one of his father's old friends, and the governor's was Middleton. Nevertheless, his father called him Jim Jr., as did most who knew him.

Fred Robbins, who worked on the copy desk, recalled: "Jim Jr. liked to have a good time in those days, like anyone else that age. It was a little hard to get him up in the morning, though.

"When he wasn't at work on time, someone would call to get him out of bed, and he would slip out of the house and down to the office without breakfast."

Jim Jr. subsequently worked in the advertising and circulation departments and was named general manager of the paper in 1931. Senior employees remembered the governor often looking over his son's shoulder, and then openly reversing his decisions. The governor, it seemed, wanted to show everyone that he was still in charge.

Daytonians tolerated the cold to attend a 1935 broadcast of the Miami Valley's first radio station.

But young Jim Cox had interests beyond newspapers. He was fascinated with the new technologies of the time, one of which was radio. Some say it was he who talked his 67-year-old father into bringing a radio station to Dayton. Be that as it may, once the decision was made, he was given the job of getting it on the air.

With radio station licenses being scarce, the Cox interests in 1934 bought a station in Painesville, Ohio, closed it down and transferred the license to Dayton.

In Chicago, J. Leonard Reinsch spotted a blind ad in Broadcasting magazine, which said, "Manager to direct a new station to be built in Dayton, Ohio." He immediately applied for the job.

At 26, he was the youngest applicant, but he got the job. Despite his youth, he had been in the business for 10 years, starting as an announcer with WLS while still in high school. At the time of his hire in Dayton he was working as a consultant in setting up a radio journalism curriculum for Northwestern University.

Governor Cox had been impressed with

Reinsch's thesis on radio advertising, but he was even more so when his new young manager told him that his architect didn't know anything about radio station construction.

Reinsch literally came in with a new broom, which he and the station's chief engineer used to sweep the floor of the building so they could lay out studios and offices with colored chalk. The architect's plans were changed.

Radio technician Ernie Adams, only 20, arrived in Dayton about the same time as Reinsch. In 1936, Adams was named chief engineer, probably the youngest in the country. He and Reinsch would work together for the next 40 years.

Adams said the National Broadcasting Company had helped Governor Cox find a frequency and sent engineers to help with the construction of twin directional antenna towers.

"Directional towers were brand new," Adams said, "and, while the theory was good, it didn't work too well. Because stations in New Hampshire, Savannah and Council Bluffs, Iowa, were on the same frequency as Dayton, we had to adjust our antenna and power output at different times of the day so we wouldn't interfere with each other's signals."

With the call letters WHIO, the first Cox radio station went on the air at 1260 kilocycles on Saturday evening, February 9, 1935. The station called itself an affiliate of the *Dayton Daily News.*

Governor Cox was to appear on the inaugural program. Years later, Reinsch recalled: "The governor asked me how long he should speak. I told him about 60 to 90 seconds. He looked me in the eye and said, 'Young man, I don't get started in 90 seconds.'"

After Reinsch said a long speech would drive away the audience, the governor agreed to cut it short. In two minutes, he delivered this eloquent dedication:

"The voice of radio as we hear it this evening takes its flight through the heavens in a historic setting. The antennas of the new station rise imperiously between the banks of the Great Miami and Mad rivers.

"Here it was that Tecumseh, the greatest Indian of all time — statesman, orator, warrior — followed the pursuits of peace and combat. Within sight are the fields now historic where Wilbur and Orville Wright gave to man the wings of the air that have carried him around the planet.

"In this inspirational scene we build a giant structure of steel and wires and insulators and all the magic devices of this scientific age. And now it takes the tongue of man and the melodies of poetry and music.

"Birth is always a solemn thing, and our emotions are deeply stirred as WHIO is announced as a new thing of life. May I express this christening sentiment — that the voice of this Miami Valley empire will always be an instrument of dignity, culture and

On December 1, 1934, these pioneers had gathered for the groundbreaking of WHIO, Gov. Cox's entry into radio when it was in its infancy: (L-R) Robert Lingle, chief engineer; Chuck Gay, *Dayton Daily News* reporter who later became WHIO program director; James M. Cox Jr.; Ernie Steiner, business manager; and J. Leonard Reinsch, station manager.

practical service; that it will carry the light of joy to places that are dark; that it will build a love of goodness and beauty; that it will plant in the hearts of men a philosophy that will help them to see Divinity in sunshine and shadow; that it will sense its obligation to the more than a million people who are by common interest to be our immediate radio fireside.

"In brief, may WHIO in its long watches of the night and its endless days be conscious of its duty to God and humanity."

To take care of those interludes in early radio, the station had an organ studio, with a mighty Wurlitzer. Even though they weren't seen by their audience, the announcers wore tuxedos.

"One time we had the Dayton Philharmonic orchestra at the studio," Adams said, "when something went wrong at the transmitter and we lost 10 or 15 minutes of the broadcast. That was when the chief engineer left and I replaced him. The governor's wife enjoyed listening to the orchestra, but she was critical of the reception she was getting. We brought her down to the studio one day and put her in a booth that had a really high-quality speaker.

"After she listened in there for a while, she said, 'Golly, why doesn't it sound that way at home?' I asked her what kind of radio she had. There weren't any little radios in those days. They were all big, but we convinced her to get a better one.

"There was a funny incident involving a drummer who played with a band in the basement of one of the local night spots. He complained to the bandleader that we weren't picking him up on WHIO radio. 'Can you get a mike a little closer to him?' the bandleader asked.

"We talked to the drummer, who said, 'Yeah, my mother says she can't hear the drums.' Hearing this, the leader said, 'Oh, forget about it.'"

WHIO's first air scout, in 1936, was an open cockpit biplane. The high-flying announcer watched for a waving blanket on the roof of the old Miami Hotel for "on" and "off" air cues.

Discovering an Editor

Governor Cox patted himself on the back when Walter Locke became editor of the *Dayton Daily News* in 1927.

"I take a modest pride in . . . discovering him," Cox wrote in his 1946 autobiography. After reading articles by Locke in various magazines, including the New Republic, he wrote a New Republic staffer and asked, "Who is this brilliant man Locke?"

He learned that Locke worked for the *Nebraska State Journal*, and would have gone to Chicago or New York but for fear of losing his editorial independence.

The governor began wooing Locke, who worried about his freedom as an editor working for a former politician. Not only that, he wasn't optimistic about the future of newspaper editorial pages, believing that a newspaper without an editorial philosophy would be less likely to upset its paying customers — readers and advertisers.

After Cox said that was nonsense, and assured the reluctant Nebraskan there would be no interference, Locke took the job as an "experiment." The experiment continued for 26 years, until Jim Fain became editor of the paper on December 7, 1953.

Knowing that his editorials often brought criticism to his boss, Locke wrote in 1938:

"He must have felt a thousand times like wringing my neck, for naturally a man of his power cannot always have been satisfied with the workings of my mind. But he has kept the faith. Never a finger has been laid on me. In times when the risks to be run seemed greater than I felt I had a right to impose on another man's property, I found him with the courage I might have lacked."

On Locke's 25th anniversary with the paper, the governor said of the man from Nebraska: "He and I have not always thought alike in our economic and social philosophies, but that has made no difference to either of us. The good-natured discussions growing out of all this develops usually into a useful research of the minds of both. In the 25 years of our association there has never been an unpleasant word passed by or between us. It has been a comradeship."

Thirty years after becoming editor of the *Dayton Daily News*, retiree Walter Locke (R) attended the 1957 dedication of the new building. With him are Bob Wolfe (L), executive vice president and general manager of Dayton Newspapers, Inc.; Jim Cox Jr. and his nephew, nine-year old Jim Kennedy.

Georgia on His Mind

Calling it "the rounding out of a dream," Governor Cox moved into the heart of the South in December 1939, with the purchase of *The Atlanta Journal* and the *Atlanta Georgian*.

He immediately shut down the *Georgian*, which had been owned by William Randolph Hearst. The *Journal* was the prize he was really after.

"I wouldn't know of another property in America I would want outside of this one," he wrote an acquaintance. "Georgia is a great empire with an inescapable progress of agricultural development. That appeals strongly to me. The town is progressing more than any city in the South."

Although it was not generally known, the *Journal* had been losing money for years. Between 1934 and 1939, its losses were $926,513. The *Georgian* had never been successful, and lost money every year of its existence.

The governor, only three months shy of his 70th birthday, said he never intended to create a centralized form of "chain journalism," adding, "Now that I had newspaper properties in Ohio, Georgia and Florida, each journal was encouraged to maintain its own personality under its own staff."

"Them lyin' Atlanta newspapers" was a theme of Georgia Governor "Ole Gene" Talmadge, under relentless attack for his racism.

John A. Brice, a cousin of Hoke Smith, a senator Cox had admired in his Washington days, was named president of the Journal Company. He served until his death in 1945 and was succeeded by George C. Biggers, a talented executive with a background in both editorial and business.

President Roosevelt, who had made Warm Springs, Georgia, his "little White House," wired Cox: "Accept my hearty congratulations as you enlarge your activities and broaden the field of your influence. Just short of a score of years ago you and I were together fighting side by side. In the years that have intervened we have been active in widely different fields. Now, happily, I feel we are brought closer by the bond of union which your entry into my other state — Georgia — symbolizes. All success and happiness to you as an old friend and now as a fellow Georgian."

Cox often said he came to Atlanta with "Gone With the Wind." The world premiere performance came a day or two after the acquisition of the *Journal*. Some wag remarked that Cox bought the newspaper to get a ticket to the show.

Margaret Mitchell, who wrote the best-selling classic, had worked on the *Journal*'s Sunday magazine. Called Peggy by her friends, she remained close with her former newspaper colleagues for the rest of her life. To the governor, she was that "grand little woman."

Cox praised everything about the *Journal*, from its slogan, "Covers Dixie Like the Dew," to its reputation, saying, "People believed in it. It had always dealt with them in good faith, and this made it a tremendously useful instrument in the governmental reforms that the public interest gravely required."

The paper quickly went on the attack against the racist Eugene Talmadge, who was seeking re-election as governor. Cox was forthright about his feelings toward the gallus-snapping politician, known to his cronies as "Ole Gene," saying, "I doubt whether in all the history of our American commonwealths there was ever a more dangerous and disgraceful regime than that of Eugene Talmadge."

When Talmadge would speak in the small towns of rural Georgia, some of his supporters would climb trees to see and hear him. They were called roosters.

As their hero would take off his jacket, roll up his sleeves and snap his red galluses, a rooster would yell, "Tell 'em about them lyin' Atlanta newspapers, Gene!"

"I'm a-comin' to that, boys," Talmadge would respond.

"Gene, they say you stole money," another rooster would shout.

"I stole it for you boys," came the answer. "Besides, I don't want no votes from no town with a streetcar," he would say.

The streetcar remark was a direct slap at Atlanta, because under the county unit rule system in Georgia, less-populated counties had almost as many unit votes as metropolitan ones. The statewide popular vote was meaningless.

Exposing Talmadge's misdeeds, the *Journal* strongly supported the candidacy of Ellis Arnall, a 35-year-old lawyer who had served as the state's attorney general. Arnall won the election and instituted reform. However, by law, he couldn't succeed himself, and Talmadge, preying on fears of racial integration and Yankee unions, was returned to office four years later.

Gov. Cox and famed author Margaret Mitchell, who once worked on *The Atlanta Journal*'s Sunday magazine.

George Biggers, executive vice president and general manager of *The Atlanta Journal*, wishes pilot George R. Cushing and his crew "Godspeed" as they prepare to carry the first air express editions of the *Journal* to Augusta and Savannah.

Welcome South, Brother

Marcus Bartlett (L) and Frank Crowther (of the Red Cross) hammed it up to promote WSB's music leadership. Bartlett was hired in 1930 to play the piano and tell bedtime stories on WSB. He retired 45 years later as an officer of Cox Broadcasting Corporation.

As part of *The Atlanta Journal* deal, Governor Cox also got WSB, the South's first radio station, whose call letters stand for the friendly salutation, "Welcome South, Brother."

WSB was a real pioneer. The *Journal* was awarded the broadcasting license in 1922, just two years after KDKA-Pittsburgh, the nation's first commercial radio station, went on the air.

WSB began broadcasting with 100 watts of power, less than what is in most of today's light bulbs. Metropolitan Opera star Rosa Ponselle, making her radio debut, reportedly sang with such force that she blew the transmitter off the air.

WSB joined the infant NBC network in 1926, and, by the time Cox took over, the station was a 50,000-watt powerhouse that could be heard throughout the United States.

Unlike Dayton, where Cox had to start from scratch, WSB came with a group of talented reporters. That talent had an opportunity to prove itself to the new owner with its outstanding coverage of the world premiere of "Gone With the Wind."

As a parade featuring film stars of the cast — Clark Gable, Vivian Leigh, Olivia De Havilland and others — wound its way from the Georgian Terrace hotel to the Loew's Grand theater, a half-dozen WSB reporters were stationed along the parade route.

Among those covering the spectacle were Marcus Bartlett, who would retire as an executive vice president of the Cox Broadcasting Corporation, and Douglas Edwards, who would end up in New York as a CBS news anchor.

Although not yet an employee, Bartlett first went on the air with WSB in 1926, as a piano player in a dance band. In 1930, the station was looking for someone who could play the piano and tell bedtime stories at the same time. Bartlett auditioned and got the job, but for years he was classified a temporary employee.

In the early days, radio stations did not carry commercials. No one was sure radio was here to stay, Bartlett said half-jokingly. He delivered one of WSB's first commercials in 1930. It was for the Book House Story Company, publisher of a series of children's books. For a teller of bedtime stories, it was a natural fit.

"One of the things I enjoyed as a radio reporter was interviewing celebrities," Bartlett recalled.

"I'm not a celebrity seeker, but I enjoyed meeting interesting people. Big bands were popular in the 1930s and 1940s and when Fred Waring and his Pennyslvanians came to town, I was assigned to interview Waring himself.

"After I questioned him in his sleeping car at the railroad station, he invited me to see one of his shows from backstage. Afterward, I accompanied him to his dressing room, where he showed me a new invention that he was ready to put on the market.

"He put the device together, pushed some celery and fruit and other things into it, and turned it on. Everything was shaken up. It was the prototype of the famous Waring blender."

J. Leonard Reinsch, who had put WHIO-Dayton on the air, came to Atlanta to manage the governor's newest radio property. "I didn't know what was going to happen to me," Bartlett said, "but to my relief, Leonard said, 'I want you to stay on. You're going to be my program director,' and he put me on the payroll on a permanent basis.

"Leonard was the kind of person who gave you responsibility and expected you to carry it out. He wanted an accounting, of course. He wanted to know about everything you were doing. He could absorb more information in a short time than anybody I ever knew. He was ahead of his time, actually, because he had visions far beyond what we were capable of doing in those days."

Reinsch hired Elmo Ellis right out the University of Alabama and made him WSB's publicity and promotion director. Ellis had applied for a job in the *Journal*'s editorial department, but because he had done some radio work in college, his application was sent over to WSB.

"They had a very open policy about allowing me to do whatever I wanted, in addition to my publicity and promotion work," Ellis said, "so I very quickly got into writing and directing various types of radio programs.

"Leonard was an exciting person to work for. He always was bubbling over with ideas. He would give you an assignment with a minimum of instructions, and leave it up to you to figure out how to do it. But I loved that. That's the kind of person I wanted to work with."

Ellis went off to World War II, and did radio shows for the Army. He produced several programs for the highly popular Glenn Miller and his orchestra and, for a while, roomed with a young actor named William Holden. After the war, Holden tried to get Ellis to come to Hollywood.

"That was a different world," Ellis said. "I felt more comfortable in a broadcasting environment. Holden and I exchanged letters for a time, but, you know, our communicating gradually faded away over the years."

But Ellis did not return to WSB, at least not right away. While in the Army, he wrote a show for "We the People," a popular radio program. He later accepted an invitation to come to New York and work full-time for "We the People."

"By that time I was married," Ellis said, "and my wife and I went to New York

Elmo Ellis, producer of "Reveille in Dixie during World War II," researched his subject first-hand. Later, the industry credited him with "removing the rust from radio."

together. It was a great adventure, but Marc Bartlett kept in touch. We had been in New York about a year and a half when he called and said, 'Elmo, we're getting ready to go into television. Don't you want to come back for that?'

"My wife and I wanted to start a family, and we knew we didn't want to do it in Manhattan. We accepted Marc's invitation and came back. It was the start of a wonderful new career."

Ellis spent a few years as a writer-producer for WSB-TV, but his wonderful new career really was in radio. In 1952, he was asked to become program director for WSB radio.

"Frankly, I was reluctant to do it," he said, "because I was enjoying television, and it was obvious that the future of television was so bright and so unlimited. But it really was a challenge for me. John Outlar, who at the time was general manager of both television and radio, told me, 'See if you can come back and pump some life into radio,' but he put a little addendum to that, saying, 'Of course we don't have any money to spend.'

"My approach was to reinvent radio, and make it a strong, community-oriented operation. I decided to involve the public in ways they had never been involved before. To do that, I created interactive radio and it worked.

"We had the listeners calling us, telling us what kind of program they would like to hear in the next hour, requesting favorite musical numbers, and voting on all sorts of things for which we had sought responses.

"There was no tape delay in those days. We trusted the good taste of the public. If you operate on a level where you ask people to be nice, they will accommodate you. The reason we hear so much junk on radio today is that no one is expected to be nice. We did talk radio, not hate radio.

"I worked very much on programs for drive-time. We were one of the first stations in the United States to broadcast traffic reports. And we were among the first to hire an airplane to go upstairs and let us know what the traffic looked like. I remember our first sponsor was The Coca-Cola Company.

"Broadcast Music Incorporated (BMI) asked me to go around the country to program clinics and tell other broadcasters what we were doing at WSB. I visited 40 states, Puerto Rico, Canada and Mexico. BMI issued a booklet, called 'Removing the Rust from Radio,' which was condensed from an article I had written for *Broadcasting* magazine."

In the article, Ellis said broadcasters should find out what listeners want and dare to be different. He advised taking the microphone to the people, covering the sounds of the community and talking with people from all walks of life.

One of Ellis' programs, "You and Your Health," helped bring WSB the Peabody Award in 1953. He received a personal Peabody in 1966 for his contributions to broadcasting. Three years later, President Richard M. Nixon commended him for a WSB radio campaign to raise school lunch money for needy youngsters.

During the Cuban missile crisis in 1962, WSB radio was one of six stations asked by the U.S. government to carry "Voice of America" programs in Spanish. All advertising was canceled and station personnel each evening answered calls that came in on 15 telephones. In 1963, WSB radio and WSB-TV became only the third stations in the nation to win the "Gold Mike Award," presented by the Broadcasting Pioneers for their contributions to the industry.

Ellis retired in 1982 as a vice president of Cox Broadcasting.

Looking back, Ellis said, "Rather than being driven to the wall by television, radio got off its podium, dropped its pomposity and put on its roller skates. It became mobile and started rolling around the country, mingling with citizens, collecting and reflecting reactions and opinions. Radio fought successfully for its life by taking off its tie and tails and slipping into sports clothes."

Another kind of radio — frequency modulation or FM — was pretty much in its infancy in the 1940s and 1950s, but when it matured and grew strong, it would surpass AM as the listeners' choice. It was described as "radio receptivity with virtually no static." Cox had been a pioneer when it put the South's first FM radio station on the air in 1948, followed shortly thereafter by the Miami Valley's first FM.

Cox Broadcasting chief engineer Ernie Adams said there was not a whole lot of interest in it at first because very few people owned FM receivers. There really wasn't any programming, except for playing records, he said.

Stan Mouse said sales representatives in Dayton were not allowed to sell commercials on WHIO-FM Dayton. "It was a beautiful music station, playing what later became known as elevator music," Mouse said.

"But, I'll tell you, within three years after we started selling commercial slots, we were the top-rated FM station in the market, and within five years WHIO-FM was rated higher than our AM station."

Eventually, FM became a strong segment of radio broadcasting everywhere. As usual, WSB-Atlanta was the South's pioneer and leader. On May 15, 1973, WSB-FM began broadcasting 24 hours a day.

From Europe in 1944, Wright Bryan (C), editor of *The Atlanta Journal*, broadcast the first report of D-Day to a national radio audience. After returning, he talked about the experience with George Biggers (L), president of The Journal Company (which owned WSB), and Jim Cox Jr.

Expanding in Dayton

In late 1948, fifty years after becoming the owner-publisher of the *Dayton Daily News*, Governor Cox acquired two old hometown opponents — the morning *Journal* and the afternoon *Herald*.

The year 1949 opened with a new newspaper in Dayton, the morning *Journal Herald*. The move left Cox's beloved *Daily News* alone in the afternoon field. With little or no television at that time, afternoon newspapers outsold the a.m.'s in industrial markets like Dayton, where factory workers were frequently home before 5 p.m.

Lewis B. Rock had been the owner of the *Journal* and the *Herald*. When his long-time conservative editor, Dwight Young, whom everyone called "Deacon," learned of the deal, he told Rock he would retire when the sale was consummated.

Although Young was nearing his 65th birthday, normal retirement age, Rock told him he was confident Governor Cox would want him to stay on.

Recalling the conversation years later, Young wrote, "I said that I had no desire to work for a new publisher. My mind is made up."

"The next morning, before I left home," Young continued, "I received a telephone call from Governor Cox, asking me to have breakfast with him at Trailsend. As I entered the living room, the governor greeted me with: 'What's this I hear about your thinking of retirement?'

"'That's no way for a good newspaperman to talk. Fellows like you and me have no business talking of retirement. I hope to die with my boots on. I advise you to do likewise.'

"When I explained to him that as an editor I had worked for five different publishers and that, approaching 65, I didn't think I felt like going through the experience of breaking in with yet another, he promptly answered, 'That's an easy problem to settle. If you occupied both posts, couldn't Editor Young get along with Publisher Young?'

"'Yes, governor, I think he could,' I answered, 'but unfortunately he still would have Owner Cox to deal with.'

"It was then that Governor Cox paid me the greatest compliment of my entire newspaper career. With right hand outstretched, looking at me straight, eye to eye, he answered:

"'Deacon, I can assure that the new owner of the *Journal Herald* will not interfere in

Lewis B. Rock sold his morning Journal and afternoon Herald to competitor Cox in 1948, who combined them into a morning paper and gave Daytonians Cox coverage all day.

the smallest degree with your operation of the paper. I am sure you will not always do things the way I personally would do them, but you never will know it from anything I may say or do.'"

The governor kept his promise and never stepped foot in Young's office. For almost six years the *Daily News* and the *Journal Herald* operated in different plants, with separate composing and press rooms. The two papers did not share a common press until 1956, when a new Dayton Newspapers building was dedicated.

Young loved to tell the story of a proposed meeting between Governor Cox and Ohio Senator Bob Taft. Mutual friends of the two Ohio political giants, including Young, had attempted to get them together, but the governor, partisan to the end, declined, telling Young: "You know of my admiration for Bob Taft. He is perhaps our country's outstanding statesman. But he is the leader of the Republican Party, and I am a Democrat who has been signally honored by my party. I can think of no good that could come from such a meeting."

When this writer went to work as a reporter at the *Journal Herald* in June 1949, there was still resentment about the merger of the two papers, and also against Governor Cox and the *Daily News*. After all, they had been enemies for as long as anyone on the staff could remember.

Deacon Young used to come down to the editorial department every now and then with "great news." I always hoped he was going to announce a pay increase, since my salary was $47.50 per week. Instead, with great gusto, he would announce the latest circulation figures.

The *Journal Herald* opened with a paid circulation in the neighborhood of 35,000. I remember Young's great joy when it cracked 50,000.

Young retired as editor and publisher of the *Journal Herald* in 1959. He was succeeded by Glenn Thompson, who came to the job after 36 years with the *Cincinnati Enquirer*.

As a city hall reporter for the Dayton Daily News *in the mid-1950s, I accompanied Dayton's mayor and city commissioners to Trailsend, where Governor Cox was to be presented with a framed copy of a resolution naming the municipal airport after him.*

The governor was sitting in an overstuffed chair in his library. As Mayor Louis Lohrey was reading aloud the resolution, someone started talking in a far corner of the room.

"Would you be quiet back there?" the Governor exclaimed. "They are trying to name an airport after me."

After Lohrey finished, Governor Cox became emotional and said, "This is the greatest honor I have received since being nominated for president of the United States."

I was back in the newsroom writing the story when Jim Cox Jr. called. "'Chuck,' he said, "the Governor got carried away today. I think having an airport named after you hardly compares with being nominated for president. Let's not embarrass the old man."

The quotation was not used.

—CHUCK GLOVER

A Birthday Present

In March 1950, Governor Cox bought himself a birthday present. It was *The Atlanta Constitution*, the newspaper of Henry Grady, Joel Chandler Harris and Ralph McGill.

The treatment of the acquisition by the *Constitution* and the Cox-owned *Journal* was bizarre. Neither paper printed a news story about the change of ownership.

On Sunday, March 19, only 13 days shy of the governor's 80th birthday, both papers printed a front-page "statement," signed by Governor Cox and Clark Howell, president and publisher of the Constitution Publishing Company.

It said, in part: "Rumors persist that the two Atlanta newspapers are going to be merged. We think the people are entitled to know the facts.

"It is true that we have reached an agreement toward merging the *Constitution* and the *Journal*. This agreement is subject to the approval of certain government agencies. It is assumed this approval will be forthcoming without undue delay.

"The effect of this merger, should it be accomplished, will be the continuance of the publication of the *Constitution* in the morning field and the *Journal* in the evening field. We are looking forward to the consolidation of the Sunday *Journal* and Sunday *Constitution*, the combined publication to retain all the best features and writers now carried in each."

The statement went on to say that the editorial policies of the two papers would remain independent and that Howell would continue as publisher of the *Constitution*.

The final order authorizing the consolidation of the newspapers was signed in Fulton County Superior Court on May 31, 1950. Under the agreement, Cox had to turn back to the FCC a construction permit for radio station WCON, a property of the *Constitution*.

The first combined Sunday paper rolled from the presses of both plants on June 4, 1950. Some 475,000 copies were printed. Five weeks later, the editors of the two newspapers told the members of the Atlanta Kiwanis Club the merger of the *Journal* and *Constitution* would mean greater coverage and more community service.

Journal editor Wright Bryan quoted Governor Cox as saying that the directors of the new company must remember the great traditions of the two papers, and must establish new traditions in keeping with those of the past.

Ralph McGill, editor of the *Constitution*, said "Governor Cox believes that well-known newspaper chains have made a mistake in trying to impose overall news and

Mementos of Joel Chandler Harris, author of the "Uncle Remus Tales" and one of the most famous writers at *The Atlanta Constitution* following the Civil War.

editorial policies," adding that "the governor thinks such a practice is contrary to the public good and is also bad business."

Calvin Cox, a 37-year editorial department veteran of Atlanta Newspapers, recalled, "After the merger the papers continued to be unrelenting foes six days out of the week and part-time on Sunday. Operating in separate newsrooms, the staffs gave each other no quarter and scant 'hellos' for more than 30 years. There was no exchange or trading of information."

Jack Tarver, associate editor of the *Constitution*, who had been hired by McGill in 1943, was in South America on a fellowship when the consolidation occurred. Upon his return, Howell told him the "bad news."

"I had a couple of job offers," Tarver said. "One came from the owner of a Houston newspaper, who obviously knew about the merger before it became public. There was an editorship open and I was invited to come out there and talk about it."

Before he could go, George Biggers, who had been named president of Atlanta Newspapers Incorporated, told Tarver the governor wanted to see him and Ralph McGill. The two traveled to Miami, and met with their new boss in the *Miami News* tower.

"We arrived early," Tarver recalled, "and went to the top floor of the building, where Governor Cox was waiting for us. He said, 'I know how you boys feel; you feel like you've been sold out. I won't lie to you; you have been, but just remember I bought you because I wanted you. I want the *Constitution* to grow and I want you fellows to build it.'"

At the time the *Constitution* was sold to Cox, Clark Howell didn't own the paper, Tarver said. The bank did. The *Constitution* had been the most profitable newspaper in town prior to 1950, but its earnings were declining. A costly television venture had put the company deep in debt. According to Tarver, large demand notes kept Howell going to the bank every week.

Proud to have McGill working for him, the governor quickly made it clear he wanted to showcase his new columnist. After the first combined Sunday edition was published, Cox called Tarver and asked, "Where did you run McGill?"

"He's back on the editorial page," Tarver responded.

"No, I want him on the front page," the governor emphasized, and on the front page McGill remained until his death.

"We never had any real trouble with the governor on anything we did," Tarver said. "During the 1952 presidential race between General Eisenhower and Adlai Stevenson, McGill wrote some columns very favorable to Eisenhower, which caused the governor some concern.

"He telephoned me one day and said, 'Jack, I thought Ralph was a Democrat. He's been writing an awful lot about Eisenhower.'

"I said, 'Governor, don't worry about it; he's going to be our Democrat.' And Ralph, although he admired Eisenhower, came out for Stevenson."

Biggers, an ex-sportswriter, soon moved Tarver into the executive suite, naming him general manager.

In 1950, George Biggers became president of Atlanta Newspapers.

Associate Editor of *The Atlanta Constitution*, Jack Tarver moved Ralph McGill's column to the front page to satisfy the new owner, Gov. Cox.

The Eyes of the South

Television, the technology that would change American society forever, made its dramatic debut with the Cox organization in Atlanta on September 29, 1948.

At eight o'clock that night, WSB-TV, calling itself the "Eyes of the South," went on the air with an American flag waving in the breeze as "The Star-Spangled Banner" played.

Leonard Reinsch introduced Jim Cox Jr., who praised the "spirit, the aggressiveness and high intelligence of the people of the area."

Viewers were entertained by the Baptist Hour Choir, Ace Richman's "Sunshine Boys" and a marionette show. There was a local news report, a summation of national and international news and interviews with Atlanta area sports celebrities.

After a movie was shown, the evening ended with a listing of programs that would be broadcast the next day, followed by the National Anthem. The South's first television station had successfully completed Day One of its existence. Since then, the days "on the air" have continued unbroken.

Atlanta area residents began buying television sets four months before WSB-TV began broadcasting, and approximately 2,500 receivers were in homes when the station went on the air.

WSB-TV's first mobile unit took Atlantans to the scene of home-town action, with Emmitt Kelley, Oliver Heely and Gordon Swann at the controls. Gov. Cox put "The South's First TV Station" on the air in 1948.

After watching a closed-circuit demonstration telecast of a local high school football game, Ed Danforth, veteran sports editor of *The Atlanta Journal*, wrote:

"The whole show was interesting, but it left some of us in a fine state. Just as we were beginning to believe that radio was on the level, they show us a little machine with its back to the game putting pictures on a little screen . . . moving pictures . . . of what we were looking at with our eyes.

"Once again, I am disturbed over what can be done with nothing but electricity. Frankly, I am scared of the thing and may never have one in my house."

The early pioneers in television could have taken a cue from song-and-dance man Al Jolson and said, "You ain't seen nothin' yet," because that certainly turned out to be the case.

Danforth wasn't the only one who wasn't sure about television. Governor Cox was another. When the second Cox television station – WHIO-TV, Dayton — was being built, he didn't hide his doubts.

Ernie Adams, retired chief engineer of Cox Broadcasting, recalled a story Jim Cox Jr.

passed on to him. "Jim told me," Adams said, "that after he and the governor had completed a tour of the station, his father turned around, looked back at the building and asked, 'Who authorized all of this?'

"Well, I guess I did, Governor," Jim said.

"You know, Ernie, he fired me," Jim laughed. "I was out of work for two weeks."

When "White Columns," WSB radio and television's new home, was being built in Atlanta in the mid-1950s, Governor Cox came by, took one look and said, "Stop everything!"

"He was not getting what he thought he was getting," explained Marcus Bartlett, WSB-TV station manager at the time. Leonard Reinsch and Jim Cox had told him that he was going to get a representation of the Old South in some way or another.

"I believe he thought he was getting a replica of the governor's mansion in Milledgeville, but that was not what he saw. So, for three weeks, nothing happened. Finally, Jim and Leonard convinced Governor Cox that we were building a structure that, in effect, was Tara Hall of "Gone With the Wind" fame, and that it would be a memorial to him. He accepted that and construction resumed."

After White Columns was finished, the governor would come in and sit in a big lobby chair that was covered with red velvet. It was right at the door. He would sit there and tell anyone who would listen how he had built the building.

Adams treasures a personal note Governor Cox sent him in October 1956. With his hearing deteriorating, the old man asked Adams to get him something that would help him hear better. He did, and after several months had passed, the governor sent him the following:

"This is a belated acknowledgment of the hearing device which you sent here some time ago. It is the best thing I have seen of its kind, and I prize it, not only for its worth, but because it came from you."

Stan Mouse, a WHIO sales executive at the time, said that, shortly after WHIO-TV went on the air in 1949, he went to the station one morning to deliver copy to an

For 14 years, WHIO radio had brought Daytonians innovative programming, such as "Man on the Street" interviews, but Gov. Cox was still leery of broadcasting when he put WHIO-TV on the air in 1949.

International star Dick Van Dyke (L) was a WSB-TV employee in the late 1940s as one of "The Merry Mutes."

Curious crowds saw "Faximile" transmit anything that could be put on paper, in the lobby of *The Atlanta Journal*, when WSB-TV experimented with the communication device during 1948. Facsimile was ahead of its time; the national push was behind television.

announcer and found Governor Cox sitting on the front steps.

"As I approached him, I said, 'Good morning, Governor,' Mouse said.

"'Good morning, young man,' he replied, and then looked up at me and said, 'I don't think this television thing is ever going to make it.'

"I knew Jim Jr. a lot better than the governor because broadcasting was his baby. When he was having bad TV reception, he would call me and say, 'Mouse, what the hell is going on with my television set?'

"So, we would adjust his set. One day he asked me to come to his office in the *Daily News* building. Telling me he was going out of town, he said, 'Here is the key to my house. Drop by every three or four weeks and see how everything is. I'll call you before I come back so you can make sure all the TVs are working well.'

"Boy, I'll tell you, I had the keys to Jim Cox's house and I was always afraid something would be missing and they would look at me and say, 'What the hell?' It was unbelievable. I don't know why he trusted me that much, but he did.

"When I was discharged from the Army Air Corps at the end of World War II, my dream was to be a radio announcer. But when I visited WHIO, I saw the announcers driving used Fords and the sales guys riding around in Buicks. That's when I applied for a position in sales.

"You didn't have to be a brain surgeon to sell television advertising in those days. Every time they promoted me I took a cut in pay. I was losing all those commissions, but, obviously, things worked out well for me."

Mouse quickly climbed the promotion ladder, eventually becoming president of the Miami Valley Broadcasting Corp., in Ohio, and later serving twice as president of Cox Broadcasting in Atlanta.

In the early days of television all shows were in black and white and there was no taping. Live television produced some hilarious moments. In Dayton, WHIO-TV announcer Ted Ryan was demonstrating an unbreakable watch for a local jewelry store.

Holding the watch in the air, he said, "You can take this watch and drop it, and it won't break." He opened his hand, and when the watch hit the floor, it came apart with springs flying everywhere.

"I had a guy come in one time," Mouse recalled, "who was going to shoot a lit cigarette from his daughter's mouth. We're doing this thing, and the guy is aiming. All of a sudden I see the end of his rifle jumping around.

"He's excited. He's never been on television before. I say to myself, 'We're gonna kill somebody here, right on the air.' He fires, misses the cigarette and damn near the whole board that was set up to catch the bullet. After that, no more gunplay in the studio."

According to "Welcome South, Brother," a 50-year history of WSB, a frightened young actress doing a commercial on WSB-TV suddenly quit talking, stared wide-eyed at the camera and then ran from the set.

On another occasion, a bull was dragged into the studio to promote a rodeo. Startled by the bright lights, the animal became upset and began pushing things around. According to an observer, "He nearly broke up the show by proving that he wasn't house broken."

Both the Atlanta and Dayton television stations have had their share of personalities, but the two who have become most recognized nationally are Tom Brokaw, current anchor of NBC's "Nightly News," who cut his teeth at WSB-TV, and Phil Donahue, a newsman at WHIO-TV, who left the station to become a pioneer in the talk show business.

CNN's Larry King, a master of the talk show genre, made WIOD(AM), "Wonderful Isle of Dreams," a Cox radio station in Miami, a way station in his career.

He hosted a celebrity talk show at the station from 1975 to 1978, doing many programs from a boat named "Surfside Six," which was anchored in Indian Creek across from the Fontainebleau Hotel in Miami Beach.

Elmo Ellis, a retired vice president of Cox Broadcasting, said, "Larry had all the top show business people on his program — stars such as Bob Hope, Frank Sinatra and Milton Berle."

For a time, King also wrote a weekly celebrity chitchat column for the Cox-owned *Miami News.* He left WIOD for a job with Mutual Broadcasting System in Washington, D.C.

Children flocked to watch "The Woody Willow Show" each afternoon. Some of Don and Ruth Gilpin's lovable marionettes are displayed in the new home of WSB TV and Radio, built in 1998.

Dayton's New Editor

For the first time in 26 years, the *Dayton Daily News* had a new editor. James E. Fain, a 33-year-old editorial writer at *The Atlanta Journal*, was selected to replace Walter P. Locke.

Fain would be a different kind of editor than Locke. Whereas Locke was concerned only with the editorial pages, Fain would be responsible for both the news and editorial page operations.

He came to work on Pearl Harbor Day, December 7, 1953, rolled up his sleeves and began the task of energizing a somnolent newspaper. Known as Jim Ed in Georgia, he was simply Jim in Dayton.

Fain began his life with Cox in March 1948, as a copyreader at the *Journal*, but before that he had been the managing editor of a newspaper in Columbus, Georgia. After news department budget cuts, he left Columbus, feeling he needed a new beginning.

He moved up to news editor at the *Journal*. After five years in the job, he was considering going to law school, when George Biggers called him to his office, and asked if he would be willing to leave Atlanta.

Fain said he would, and when Biggers asked, "Isn't your wife from Miami?" he figured that he was bound for the troubled *Miami News*. However, Biggers said, "You could come down to the second floor and write editorials for a while. I can't raise your salary, but it might lead to something."

Fain jumped at this chance. After a year of writing editorials, he was offered the editor's job in Dayton.

"It was funny how it happened," he said. "When I was news editor at the *Journal*, the *Chicago Tribune* on an Easter Sunday ran nothing but good news on its front page. Governor Cox liked the idea and decided all his newspapers should do the same thing a year later.

"I saw it as a promotional thing that wouldn't do any harm. There was not likely to be a big story that night, although if there had been, I might have gone without the Easter front. But it occurred to me there ought to be some explanation of the good news page. So I sat down and wrote about three paragraphs about why we were doing this.

"Governor Cox read my little note and asked Biggers who wrote it. George said he didn't know, but he would find out. He finally learned that I had written the piece. Well, the old man was impressed with that, and the next time he came to Atlanta he asked to meet me.

"I went to his office, not knowing what I was dealing with. When I sat in a chair, he said, 'Pull over closer; I don't hear as well as I used to.'

"I got right up next to his big desk and we started talking. And the first thing I knew, he spit past my head. Fascinated, my eyes followed this glob until it hit the spittoon dead center. It was a beautiful shot. He was chewing tobacco as he sometimes did.

"Well, as we talked, he found out I had a little boy. He was very good at inquiring about families. When he asked about Mike's health, I told him the kid was having problems with his tonsils.

"He urged me to have them removed immediately, but I didn't much want to do that. As a matter of fact, I didn't, and Mike still has his tonsils.

"When I got home, my wife, Laura, said, 'Well, what did he want to talk about?'

"'About Mike's tonsils,' I answered."

All newspapers seem to have their share of characters, but Fain said two of the oddest he had ever encountered worked at *The Atlanta Journal* when he was on the copy desk.

"One was a copy boy," he said, "named William B. Whidby Jr., who wanted to be a writer. He would come to the office early and strip the *New York Times* teletype machine, because he figured the *Times* people really knew how to write.

"He would take the *Times* report over to his desk and copy some of it on his typewriter. He was an original; kind of unbelievable. He once wrote a memorable story about a Lone Ranger-type character. When the horse and rider encountered some startling scene, Whidby wrote, 'The horse chortled.' When he would find a word like 'chortled,' he knew he had a treasure and he would use it."

Eventually, Fain said, Whidby decided that his true calling was to make movies. He bought a camera and started filming one of his own stories, which he titled, "Ganyak, the Jungle Man." Ganyak bore an

"Jim Ed" Fain left Atlanta and became simply Jim in Dayton.

amazing resemblance to Tarzan. He also cast his girlfriend as the "Jane" character.

Whidby and his cast went into the Georgia woodlands to film "Ganyak, the Jungle Man" in a natural setting. While anxiously reviewing the rushes, Whidby discovered that Ganyak had forgotten to take off his wristwatch.

After wasting all that film, Whidby decided he needed to learn more about the mechanics and techniques of moviemaking, so, when his vacation came, he bought a train ticket to Los Angeles, where he planned to visit Hollywood.

Whidby rode a day coach from Atlanta to Los Angeles, staying up all night because he was nervous and excited. When he came back to Atlanta, he was close-mouthed and sort of abashed. "I knew him pretty well," Fain said, "so he told me, confidentially, what happened.

"He said that while walking from the Los Angeles railroad station, he asked people for directions to Hollywood. They pointed the way, but then some folks began laughing at him. Whidby didn't like the way they were behaving, so he got himself something to eat, returned to the railroad station and caught a train back to Atlanta.

"Whidby," Fain recalled, "used a booming, cathedral voice when he answered the telephone. He would say, '*The Atlanta Journal* city room, William B. Whidby Jr. speaking.'

"I do know the following actually happened. It was a Saturday afternoon and everyone had sneaked off to the Georgia Tech football game. Governor Cox called the office, got Whidby on the phone, and asked to speak to about five people in a row, only to be told, in each case, they weren't there.

" 'Well, who is this?' the governor inquired. 'Who am I talking to?'

"And the voice on the other end of the line said, 'This is William B. Whidby Jr., sir.'

" 'Whidby, what do you do there?' the governor asked.

" 'Sir, I am the copy boy for *The Atlanta Journal*,' he answered.

" 'Whidby,' the governor said, 'whatever you do, don't leave that room!' "

Fain said the second character was O. B. Keeler, *Journal* sportswriter who became famous for reporting the exploits of legendary Georgia golfer Bobby Jones. In fact, Keeler became known as Jones' Boswell, a reference to the man who recorded the life of England's Samuel Johnson.

"He was long in years and near retirement when I knew him," Fain said. "We called him 'Pappy.' He would come to work between nine and ten in the morning, brandishing his cane, and looking for a mythical Scotchman, whom he called 'McTavish.'

"He would go around the city room, yelling, 'McTavish, McTavish; where are you, McTavish?' As far as I know, he never found McTavish.

"Then, he would come by the copy desk, pound his cane hard on the desk and make some pronouncement. You never knew what it was going to be, but in the one I recall best, he declared:

" 'Gentlemen, I ask you, what has happened to this great nation, when one of our leading publications, I do not hesitate to name it, the *Saturday Evening Post*, will carry a cover article on the sonofabitch who invented bubble gum?' "

In late 1953, Fain was invited to Jim Cox Jr.'s office in Atlanta, where he again heard the same questions he had been asked earlier by Biggers and Governor Cox. Would he be willing to leave Atlanta and wasn't his wife from Miami?

"Only this time," Fain recalled, "Jim Cox said the magic words, which were: 'We have this opening in Dayton. It's for an editor.'

"He went on to say that longtime editor Walter Locke was getting on and wanted to retire. I had practically never heard of Dayton, but I said right away, 'If you want to offer me the job, I'll take it.'

"This surprised Cox, who said, 'You can't do that. First, you have to come and see the town.'

"'You don't understand,' I said. 'I'll take the job.' I was making $150 a week. I figured they must pay the editor in Dayton more than that.

"Jim drove me all around Dayton and then took me to lunch at Trailsend. Governor Cox came downstairs and asked good-naturedly, 'Is there someone around here named Jim Fain?'

"Near the end of a pleasant visit, the governor asked me about my religion. I told him my father was a Methodist preacher, and that I was a kind of backsliding Methodist.

"To my surprise, the governor said, 'When you get to Dayton, I think you probably ought to join the Episcopal church.'

"'Why?' I asked.

"He stopped for a moment and said, 'Well, it's not important.'

"I heard later that he told people all over town: 'I asked that young fellow Fain to join the Episcopal church, and he told me to go to Hell!'

"I liked the town and was eager to get the job. I found out they were going to pay me $250 a week, which I thought was all the money in the world. The governor liked to say he discovered me, but it was Jim Cox who hired me.

"I developed a great deal of respect for Governor Cox, but, at the beginning, we had some difficult times. He loved wire stories, but did not have much use for local news. After I started running local on the front page, he called me and said, 'You've got this local page on the back of the news section, and you can run local news there.' 'Well, Governor,' I said, 'some of this local news is just too important to put on the back of the section.'

"One morning, after I gave him the same routine, he got mad. 'Who do you think owns this newspaper anyway?' he said.

"'Why, Governor Cox,' I said, 'you own this newspaper, and if you want to give me an order it will be followed.'

"There was a pause, and he said, 'It hasn't come to that,' and hung up.

"My father was a great admirer of Governor Cox, having cast his first presidential ballot for Cox in 1920. When he came to town to visit me, the governor telephoned and said, 'I hear there is a VIP in town.'

Governor Cox was always driven to the Dayton Daily News *by his chauffeur, Clifford Snyder, in a pre-World War II Cadillac. The license plate was JC-1. The young reporters called it "God's Car."*

"'Well, I think so, Governor,' I responded.

"'Why don't you bring your father out here for lunch?' he said. 'I'll have Clifford down there at noon to pick you up.'

"Clifford showed up in an ancient Cadillac. He had been trying the get the governor to buy a new one, but the new models knocked the old man's hat off when he got in and out of the car.

"We had a great lunch, with pheasant, as I remember. My father was just enthralled with being in the presence of this great man. And the great man was enthralled at having someone enthralled by him. After lunch we retired to the library, where the governor and my father smoked cigars. It was a love affair between the two of them.

"As we were leaving, Governor Cox said, 'Jim, you've got a little better paper there tonight. There's not much local on the front page.'

"'Thank you, Governor,' I replied. 'I thought we had a couple of strong local stories.'

"I could say that because I knew what local stories we had working. But neither of us had seen the paper, so I hurried down to the office and looked at the final edition in a big hurry."

Long-time Montgomery County Democratic leaders became unhappy with Fain when he stopped publishing a Sunday column that was practically dictated by Al Horstman, Montgomery County's Democratic Party chairman. Even the writer, staffer Bernie Losh, was embarrassed about it.

There was a conference at Trailsend, and Fain said it was the only time he saw Governor Cox in a political mode. Fain remembered, "The guy was a master, an absolute virtuoso. It was marvelous to watch him.

"At one point, Horstman said, 'The party's not losing any vitality. The only thing we've lost is the newspaper. This young man has taken it away from the party.'

"Governor Cox looked at Horstman and said, 'This young man is a better Democrat than I ever was.'

"It just went on from there. The governor handled it gloriously. Everything was put on the table, which made it abundantly clear to them that I had Governor Cox's support in carrying out an independent newspaper policy.

"Not too long before the governor died, Mrs. Cox called my wife and invited us to dinner at Trailsend. We drove out there on a late Sunday afternoon. We ate out on the terrace, just the four of us. It was a very nice evening, with very casual conversation.

"But after a while, it was obvious that the governor was getting tired. So we got up to say goodnight, and the governor and Mrs. Cox saw us to the door. When we were outside, Laura said to me, 'Did you notice what that old man did?'

"'No,' I answered.

"'He put his arm around you.'

"'He did?'

"'He likes you.'

"'Well, I like him.'

"'You ought to tell him that sometime.'

"Apparently, it was a very poignant thing, his putting his arm around me. It's a beautiful memory for me, but one that my wife had to point out."

End of an Era

James Middleton Cox died Tuesday, July 15, 1957, at Trailsend, his home near Dayton. He was 87 years old.

Less than a month before, he had been on the roof of the new Dayton Newspapers building for its dedication. His nine-year-old grandson, Jim Kennedy, raised the American flag over the new facility.

Although in failing health, the governor continued to come to the office. During a visit July 10, he fell to his knees as he was stepping from an elevator onto the floor of the *Dayton Daily News* editorial department. People with him quickly pulled him to his feet, and took him around the corner to his office.

He told his secretary, who was behind him, "You pushed me."

Dayton Newspaper executives Bob Snyder and Bob Sherman took Governor Cox out to Trailsend in Snyder's car. "He didn't say a word during the ride," Sherman said, "but when we got to Trailsend he stepped out of the car, straightened up and walked right into the house. I remember there was a nurse there waiting for him."

A massive stroke from which he never regained consciousness followed two days later.

Three generations gathered for the 1957 dedication of the new *Dayton Daily News* building: Jim Cox Jr., Gov. James M. Cox and his grandson, Jim Kennedy. The company's founder died less than a month later.

Daughter Barbara said her mother telephoned her in Honolulu, and said, "Daddy's had a stroke and is in a coma. Come as quickly as you can, but you don't have to panic because the doctor said he won't go for several days."

"Oh, my God," Barbara said, "I went to get Jimmy out of camp, and we flew out of Honolulu. There weren't any jets in those days. We changed planes in California, but because of an engine problem, we had to land at Denver.

"I went to another airline and said, 'I must get home; my father's dying.' They accommodated me, and we finally made it to Dayton. When I arrived at Trailsend, I ran up the stairs to Daddy's room, only to have the doctor tell me, 'He waited for you. He just died.'"

With him at the time of his death were his wife, Margaretta; son, James M. Cox Jr.; daughter, Anne Cox Chambers and Dan Mahoney Jr.

Ohio Governor C. William O'Neill ordered state flags lowered to half-staff. Daytonian Charles F. Kettering, General Motors' genius-inventor, said, "There are many cities in this country that will feel this very greatly because wherever there was a Cox newspaper, there was a Cox influence. No one can evaluate the great loss to this community and this country in the death of Governor Cox."

In Washington, old friend Sam Rayburn of Texas, speaker of the House of Representatives, stepped down from his speaker's chair, and, in a voice barely above a whisper, said: "Governor Cox was a dear friend of mine for many years. He was one of the grandest men I have had the privilege of knowing."

In his will, Governor Cox urged his trustees and heirs to show "unfailing devotion to the best interests of those communities wherein my papers are located. These papers have developed until they occupy an influential position.

"As such, the power that they have should be exerted for those who have made possible their growth — the best people of all classes. The working people, by their numbers, have been a tremendous factor behind these papers in many an emergency, and I ask my trustees and children to recognize this debt."

Trailsend was sold in 1958. Two and one-half years later, Margaretta Cox, the governor's wife of 40 years, died tragically in a fire at her residence in Oakwood, a Dayton suburb. At the time of her death, she was Montgomery County chairman of the Citizens for Kennedy and Johnson.

PART TWO

The Growth Years — 1957–1988

The New Boss

After serving in the shadow of his father for almost 30 years, Jim Cox Jr. moved easily into the position of leadership with the family-owned Cox organization.

He already had direct responsibility for the company's radio and television stations, and played a growing role in watching over the seven Cox newspapers.

It wasn't long before many company executives, first in conversations with each other, and later with him, referred to Jim Cox simply as "the boss."

It was not often that Jim Cox defied his father, but one of the times he did was when he joined the United States Navy in 1942. He was 39 years old, but he didn't want World War II to pass him by. An aviation enthusiast and pilot, he served in

the Naval Air Corps. He was discharged with the rank of lieutenant commander in 1945.

He came home to find television about to burst on the scene. Although his father remained a doubter to the end, Jim Cox persuaded the governor to go ahead with television stations in Atlanta in 1948 and Dayton in 1949.

Leonard Reinsch, who had worked closely with Cox since 1934, would find attractive broadcast properties and bring them to the boss, with a recommendation for acquisition. One such property was WSOC TV-AM-FM, Charlotte, which was sold to the Cox interests in 1959 for $5.6 million.

In October 1962, a major step was taken by Cox and Reinsch, although it didn't appear to be so important at the time. However, it was a step that would have a dramatic effect on Cox prestige and prosperity — now and far into the millennium.

At Reinsch's urging, Cox approved the acquisition of community antenna television systems serving Lewistown, Lock Haven and Tyrone in the valleys of central Pennsylvania. Combined, the three systems had 11,800 subscribers. The cost was $660,000.

Amusingly, the minutes of the meeting in which the acquisition was approved state: "It appeared that this type of activity had matured enough to indicate its financial soundness and continuing place in the broadcast industry. It was felt that the company should enter this field in order to keep abreast of current conditions, including a possible place in the pay-television picture."

The first cable systems were installed in areas where the terrain made it difficult to receive a satisfactory picture from a television station. A wider selection of channels

Cox Broadcasting Corporation was honored in 1969 for community service and leadership. Chairman James M. Cox Jr. (L) accepted the "Salute to Industry Award" from Ed Sullivan, general manager of the Regency Hyatt House.

was an added attraction. Reinsch believed these two factors — better reception and more channels — would sell in metropolitan areas, no matter what the terrain.

Reinsch and the boss decided to take all the broadcast properties into a separate, publicly owned company. In September 1963, Reinsch hired Cliff Kirtland to be the financial officer for that project. Kirtland, a certified public accountant, had been in broadcasting since 1954.

"Before I was hired," Kirtland recalled, "Leonard said I had to go to Dayton to meet Jim Cox. We had a nice lunch, and he suggested I meet with Ray Sadler to talk over some financial ideas of mine. (Sadler had been a financial adviser to both Cox and the governor before him.)

"Well, I passed the Dayton test and was hired. I must say that Jim Cox was very kind to me, as everyone said he would be. I've never known a kinder, gentler and more wonderful guy than Jim Cox."

On February 6, 1964, Cox Broadcasting Corporation was formed with an original capitalization of two million shares. Cox stock was admitted for trading on the New York Stock Exchange on July 17, 1964. Cable television also was part of the new company.

White Columns in Atlanta, home of WSB TV-AM-FM, became the headquarters of Cox Broadcasting. Jim Cox was chairman of the board and Reinsch president and chief executive officer. Other officers included vice presidents Marcus Bartlett and Frank Gaither, both WSB veterans, and secretary-treasurer Kirtland.

Many television operators viewed cable television as a threat to commercial broadcasting, but Reinsch reminded them that radio did not replace newspapers, and that television did not replace radio.

Among the corporate officers responsible for directing CBC's growth in the early years were, circa 1970, (L-R) Ray Tucker, controller and assistant treasurer; Frank Gaither, executive vice president of broadcasting Marcus Bartlett, executive vice president of non-broadcasting operations and Cliff Kirtland, executive vice president, secretary and treasurer.

"We believe competition fosters excellence," Reinsch said. "By embracing new technology and new methods we learn to serve the public interest better. The communications business is the most exciting business in the world, and we'll be in the forefront of any development in the industry."

Another major player, Henry Harris, joined Cox Cable Communications as business manager on April 1, 1966. At that time, there were 20 systems — under various ownership arrangements — in Pennsylvania, Ohio, Oregon, Washington and California, with some 50,000 subscribers.

On the same day Harris started to work, the Federal Communications Commission issued a report that in essence, froze expansion of the business for the next five years.

"They were trying to protect the broadcasters," Harris said, "who felt that cable would be detrimental to their growth. As you can imagine, my first five years were less than exciting.

"Cox knew the freeze was coming, and they were building cable as far and as fast as they could, particularly in San Diego, which was the company's biggest system. Because we did all this building ahead, we were able to take the system from 23,000 to about 55,000 customers.

Henry Harris had the unenviable job of serving as business manager and then president of publicly traded Cox Cable Communications, Inc. during a government freeze on development in the late '60s.

"However, because of the freeze, we ended up with a situation in 1966 where literally a guy on one side of the street had cable, and the guy across the street did not. A California congressmen, many of whose constituents lived on the wrong side of the street, was as instrumental as anyone in getting the freeze lifted in 1972."

In 1968, Cox Cable Communications became a public company. First traded over the counter, it later moved to the American Stock Exchange. A majority of the stock was held by Cox Broadcasting Corporation. Harris became president of Cox Cable Communications in 1970.

On December 16, 1971, he told the New York City Society of Security Analysts: "Cox Cable is now the second largest company in the cable television industry, currently operating 32 systems serving more than 239,000 subscribers in 50 communities in 14 states. In the last three years both our revenues and the number of subscribers on our systems have increased more than two and one-half times, and this despite a continuing freeze by the federal government on development."

Despite his deep interest in broadcasting, Jim Cox kept a close watch over his newspapers. Jim Fain said Cox had the fastest mind he ever encountered. "A conversation with him moved on seven-league stilts," Fain recalled, "jumping quickly from subject to subject, not because of disjointedness, but simply because he understood everything you were trying to tell him with just a phrase or a sentence.

"He visited all his papers often and invariably made time for at least one lunch with me when he was in town. In about 45 minutes, he would cover the waterfront. An update of all the community problems. Major national and international questions. Local politics. Personnel in the newsroom. Circulation. Just about everything in the compass of my job and of things outside that interested him about which he wanted opinions and information.

"The boss had guts and wisdom, along with a tremendous sense of humor. He could speak eloquently with his eyes, often with an amused skepticism when he thought the speaker was being carried away.

"He is the man who stood by me in all the waves of controversy, who never flinched when some of the crusading positions of the *Dayton Daily News* threatened its community support and his fortune."

His support for his young lieutenants also was unflinching. As the newly appointed managing editor of the *Daily News* in late 1959, this writer found that out early. Barely 33 years old, I was just finding my way around my office when a syndicate salesman dropped by.

These folks were the troubadours of the business, traveling from newspaper to newspaper, singing the praises of their wares, which included everything from comics to columnists. This particular peddler's opening gambit was, "I have a feature here that I am so excited about I have had trouble sleeping nights."

After looking over this insomnia-causing item, I decided it was not for us. When I didn't respond right away, the syndicate person said, "Young man, as a new managing editor, you have to learn to make decisions."

"I just made one," I told him. "Get out of my office!"

He left in a huff, his parting words being, "I'm going to write to Jim Cox about this. You're going to be sorry for the way you treated me."

Weeks later, the boss sent me a letter the guy had written him. Mr. Cox had drawn a large question mark on the envelope. I sent back a memo, explaining what had happened. The next day, I received this answer:

"Dear Chuck, you were much more courteous to this jerk than I would have been. . . . Let's wish him well in his happy outlook on life."

In Atlanta, Jack Tarver said the boss roused quickly to anger when the independence and editorial integrity of his beloved newspapers were under attack. Then, Tarver said, he could be fiercely protective in defense even of a liberal editorial position with which, as a lifelong conservative, he reserved the right privately to disagree.

"Our first obligation is to our readers," he reassured a recently appointed young publisher (Tarver) in the early 1960s, following a belligerent visit from a delegation of the city's fat cats protesting Page One coverage of the then-widespread sit-ins and demonstrations in the civil rights era.

"Tell those guys to go to hell," he said. "It's a newspaper's job to print the news."

CBC President Leonard Reinsch foresaw the potential of cable, and the company was one of the earliest broadcasters to embrace the new technology, in 1962.

The Tiffany of Auctions

It was a rainy September day in 1946, when Manheim Auction held the nation's first autos-only sale in the heart of the Pennsylvania Dutch country.

Thirty-three automobiles were put on the block. About one third of them belonged to Arthur Walters, a Lancaster used car dealer and one of Manheim's five founding partners. The next sale offered 70 cars.

There were no employees. Besides Walters, the other partners were Jacob H. Ruhl, an insurance executive in Manheim; B.Z. Mellinger, a New Holland Ford dealer; Paul Stern, a Chrysler dealer in Manheim and Robert Schreiber, a used car dealer in Salunga.

Each of the founding partners invested $5,000 in the business. The first auctions were retail, which had the problems of bad checks and buyers changing their minds. The owners decided on wholesale auctions for dealers only, and named Ruhl the full-time manager.

Walters said, "We had to figure out from one sale to the next what would work out best. We made sure we didn't favor large dealers over smaller ones, or buyers over sellers. We founded the auction on honesty, integrity and courteous, helpful employees. Manheim has always provided a kind of trust that is not often found elsewhere."

Within a couple of years, Manheim was selling 200 cars a week, and the business was growing 35 to 50 percent annually.

With the accumulation of profits, the company in 1965 paid $1 million for a small auction at Bordentown, New Jersey. Two years later, an auction at Fredericksburg,

Manheim, established in 1945, was a pioneer among auto auctions, as well known and respected in that industry as Cox was in media.

Virginia, was acquired.

Warren Young, who later would become president of the Manheim Auction Group, was office manager at Bordentown. He said Manheim moved cars to be auctioned through three sales lanes. "Our auction at Bordentown had two," he recalled, adding, "I think at that time there were only a half-dozen auctions in the whole country that had three lanes, and none more than that. So, Manheim was a big deal."

After the death of one of the investors in 1968, Walters and Ruhl, who were now running the business, considered taking the company public on the American Stock Exchange, when they were approached by Cox.

Jake Ruhl (at mike) was a founder and the first president of what is now Manheim Auctions, Inc. To his left is another founder, Art Walters. Fritz Cassel (second from left) was the first employee.

Cliff Kirtland, vice president-finance of Cox Broadcasting Corporation at that time, said, "We had never heard of Manheim until Gene McDonald told us it might be for sale through an investment banker in Philadelphia. Gene was the top guy at Cox-owned National Auto Research Publications, publisher of the *Black Book* used car price guide. I looked at the numbers, and they looked pretty good.

"We had certain criteria for acquisitions. Manheim looked like a pretty good business. We wanted a company which emphasized service, not inventory, with low labor content, high operating margins and good growth potential, and Manheim certainly met our criteria.

"And so we had a preliminary agreement with Jake Ruhl to buy the company for $6 million. But before we could close the deal, we had to run it by Jim Cox. Leonard Reinsch and I arrived in Dayton fairly early in the morning and met with Jim, who apparently had had a rough night.

"So Leonard says, 'Jim, we have this wonderful acquisition we want to discuss with you. It's a wholesale auto auction business.'

"'An auto auction business,' Cox said.

"Leonard and I just shrank in our seats and listened to the tirade. Jim finally calmed down and said, 'All right, you guys, get out of here. Go make that stupid deal.'

"Leonard had a way with Jim. If Leonard said, 'I really want to do this,' Jim would finally say okay."

In a 1969 speech, Reinsch said, "I am sure that some of our friends raised a quizzical eyebrow when they heard we were getting into the auto auction business. But let me assure you that results in this division during the first six months as a Cox Broadcasting Corporation operation have confirmed our original evaluation of this relatively new industry as one with an impressive earnings potential.

"The auto auction business today is a fast-growing sub-industry in which more than

a million dollars a day will change hands on large, efficient lots featuring closed-circuit television, walkie-talkies, air-conditioned lounges and simultaneous operation of five or more sales lanes."

Despite what Reinsch said, he had trouble convincing security analysts to give the auto auction business much weight when it came to evaluating Cox Broadcasting stock, and it bothered him greatly.

Young, who is now retired, said, "When Cox bought Manheim, I came along for the ride." He laughed at the reaction of some Cox people when Manheim was acquired, saying, "We were black sheep. We didn't want to contaminate the rest of the company."

In the early days, almost all cars came from used car dealers, but that changed dramatically. Young estimated that currently about 60 percent come from dealers, with the rest made up of fleet, rental and leased cars.

"We've always been the biggest in the business, from the beginning to now," he said. "In 1966, we did the first factory sale for American Motors. A few years before that we began reconditioning cars. We clean up the cars and do minor body work, but we don't get into major mechanical repair."

Manheim pioneered the systems of lights that have become standard at all auto auctions. A green light means a car is in good condition; a yellow indicates there is a problem that will be announced; and a red means the car has a serious problem.

Young, who was president of Manheim from 1975 to 1992, said, "I am very proud of setting a base and helping build the company. I hired good people, who were always concerned about the bottom line. Most of those people are still here. That's my legacy."

Darryll Ceccoli, chief operating officer at Manheim, started his career as an auctioneer, selling cars, along with livestock and farm equipment, on weekends in central Pennsylvania.

"I used to go to Manheim auctions back then," he said. "It was the Tiffany of auto auctions, and still is for that matter. It was like a golfer going to the Masters. Because I got to know their people, Manheim hired me in 1975, and I was sent to Bordentown.

"It was wild and woolly in those days, with even a few fistfights, but now we have a process called arbitration. If you buy a car, and don't think it was represented properly, you can file a claim with us and we will check it out."

Darryll Ceccoli, currently chief operating officer of Manheim Auctions, started as an auctioneer and later managed NADE in Bordentown, N.J., one of the three original auctions.

Ceccoli said that, of the hundreds of auctioneers who have sold cars for Cox (they are all independent contractors) many utilize different styles. "A lot of them have gone to school to learn their trade," he said. "They talk very fast, giving the price they have and the next price they want.

"They also use filler words, and the whole thing takes on a certain rhythm, which goes something like this:

"'I've got $2,000; would you give $2,100? Would you bid $2,100? Now I've got $2,100; who'll bid $2,200? I'm looking for $2,200; who's going to give me $2,200,' and so on.

"A good auctioneer will sell a car every 45 to 60 seconds. Remember, an auction is the only forum where you can actually get more than you are asking for."

Francis L. "Fritz" Cassel, 89, Manheim Auction's first full-time employee, died July 23, 1997. He went to work for Manheim's founding auction in Manheim, Pennsylvania, in 1957, where he later became general manager. On the occasion of Manheim's 50th anniversary in 1995, Cassel made the following comments:

"We stressed quality cars. We gave dealers what they were looking for, service and equal treatment — and they had confidence in us. Tell it as it is, and be courteous. I think it was Henry Ford who said, 'You don't earn a reputation by what you do tomorrow. It's by doing what you do at the present time.' You have to build confidence. You have to build good will. If you, through your employees, give the kind of service that a person should get when he attends the auction, then he'll be back.

"Representatives from Cox told us, 'Don't expect us to tell you fellows how to run your business. You've been successful. You know how to do it, so do it.'

"I never thought the business would be this big. It's amazing to me how big it has gotten. As long as I have known Manheim, it has been a place where a dealer can get fair treatment whether he's bringing in one or 20 cars."

Trouble in Dream City

The Miami paper's former home regained life in the early 1960s as a processing center, known as Freedom Tower, to thousands of Cuban refugees fleeing Fidel Castro.

Until the second world war, the *Miami Daily News* was the leading newspaper in town, and was making money. During World War II and the Korean War, the paper was forced to cut news and feature coverage because of newsprint shortages. Some mills allocated only a fraction of the paper's requirements.

Their only competitor, the Knight-owned *Miami Herald*, was able to obtain a much larger percentage of its newsprint needs. As a result, the *Herald*, over time, seized a commanding position in the market.

From 1939 through 1947, the aggregate net profit of the *Daily News* was $2,728,261. Commencing in 1948, however, the paper suffered an unbroken string of losses.

The red ink flowed slowly at first, but it soon turned into a torrent. In an effort to make a statement and show Miamians the newspaper was in town to stay, Jim Cox Jr. authorized the construction of an expensive new building on the Miami River.

The historic *Daily News* tower, a 279-foot Miami landmark since 1925, was sold for $1.25 million, and the paper moved into its fancy new quarters on October 20, 1957.

Now deserted, the *News* tower was called by one journalist "the dowager of the boulevard." But dramatic changes in the Cuban government soon would bring new life to the building.

Howard Kleinberg, long-time employee of the *Daily News* and later editor of the paper, wrote, "In 1960, Cuban refugees fleeing Fidel Castro began pouring into Miami. The temporary processing center at Miami International Airport could not handle the volume and a new center was sought. That center turned out to be 'the dowager of the boulevard.'

"It also was given a new name — Freedom Tower. The first four floors were leased by the U.S. Department of Health, Education and Welfare. Each month, hundreds of new refugees arrived at the Tower for processing. They got there either through the Freedom Airlift or on leaky boats — much as did Haitians who began following the Cubans in to our shores a decade later.

"It is estimated that between 1962 and 1974, a total of 463,854 refugees passed through the Freedom Tower."

The *Miami Daily News* moved into its new building on October 20, 1957. Just months earlier, William Calhoun Baggs was named editor of the paper. The newsroom was overhauled and Jim Bellows, who had once been news editor of *The Atlanta Journal*, was hired from the *Detroit Free Press* to be managing editor.

Baggs was a piece of work. Kleinberg described him as "a Georgia boy with a crew cut and a permanently wry smile."

"To those of a more recent generation," Kleinberg said, "the Bill Baggs name is only that which attaches to Cape Florida State Park on Key Biscayne. But to those who knew him, who loved him, or who hated him, Bill Baggs was a giant."

Baggs' letter of application for a job on the *Daily News* is a classic, and is treasured by those fortunate enough to have a copy. From Greensboro, North Carolina, he wrote on February 20, 1946:

"The unbearable chills and nasty attitude which have resulted from this present winter blast is the prompting point of this letter, purpose of which is to be gainfully employed in that section of the country where a high temperature reading is a constant of the climate.

Howard Kleinberg, an editor of the *Miami Daily News*, turned his series of history columns into a book, *Miami, The Way We Were*, in 1985.

"The Miami area is not unfamiliar to me. Upon my return from overseas duty as a flying officer in the Army, I had the unquestionable pleasure of loafing about the redistribution center for some three months, and was later assigned to the Boca Raton Army airfield for some six months. After such orientation, there remains no doubt in my mind that the South Florida section would be an enjoyable place to live.

"I have not written to your journal's adversary, the *Herald*, because the late hours which are demanded do not appeal to my wife or to me. It seems to me that I have forever been toiling on a morning sheet, and this irregularity has been preying on my conscious of late. I would like to be employed in what are considered normal hours.

"My private life does not menace or interrupt my profession during employment hours, and after such periods of working, I regard my private life as my own concern and no one else's business. I am happy, and believingly permanently, married."

The *Daily News* managing editor turned him down with the standard reply, "We shall keep your letter on file for consideration in case of a future vacancy." However, within a year, Baggs was working at the paper as a reporter.

Don Wright, Pulitzer Prize-winning editorial cartoonist, shifted to Cox's *Palm Beach Post* after the *News* closed.

One of the first things Baggs did as editor was to change the name of the paper from the *Miami Daily News* to the *Miami News*. The Baggs-Bellows combination energized the newspaper. Talented reporters and columnists were recruited and the editorial product improved markedly. Baggs called Bellows the "blue darter" because of the way he raced around the newsroom.

The *News* had been honored with its first Pulitzer Prize in 1939, when it was awarded the Gold Medal for Public Service. A campaign against three corrupt city commissioners had forced their recall in 1938.

In the Baggs era, *Miami News* reporter Howard Smith in 1959 won the Pulitzer for national reporting for a series on the plight of South Florida's migrant workers. Another Pulitzer, this one for international reporting, was awarded to the *News* for its coverage of the Cuban missile crises.

In 1966, Don Wright was honored with his first of two Pulitzer Prizes for editorial cartooning. Wright, who started at the paper as copy aide and subsequently was a photographer, photo editor and cartoonist, became a nationally acclaimed cartoonist and is widely syndicated.

Despite these honors and a crackerjack editorial operation, the *Herald*'s growing dominance in circulation continued to attract the bulk of the market's advertising. It

was like a round robin. More advertising brought even more circulation. Despite the valiant efforts by Baggs and Bellows, *Miami News* losses mounted.

Between 1948 and 1966, the overall losses of the paper amounted to $28,377,712. Approximately 75 percent of that red ink flowed in the last 10 years of the period. On December 31, 1965, the balance sheet of the *News* showed a deficit of $24,394,370. Between January 1 and May 31, 1966, the paper lost an additional $483,588.

The Miami problem also was putting a terrible strain on the bottom lines of Cox newspapers in Atlanta, Dayton and Springfield, whose income was being used to help keep the *News* afloat.

Something had to be done. The answer was a joint operating agreement between the *News* and its archrival, the *Herald*. Under the terms of the 30-year agreement, the *News* kept its name, but gave its goodwill, circulation, advertising contracts and related intangibles to the Miami Herald Publishing Company, which agreed to print, distribute, sell advertising and promote the *News*.

The *News* also was required to give up its Sunday edition, and became a six-day-a-week paper, publishing, as before, in the afternoon. Being an afternoon paper in a changing society would continue to erode *News* circulation. Because of the growth of television and the shift of jobs from manufacturing to service-oriented businesses, the national trend showed growth in the morning field at the expense of afternoon papers.

The *News* moved from its home on the Miami River and into the *Herald* building on July 29, 1966.

Meanwhile, Baggs became a player on the international scene. He and Harry Ashmore of the *Little Rock Gazette* twice made secret visits to North Vietnam on missions of peace, which were authorized by President Lyndon Johnson. According to Kleinberg, the missions were "stealthily submarined by the President and his advisers in the White House cellar."

Editor Bill Baggs broke the news to his staff, in 1966, that the *Miami Daily News* had a joint operating agreement with archrival *Miami Herald*.

Baggs also became deeply involved in the civil rights struggle, and, working in close relationship with the leaders of the Miami chapter of the NAACP, helped integrate Miami's two largest department stores.

Stricken with respiratory problems, Baggs' health declined noticeably. Alarmed, his friends and associates urged him to go home and rest, but he would not listen. Exhausted, he finally collapsed. A few days later, on January 7, 1969, he died of pneumonia. He was 48 years old.

I recall the *News* staff gathering outside the newspaper office on the day of Baggs' funeral. A light rain was falling. Jim Cox, wearing a trench coat, came out of the building, and said, "Let's go do it." We all followed him to the nearby church.

Young Dan — and Me

Following his graduation from the University of Virginia Law School, Daniel J. Mahoney Jr. began his career with the Cox organization as a police reporter at the Springfield, Ohio, *News* in 1953.

Newspapers were in his blood. His father was the long-time publisher of the *Miami News*. Those who knew both father and son said the elder Mahoney was as flamboyant as his son was soft-spoken.

Tall and slim, young Mahoney had been captain of the polo team at Yale. In 1955 he came to Dayton Newspapers, Inc., publisher of the morning *Journal Herald* and the afternoon *Daily News*, as Jim Cox's executive assistant. Some young reporters used to call him "best of breed."

But Mahoney was more than a dilettante. He believed in hard-nosed but responsible newspapers, and he glowed when they struck a blow for the public good. He had great influence behind the scenes, pushing for higher wages and improved benefits for salaried employees, which came to pass.

When Mahoney's friends at the Hunt and Polo Club and the Moraine Country Club in the affluent southern suburbs of Dayton would say that *Dayton Daily News* editor Jim Fain must be some sort of Communist because of his liberal views, Mahoney would defend Fain.

Some reporters called Dan Mahoney Jr., a former captain of a polo team, the "best of breed."

In fact, he got Fain in the Moraine Club, so its members could see that he didn't have horns. As the years passed, Mahoney's friends would say, "You know, Jim has mellowed. He's different now." Of course, Fain hadn't changed, but they had.

Fain said Mahoney was a good judge of talent, adding, "His management style was to pick good people, delegate and leave them alone."

This writer was a *Daily News* reporter when he first met Dan. After several years as a staff writer on the *Journal Herald*, I had gone to work for the *Daily News* in December 1951, and ended up covering the city hall beat for almost six years.

I became assistant managing editor of the paper in 1958, and managing editor a year later. In 1964, Mahoney asked me to come to the executive offices as assistant business manager, a newly created title in the "mahogany jungle." Assistant business manager would become the entry job to the executive suite for a number of people from the editorial department.

Bob Sherman, the business manager, was off building a newsprint mill in Georgia. He became president of Cox Newsprint, and in 1966 I was made business manager in Dayton. One of the duties of the job was negotiating labor contracts with the eight or nine unions in the plant.

In many ways, it was a thankless task. You were almost always in an adversarial position and, if you made a commitment, you couldn't change it without losing credibility, even if it was a bad decision on your part.

Many of the negotiations were as ritualistic as the mating dance of the great blue heron. I remember one that historically took more than 20 meetings between labor and management to reach agreement on a contract.

At our first meeting to negotiate a new contract, I told the union representatives, "Look, it always has taken us 20 or more sessions to get this done. We both have a pretty good idea of where we're going to end up in this negotiation. Why don't we try to wrap it up in, say, five or six meetings and save a lot of time?"

It worked. At least I thought it did. A tentative agreement was reached after seven meetings, and the union negotiators took it to their membership for a vote. It was rejected. The reasoning was: "If the company was willing to offer us this much in only seven meetings, there must be more there. Let's go back and try to get it."

So we had another 13 or 14 sessions, and, of course, there wasn't any more there. With the exception of some cosmetic language, we ended up with the same deal. But the union membership was satisfied. After all, it had taken them more than 20 meetings to wring an acceptable agreement from the company.

Dan Mahoney was named president of Dayton Newspapers in 1968, with the added responsibility for the morning *Springfield Sun* and the afternoon *News*, and I continued to negotiate labor contracts.

There was a great deal of labor unrest in the newspaper business in the 1960s and early 1970s, with new technology threatening jobs. On the management side, the new technology was desperately needed to offset rising newsprint and production costs. Also, the competition for the advertising dollar was growing more intense by the day.

Some newspaper crafts — stereotyping for one — disappeared altogether. Stereotypers cast the heavy lead press plates on giant, smoking machines that occasionally squirted hot lead on the operators. The entire hot metal process, from Linotypes to letter presses, went the way of the buggy whip.

It was a terrible dilemma, but Cox and other newspaper companies resolved many of their labor problems by offering employee buyouts and guaranteeing jobs. Many workers became proficient in new skills, but the size of the remaining production force was gradually reduced by normal attrition.

In early 1972, David Easterly, who was city editor of the *Daily News*, became assistant business manager. Later that year, he moved up to business manager as I replaced the retiring Robert C. Snyder as executive vice president and general manager of Dayton Newspapers.

Mahoney's dream was to return to Florida, where he had grown up. He used to winter in Miami and spend his summers at the family ranch in the shadow of Idaho's Sawtooth Mountains. Some of his friends said Dan seemed most at ease sitting on a horse in Idaho.

His dream was realized in October 1975, when he became publisher of *The Palm Beach Post*, *Evening Times* and *Daily News*. I succeeded Dan as president in Dayton and Easterly was named executive president and general manager.

I became a director of Cox Enterprises in 1976, and moved to Atlanta in January of the following year as president of Cox Enterprises. Easterly replaced me as president in Dayton.

David Easterly (foreground), as city editor in Dayton circa 1971, is now president and chief operating officer of Cox Enterprises.

The Green Kid in the Green Suit

Ralph Emerson McGill, a son of Soddy, Tennessee, came to *The Atlanta Constitution* from the *Nashville Banner* in 1929, to become assistant sports editor.

He arrived wearing a green suit, and McGill would later say, "I was just about as green as that suit." He forgot to ask the sports editor how much money he would make, confessing, "I was too ashamed to call back and ask."

He had been a football guard at Vanderbilt University. Newsroom jokesters would sometimes tease him, and ask, "Mac, how many games did you play without a helmet?"

McGill became executive editor of the *Constitution* in 1938, and editor in 1942, but he was not one to repose in an ivory tower and think great thoughts. First and foremost, he was reporter with a lyrical writing style, who often went to the scene of the action.

Ralph McGill's reports from his farm tour in Georgia led to his winning the Rosenwald Fellowship (1935–36).

He covered the United Nations charter meeting in San Francisco, the post-World War II war crimes trial at Nuremberg, and accompanied Vice President Nixon on his 1959 trip to Russia. Much of his reporting appeared in his daily column, which ran on the front page of the *Constitution*.

In the early hours of Sunday, October 13, 1958, the quiet of midtown Atlanta was shattered by dynamite blasts that almost wrecked the Reform Jewish Temple on Peachtree Street. The Temple and its renowned rabbi, Jacob Rothschild, had taken a leading role in the Atlanta civil rights struggle. Damage was estimated at more than $200,000.

McGill biographer Harold Martin said the *Constitution* editor returned to his office Sunday afternoon from the North Georgia mountains and "in twenty minutes of furious, uninterrupted writing, produced three typewritten pages that smoked with anger and shame."

The column, which was entitled "A Church. A School," said in part:

"Dynamite in great quantity ripped a beautiful temple of worship in Atlanta. It followed hard on the heels of a like destruction of a handsome high school in Clinton, Tennessee.

"The same rabid, mad-dog minds were, without question, behind both. They are also the source of previous bombings in Florida, Alabama and South Carolina. The schoolhouses and the church were the targets of diseased, hate-filled minds.

"Let us face the facts. This is a harvest. It is a crop of things sown.

"It is the harvest of defiance of courts and the encouragement of citizens to defy the law on the part of many Southern politicians. This too is the harvest of those so-called Christian ministers, who have chosen to preach hate instead of compassion."

When McGill won the 1958 Pulitzer Prize for editorial writing, the column was cited as an example of his work. Just a year later, *Constitution* reporter Jack Nelson was awarded a Pulitzer for his exposé of monstrous conditions at the Milledgeville, Georgia, Hospital for the Insane.

McGill's courageous stand for racial justice brought hate calls and poisonous mail. His life was threatened and, one time, there were gunshots fired outside his home. He came to be known as "the conscience of the South," and was an acquaintance of presidents and prime ministers, poets and preachers, and scientists and sports heroes.

McGill was named publisher of the *Constitution* in 1960, but he continued to write his front-page column. Eugene Patterson, a former *Atlanta Journal* editorial writer, succeeded McGill as editor of the *Constitution*.

McGill's 1958 Pulitzer Prize was based, in part, on his column "that smoked with anger and shame" over the bombing of the Reform Jewish Temple in Atlanta. A detective examines the ruins.

Patterson, a member of the United States Civil Rights Commission and a vigorous advocate of racial justice, won a Pulitzer Prize in 1967 for editorial writing. He resigned from the paper a year later, following a dispute with General Manager Jack Tarver. Patterson moved on to become managing editor of the *Washington Post* and chairman and CEO of the *St. Petersburg* (Florida) *Times*.

"Ralph was a most unusual guy," Tarver said. "He used to visit me when I was in Macon, and say, 'I'm going to get you up in Atlanta.' I would tell him, 'Ralph, I'm not sure I want to go.'

"After circumstances changed in Macon, Ralph telephoned me and said there was an opening for an associate editor's job at the *Constitution*. 'I hate to tell you,' he said, 'but $150 a week is all we can give you.'

" 'Okay,' I said, 'I'll come for $150.' When I got my first paycheck, it was for $160, so I asked Ralph what happened. He smiled, and said, 'Oh, I went to Clark Howell (*Constitution* publisher) and told him the *Journal* had offered you $160. He told me go ahead and pay you $160.' It was 1943, and that was my start."

When Atlanta's Dr. Martin Luther King Jr. was assassinated in Memphis on April 4, 1968, McGill wrote: "White slaves killed Dr. Martin Luther King in Memphis. At the moment the triggerman fired, Martin Luther King was a free man.

"The white killer (or killers) was a slave to fear, a slave to his own sense of inferiority, a slave to hatred, a slave to all the bloody instincts that surge in a brain when a human being decides to become a beast. In the wake of this disaster in Memphis, a great many such slaves must consider if they wish to continue serving their masters of fear, hate and beastliness."

Those of us attending the funeral of *Miami News* editor Bill Baggs in January 1969 found McGill inconsolable. Despite the difference in their ages — Baggs was 48, McGill was 70 — the two warriors in the civil rights battle had become unusually close.

It seemed he was having great difficulty accepting Baggs' death. "He was so young," McGill said in Miami. "What a waste, what a waste."

Less than a month later, McGill was dead. Some wondered if the burden of Baggs' death had hastened his passing. No matter, the South's journalistic giant was gone.

He died of a heart attack on February 3, 1969, two days before his 71st birthday, while he and his wife were visiting friends. Condolences and tributes came from across the nation. President Richard Nixon said:

"There is a kind of courage which not only calls forth praise from friends, but also elicits respect from adversaries. It was this kind of courage, intellectual and moral, that distinguished Ralph McGill."

Former President Lyndon Johnson said McGill's "eloquent voice was the voice of a nation's conscience. America, which needed him so badly, will miss him deeply."

Perhaps the most moving tribute came from Dr. Albert M. Davis, former president of the Atlanta chapter of the National Association for the Advancement of Colored People, who said:

"Tonight is a time of mourning for all of us. Ralph McGill was the force that changed the South. He interpreted the voice of all people who suffered, not only Negroes, but all people who wanted freedom. He was the only voice we had for 25 years.

"If anyone brought the South back into the Union, it was Mr. McGill. We call Martin Luther King a prophet, but Mr. McGill was a greater one because he didn't have to be."

"Ralph McGill was present at the inaugural ball which ushered in the first administration of President Dwight D. Eisenhower in January 1953 — just in time to handle a delicate social crisis.

"Among the celebrities at the ball was actress June Lockhart and a young executive to whom she was engaged.

"Miss Lockhart was glamorously gowned and understandably eager to be in the lead dance. The only trouble was that her date's divorce from an earlier wife had not become final, and he did not think it seemly of him to be seen on television leading the dance with Miss Lockhart.

"'Let me take your place,' McGill suggested.

"As they danced and television cameras whirred, McGill murmured to Miss Lockhart: 'In 47 states, people are seeing us and saying, 'Who is that old man June Lockhart is dancing with?'

"'But in one state, the state of Georgia, they are saying, 'Who is that beautiful young girl Ralph McGill is dancing with?'"

— *Celestine Sibley,* Atlanta Constitution

Presidential Endorsements

The 1960 presidential race between Richard M. Nixon and John F. Kennedy was the first to be held after the death of Governor Cox, who had presided over the affairs of his newspapers for well over half a century.

But now Jim Cox, a conservative, was the boss and he scheduled a meeting in Atlanta with his liberal editors in Atlanta, Dayton and Miami to discuss an endorsement. This was new. *Dayton Daily News* editor Jim Fain said he had never cleared a presidential endorsement with the governor.

In 1956, while the governor was still alive, Bob Wolfe, executive vice president and general manager of the *Daily News*, told Fain, "I want you to clear your presidential endorsement with Jim Cox."

Cox was a fan and a friend of President Dwight Eisenhower, who was seeking a second term. "I called Jim," Fain said, "and told him we were going to endorse Adlai Stevenson, and he just sort of answered, 'Well, that's okay, go ahead.'"

"McGill (*Atlanta Constitution*), Bill Baggs (*Miami News*) and I were working the phones fairly anxiously the summer of 1960, because Nixon was wooing the hell out of Jim. Politicians love to get papers that had never endorsed a candidate in their

Cox Broadcasting Corporation drew Washington's A-list to a tribute in 1970 to Georgia Senator Richard B. Russell (right), the "Dean of the Senate." Leonard Reinsch and Jim Cox Jr. flank President Richard Nixon. In 1972, Chairman Cox let newspaper editors know he preferred the incumbent Nixon over Democrat George McGovern in the upcoming election.

party. It had reached the point where Nixon wouldn't go to the bathroom without asking Jim Cox.

"In that period, Jim invited my wife, Laura, and me to dinner at his house on one of those islands between Miami and Miami Beach. While we were sitting at the dinner table, he started talking about Nixon, and it sounded to me like he was getting ready to say we were going to endorse Nixon.

"I said to him, 'Jim, if you think you are going to want to endorse Nixon, I need a little time because you can't turn editorial policy around like a ship in a bathtub.'

"And he looked at me and said, 'You sonofabitch, I haven't told you who to endorse and you're already threatening to quit.' I thought about that for a minute. I wasn't threatening to quit. I would not have quit. I would have endorsed Nixon if he told me to do it, but I would not have stayed with the paper later."

Fain reported to Baggs and McGill that things looked grim. The meeting was scheduled in Atlanta and was attended by Fain, McGill, Baggs and Jack Spalding, editor of *The Atlanta Journal*. The Republican editors of the *Dayton Journal Herald* and the *Springfield Sun* were not invited.

"Jim, accompanied by Jack Tarver, walked into the Atlanta Newspapers boardroom," Fain said, "and he's got this typewritten manuscript in his hands. He passes out copies and says, 'This is an editorial on the presidential endorsement.'

"Well, I had talked to him seriously about Kennedy. I remember one of the things I said to him was, 'As much as anything, it comes down to a question of personal character. Nixon is not a guy you would want in the next foxhole.'

"He could understand that. He was very proud of his service in the Navy, and he knew Kennedy had served honorably.

"We all flipped to the last sheet of the handout and it said Kennedy. McGill roared, 'Jim, this is a magnificent editorial!' He went on to say it was one of the best pieces of writing he had ever seen.

"I was sitting there thinking, 'Damn, are we all going to run the same canned editorial?' Baggs was thinking the same thing. We could have killed McGill.

"After he keeps buttering up the boss, I started saying that we would have to couch the endorsement somewhat differently for the Dayton market, and Baggs starts saying the same kind of thing. At that point, Jim said, 'I don't care what you say as long as it comes out the same.'"

What happened in 1972 had more serious consequences. The race was between Nixon and Democratic nominee George McGovern. Jim Cox could not stand McGovern, considering him weak and wishy-washy. The boss issued a memo, stating his preference for the incumbent President Nixon. That was not a problem for Fain and the editors in Atlanta who had already decided to hold their noses and endorse Nixon.

However, Gregory Favre, editor of *The Palm Beach Post-Times*, felt he had gone too far out on a limb with his anti-Nixon editorial position to turn back. He endorsed Nixon and resigned.

I was in Jim Cox's office when Favre's letter arrived. After reading it, the boss handed it to me and said, "Well, I respect him for sticking to his principles." He then called in his secretary and dictated a friendly response. Favre went on to become the editor of the *Sacramento Bee*.

Bay Area Bonanza

KTVU(TV), serving Oakland-San Francisco, was a choice station in a prime market and everybody wanted it. But it was Leonard Reinsch who brought it into Cox.

Reinsch, chief of all of Cox's broadcasting properties, began private talks with the station's license co-holders in 1962. They were in a bit of trouble with the Federal Communications Commission, and concerned about the license not being renewed.

Reinsch's mission was to convince them he could get the license transferred to Cox. Cliff Kirtland, Reinsch's chief financial officer at the time, said: "They decided they had better sell to somebody who could make sure the value of the license was retained.

"And so in 1963 Leonard made a deal with them to buy KTVU(TV) for $12.6 million. What a bargain! The station was an independent, which meant it had no network affiliation. The three network-affiliated stations dominated the town.

"We had trouble competing in programming. One of the early things we did was build a strong nightly news show and telecast it at 10 p.m., an hour ahead of the network stations, which helped increase our audience.

"After we bought the rights to televise the games of the San Francisco Giants and the football 49ers, our audience improved dramatically, and we were on our way to being strong competitors in the country's fifth largest market."

Just how much of a bargain KTVU(TV) was became evident a year later when the newly formed Cox Broadcasting Corporation paid $20.5 million for television station WIIC(TV) in Pittsburgh, an NBC affiliate formerly owned by the *Pittsburgh Post-Gazette* and the city's Brennen family.

The corporation's 1965 annual report noted that WIIC(TV)'s first full year of operating under Cox ownership brought about "the most productive 365 days in the station's eight-year history," as the overall viewing audience increased 13 percent.

In five years — from 1960 through 1964 — revenues from Cox Broadcasting increased from $8.7 million to more than $20 million, and its net income rose from $1.1 million to almost $4 million. Cox Broadcasting's 1966 annual report showed operating revenues of $37.7 million, of which television produced 69 percent, radio 14 percent, technical publishing 12 percent and cable 5 percent. Some of the key technical publications were Electronic Products, Industrial Machinery News Black Book, and

Televising San Francisco 49ers games put points on KTVU's ratings scoreboard. In 1998, KTVU is celebrating its 40th anniversary.

Floor Covering Weekly. Cox sold its publishing division in 1980 for $26 million in cash.

Almost 8 million black and white and 1.4 million color television sets were sold in the United States in 1964. With more than 64 million sets in operation at year's end, television had penetrated 93 percent of the nation's households.

Reinsch retired as president of Cox Broadcasting at the end of 1975, and Kirtland succeeded him. He was elected chairman of the company on June 10, 1981.

Some of the popular programs of that era were "Gunsmoke," "What's My Line," "The Fugitive," "The Andy Griffith Show," "I Love Lucy," "The Twilight Zone," "Gilligan's Island," "Bonanza," "Perry Mason," "Playhouse 90" and "Alfred Hitchcock Presents."

In 1961, WSB-TV, Atlanta, sponsored its first "Salute 2 America Parade," which became the nation's largest Independence Day celebration. It's still going strong 37 years later. Among the grand marshals in the early years were Bob Hope, John Wayne, Raymond Burr and Dr. Billy Graham.

In 1966, Cox television stations in Dayton, Atlanta and Pittsburgh were the first in their markets to originate local, live-color telecasting. KTVU(TV), Oakland-San Francisco, and WSOC-TV, Charlotte, followed with full color in 1967. By the end of that year, 11 million, or 20 percent, of the country's households had color sets.

Cox Broadcasting acquired Bing Crosby Productions (BCP) in 1967, which was in the business of making movies and television series. Kirtland said he met with Crosby for the closing.

Classic channels still run Cox's "Hogan's Heroes," produced in the 1970s.

"'Bing,' I told him, 'we've agreed on everything. The lawyers are satisfied, but there is one demand I have to make before I can sign these papers on behalf of my company.'"

"'What in the world is that?' he asked.

"'I'd like to have an invitation to the Bing Crosby Pro-Am Golf Tournament at Pebble Beach,' which he called the 'clam bake.'

"He laughed and said, 'Deal.' So I was invited there for years.

"After Bing died on a golf course in 1977, his widow, Kathy, who was the executor of his estate, telephoned one day and said she wanted to examine our books because of the Cox Broadcasting stock she had inherited from her husband.

"She came to White Columns in Atlanta, all by herself. We sat her down in an office, and gave her all sorts of ledgers and other financial information. After two hours of going over everything, she announced she was satisfied the company was being run right and departed."

Cox Broadcasting began phasing out Bing Crosby Productions in 1979 but continued to market the company's inventory. Today, classic channels still are running BCP's World War II comedy "Hogan's Heroes," and the theatrical movie "Walking Tall" lives on through television. "Walking Tall" — based on the true story of a crusading Tennessee sheriff — was so successful that it was followed by two sequels.

Rolling Your Own

For years American newspaper publishers relied almost solely on the Canadians for their most basic raw material — newsprint. Second only to payroll, newsprint is the highest cost item in the business.

The black spruce trees of Canada, with their fine short fibers, produced some of the best newsprint in the world. The sheet was pure white and without blemishes.

Because of this, Canadian manufacturers regularly established the world market price for newsprint. It seemed that whenever newspapers would come up with some cost-saving new technology, the savings would be offset by another newsprint price increase.

Southern loblolly pine, with its long coarse fibers, usually was associated with cheap paper. The pulp magazines of the 1930s and 1940s were so named because the wood fibers could be seen in the coarse, slightly-yellowish pages.

Canadian trees used in the manufacture of newsprint reached maturity in 70 to 80 years, while Southern loblolly was ready to cut in 20 to 22 years. This meant that the

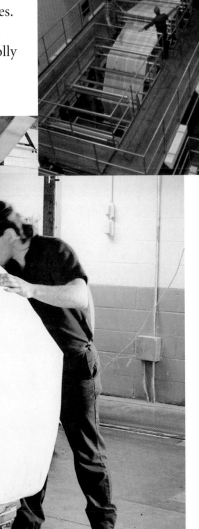

First the good news: higher newsprint usage means advertising is healthy and readership is up. But newsprint is second only to payroll as a cost.

Southern trees could be grown and harvested similar to a farm crop, but newspapers could not live with the poor quality of paper produced from those trees.

In the early 1960s Cox was in the forefront of a move to disprove that belief by making acceptable newsprint from Southern pine. Under the leadership of Bob Sherman, who became president of newly formed Cox Newsprint, a mill was built near Augusta, Georgia, in 1965–1966, at a cost of $27 million.

Carl Gross, who worked with Sherman in arranging financing for the project, said, "The mill was built next door to a plant owned by the Continental Can Company. They produced wood pulp, which they used for themselves, but they also sold us a certain amount. We also shared a power plant. It was an ideal arrangement."

The newsprint machine installed was absolutely state of the art, producing a 27-foot-wide sheet at 3,000 feet a minute. It was capable of turning out 200,000 tons of newsprint a year.

"Many of the old Canadian machines were narrow and slow," Sherman said. "By ourselves, we could out-produce four or five of them. We were the first ones to take a shot at refining the loblolly pine for quality newsprint. Some said it would be impossible. We used stone grinding and new mechanical refiners to break down the coarse wood fibers and then mixed in kraft, which is made up of cooked wood chips.

"We ended up with a stronger sheet than the Canadians, but it also was a bit coarser. We had to work to bring up the brightness because of the tar and pitch in loblolly. Nevertheless, we were the first to successfully operate a big wide machine on Southern pine."

To assure a continuing wood supply, a new company, Cox Woodlands, which Sherman also presided over, acquired 96,000 acres of timberland, which included Clarendon Plantation with its 5,000 acres and stately mansion near Beaufort, South Carolina.

"One day I invited Jim Cox to visit Clarendon," Sherman said, "telling him, 'I really want to show you this place.' After the tour, I remember him standing on the front porch and telling me: 'Bob, every Navy pilot has his own airplane and most of them have quirks about their aircraft.

"'When you had your own plane in the Navy, you could take chewing gum out of your mouth, for example, and stick it somewhere in the cockpit. That meant the plane belonged to you, so to speak.'

"Chewing gum at the time, he walked out to one of the big trees in the front yard, took the gum out of his mouth and said, 'I'm going to put my gum on this tree. This place belongs to us.'"

Cox Newsprint, however, was to have a short life. In March 1968, the mill was sold to the Abitibi Paper Company, after the Canadian newsprint manufacturer literally made Cox an offer it could not refuse. The return on the investment was huge. "They beat us over the head with cash," Sherman said.

Abitibi also signed a long-term contract to supply Cox with newsprint from the Augusta mill. The purchase included the thousands of acres of Cox timberlands, with one exception — Clarendon Plantation. Jim Cox's gum had stuck well.

Palm Beach

The Palm Beach Post was the centerpiece of a group of newspapers acquired by Cox Enterprises in June 1969.

The $25 million transaction with Perry Publications, Inc. also included the *Palm Beach Times*, the *Palm Beach Daily News*, the weekly *Delray Beach News Journal*, Palm Beach Life magazine and a substantial minority position in the *Daytona Beach News-Journal*.

It was the Cox organization's first newspaper purchase since *The Atlanta Constitution* was acquired in 1950.

Cox Enterprises Chairman Jim Cox Jr. issued the following statement:

"Becoming part of the thriving West Palm Beach region is a pleasure and a privilege for me and my associates. We will labor diligently to give the area outstanding newspapers.

"Believing that editorial freedom with responsibility is the first precept of good newspapering, your editors will strive for total objectivity in the news columns and speak from the editorial pages without fear or favor.

"There is no such thing as a home office for Cox newspapers. Each newspaper is autonomous and has its own separate and distinct editorial voice. Our newspapers here will concern themselves with the advancement of this area first, last and always. We hope to earn your respect and support."

Bob Sherman, 59, was named president of Palm Beach Newspapers, Inc. A Cox employee since 1928, he started with Cox as a salesman in the classified advertising department of the *Dayton Daily News*. Gregory Favre, managing editor of the *Dayton Daily News*, was appointed editor of the *Post* and *Times*.

The *Post* was a morning paper and the *Times* an afternoon. The primary circulation area of the two papers was in West Palm Beach and is environs. The *Daily News*, called "The Shiny Sheet" because of its heavy, slick newsprint stock, covered the social affairs of wealthy residents on the island of Palm Beach itself, who made the town their winter playground.

The *Post* traced its ancestry to the

The Palm Beach Post made headlines of its own in 1988 as the fastest-growing major newspaper in the country. The paper had 2,500 vending machines throughout South Florida.

Palm Beach County, a weekly newspaper founded in 1908. It became a daily publication in 1916 and changed its name to *The Palm Beach Post.* The *Times* began publishing in 1922.

Established in 1906, Palm Beach Life magazine billed itself as "America's Oldest Society Journal." The Shiny Sheet came along in 1907.

Jim Cox was right about there being no home office for Cox newspapers, but that was true only as far as editorial direction was concerned. Just a year earlier in 1968, a new private company — Cox Enterprises, Inc. (CEI) — had been formed to centralize the financial operations of the individual newspaper corporations. CEI officers were Jim Cox Jr., chairman; Jack Tarver, president; and Bob Sherman, executive vice president.

Also under CEI's umbrella were an Atlanta-based trucking company, which was later sold, and extensive land holdings in South Carolina, New Mexico, Texas and Hawaii.

The CEI reorganization statement said, "The financial resources and needs of the various corporations have been reviewed as a whole by management and the members of the Cox family, and there have been frequent inter-company financial transactions between them. This has proved in some instances to be awkward and disadvantageous."

It went on to say CEI would be the central organization to perform overall planning and management, which would "result in more direct and clearer lines of responsibility for each of the total enterprise's operations."

Carl Gross, a former chief financial officer of Cox Enterprises, said that when he first came to work at Dayton Newspapers, Inc. in 1965, there were no budgets or expansion plans.

"In most cases," he said, "no expansion was considered until enough cash built up to pay for it. We had good operators," he said, "but many of them were flying by the seat of their pants. Without budgets, there was no control.

"The formation of CEI created a home base where the cash could flow in, and made it possible for us to have consolidated financial statements for all of our operations. We could present these statements to the big banks and lenders and borrow the money we needed.

"That was essential when we did Palm Beach and other later acquisitions. The creation of CEI was a key part in the history of the company. That was the beginning. Had we not done that, I'm not sure what would have happened."

The only magazine produced by Cox underwent a metamorphosis in 1989 from its languid coverage of the social scene to a bold, contemporary design.

Carl Gross introduced budgeting after joining the company in Dayton in 1965.

Cable's Great Leap Forward

Explosive is the best word to describe Cox's cable growth in the 1970s. At the beginning of the decade the company had 175,000 subscribers and earned $1.3 million from operating revenues of $9.4 million.

Growth in core cable business increased Cox's revenues 10 percent over 1996 to $1.6 billion. Operating cash flow, a key indicator of financial performance, increased 10 percent over 1996 to $609.8 million.

At the second annual meeting in 1970, J. Leonard Reinsch, by then chairman of Cox Cable Communications, told shareholders that the company's belief in an expanding future for cable television was even stronger. He said the company would continue its policy of orderly development of systems and profits.

Here are the some of the highlights of what that policy produced in the seventh decade of the twentieth century:

April 16, 1970 — Cox Cable agreed to buy the cable television system in Lubbock, Texas, for $3 million. The system served 5,000 subscribers and its cable plant passed 38,000 of Lubbock's 51,500 homes. Reinsch said the company expected the system to add 2,000 subscribers a year for each of the next three years.

March 19, 1971 — Henry Harris, new president of Cox Cable, announced at the company's third annual meeting that in 1970 subscribers increased 13 percent over the previous year, bringing the total to 197,000. He also reported that Cox Cable stock would move from trading over the counter to the American Stock Exchange, beginning March 30.

March 29, 1971 — An agreement in principle was reached to acquire a cable television system serving 28,000 subscribers in Santa Barbara, California, and surrounding communities. It was believed to be the second largest system in the nation. Cox Cable operated the country's largest system at San Diego,

Cox Cable was publicly traded from 1968 to 1977, rewarding shareholders with explosive growth.

COX CABLE COMMUNICATIONS, INC.

1974 ANNUAL REPORT

which had 49,000 customers. With its 239,000 subscribers, Cox was the nation's second largest cable television firm.

January 27, 1972 — The company reported record revenues and income for 1971. Revenues totaled $13,457,437, up 28 percent from the previous year, and net income climbed to $1,362,728. More than $2.5 million was spent upgrading the company's present systems. Subscribers increased to 242,000.

December 10, 1973 — A majority interest was acquired in Greater Hartford CATV, Inc., holder of five cable television franchises in the Connecticut communities of Manchester, Glastonbury, Rocky Hill, Wethersfield and Newington, which had a combined total of 40,000 homes. It was forecast that cable would be in 50 percent of the homes within four years.

September 9, 1974 — Cox Cable of Norfolk, and Cox Cable of Portsmouth were awarded franchises to build and operate cable television systems in the two Virginia cities. Cox was a 60 percent stockholder in the two subsidiary companies. Together, the two markets had 120,000 homes. More than 1,000 miles of cable plant would have to be built. Cox Cable now had 330,000 subscribers.

September 12, 1974 — The company was awarded a franchise to build and operate a cable television system in Spokane, Washington, a city of 60,000 homes.

September 9, 1975 — Television Cable Company, Inc. was acquired for $3 million. The transaction added cable television systems in Myrtle Beach, Conway, Myrtle Beach Air Force Base and Horry County, South Carolina.

The systems served more than 7,000 residential customers and 12,000 hotel and motel rooms in Myrtle Beach resorts. The acquisition took Cox Cable's subscriber count to 367,000.

January 28, 1976 — Cox Cable reported another year of record earnings. Net income for 1975 rose to $2,849,801, an increase of 34 percent over 1974. Revenues were $29,307,442, up 24 percent.

July 20, 1976 — An agreement was reached with Davis Communications, Inc. to buy the cable television system serving Pensacola, Florida. The system, which began operations in 1970, passed 22,000 homes and served 2,000 customers. Cox Cable Communications' president Harris said the system not only had substantial growth remaining within the presently wired areas, but service could be offered to 25,000 additional homes in an area not currently passed by cable.

July 15, 1977 — Cox Cable acquired the Humboldt Video Company and its 12,000

The first remote control devices for television sets began selling in the early 1970s. Jim Robbins, president of Cox Communications, Inc., remembered that the first ones had a long, ugly cord attached to the TV.

"Continental Cable, where I worked at the time, was getting a dollar a month for them. People would trip over the cord or it would get chopped up by the vacuum cleaner, but it was $12 a year in revenue for a business selling for $4.95 a month.

"If someone wanted to be a real couch potato, we were going to make it possible for them."

subscribers in Eureka, Arcata, McKinleyville and Humboldt County, California. With 40 owned and operated systems, Cox Cable's subscribers now numbered 460,000.

July 22, 1977 — Cox Cable Communications became a wholly owned subsidiary of the Cox Broadcasting Corporation as shareholders of the two publicly traded companies voted to approve the merger.

Harris, who would continue as president of Cox Cable, and Stanley G. Mouse, a group vice president of broadcasting, were named executive vice presidents of the corporation.

January 6, 1978 — In a special referendum, Cox Cable won the right to build a cable television system in Cedar Rapids, Iowa. Iowa was one of several states that required a vote of citizens to grant a cable television franchise. With 37,000 homes, Cedar Rapids became the second major system that Cox Cable would develop in Iowa. The company presently provided service to more than 12,000 customers in Davenport and Bettendorf.

February 17, 1978 — The Larry Campbell family of Roanoke, Virginia, became the company's 500,000th cable television customer. The Campbells, new subscribers to the Cox-owned Roanoke Valley system, were presented with a color television set. In making the announcement, Harris observed that Cox Cable systems ranged in size from a 900-subscriber system in Michigan to the largest system in the nation — Mission Cable in San Diego, which served 150,000 customers.

Up front for Cox Cable's 1970 shareholders' meeting were Chairman Leonard Reinsch, Executive Vice President Marcus Bartlett and Vice President and Treasurer Henry Harris.

March 20, 1978 — The company announced the acquisition of an 85 percent interest in Cable Systems of Louisiana, which held the cable television franchise for the unincorporated areas of Jefferson Parish, which was adjacent to New Orleans. The franchise area contained 130,000 homes, and it was the principal suburban bedroom community of New Orleans. Harris estimated it would take 1,000 miles of plant to completely wire the parish.

June 1, 1978 — For $8 million cash, Cox Cable purchased the University City Television Cable Company, serving 26,000 customers in Gainesville, Florida, and surrounding areas.

July 12, 1978 — After examining proposals from seven cable television companies, the city council of Fort Wayne, Indiana, voted to award a franchise to build and operate a cable television system in their city to Citizens Cable of Fort Wayne, an 80 percent-owned subsidiary of Cox Cable.

November 10, 1978 — Residents of Yakima, Washington, voted a special referendum and selected Cox Cable over four other applicants as the company best qualified to construct and operate a cable television system in their city. With 44 franchises in 17 states, Cox Cable had 572,000 subscribers.

December 11, 1978 — Beating out five competitors, Cox Cable was awarded a cable franchise by the city council of St. Clair Shores, Michigan. The Cox bid proposed building a 184-mile, 35-channel cable system that would pass all 26,000 homes in the city.

April 4, 1979 — Cox Cable of Oklahoma and Pan Oklahoma Communications, 80 percent-owned by Cox Cable Communications, were selected by Oklahoma City voters to develop cable television systems in their city. Responding to the Oklahoma City Council's request for a proposal that would divide the city into four quadrants, Cox Cable of Oklahoma won the right to develop cable in three sections.

Pan Oklahoma Communications, formed to provide local minority ownership of a cable television system, would provide service to the remaining fourth of

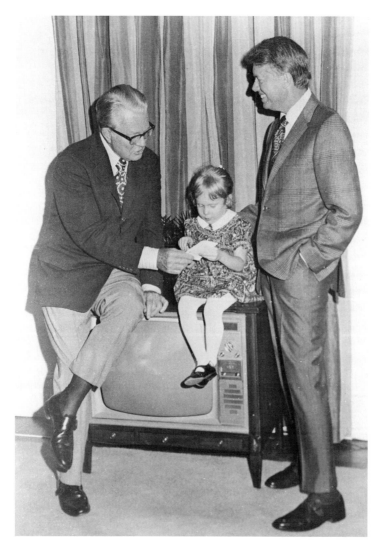

In 1971, Georgia Governor Jimmy Carter was present when the Governor's Mansion was connected to Cox's Atlanta cable system. CCI Chairman Leonard Reinsch presented a cable channel guide to four-year-old Amy Carter.

Oklahoma City. When completed in 40 months, the 35-channel network would be one of the nation's largest, comprising more than 1,800 miles of cable plant and passing 160,000 homes.

October 19, 1979 — Eastbank Cable TV, Inc. was purchased, giving Cox Cable 9,000 new cable subscribers in Harrhan and Kenner in Jefferson Parish, Louisiana. Cox now had 670,000 cable television customers in 19 states.

Harris left Cox Cable Communications in 1979 to form a new cable company, MetroVision, Inc., for the Newhouse organization.

A Voice in the City of Angels

Cox Broadcasting announced in July 1972 that an agreement in principle had been reached to buy radio station KFI-AM, Los Angeles, the most powerful clear channel station in the West.

Approved by the Federal Communications Commission in April 1973, the transaction was completed the following month when Cox handed over $15.1 million to the trustees of the Earl C. Anthony Trust.

KFI, a 50,000-watt powerhouse serving the vast Los Angeles metropolitan area, was a radio pioneer, having gone on the air on April 16, 1922. A 1972 article highlighting 50 years of KFI said:

"Jack Benny, Amos and Andy, Fibber McGee and Molly, Burns and Allen, Edgar Bergen and Charlie McCarthy, Bob Hope, Ed Wynn, Red Skelton, Rudy Valley, Jimmy Durante — and more — the biggest names in show business, some of the greatest stars of all time, claimed their fame through radio. And KFI was the station that beamed these stars when they shone brightest to all of Southern California.

Jim Wesley reported for WSB in 1957. In 1972, he headed Cox's new Los Angeles station, KFI.

"Early radio listening offered many other unexpected pleasures. Sometimes a favorite program was suddenly interrupted by another wandering broadcast. Aimee Semple McPherson, the famed evangelist, often wandered off her own station's frequency and on to programs being broadcast by KFI.

"Her rationale was, 'You cannot expect the Almighty to abide by your wave length nonsense. When I offer my prayers to Him, I must fit into his wave reception.'"

Named vice president and general manager of KFI was 18-year Cox Broadcasting veteran Jim Wesley, who had held the same title at Cox-owned WIOD-AM and WAIA-FM, Miami.

Early KFI highlights:

July 30, 1923 — Broadcast a banquet from the Ambassador Hotel, honoring Gen. John J. Pershing, World War I commander of the American Expeditionary Force to France.

February 24, 1924 — Broadcast the opera "Carmen" from the Philharmonic Auditorium.

May 3, 1924 — Had to leave the air because of an SOS sent by the oil tanker "Frank Buck." Off the air from 9:18 p.m. until 10:10 p.m.

October 28, 1924 — First continental broadcast of a speech by President Calvin Coolidge from the U.S. Chamber of Commerce building in Washington, D.C.

August 1925 — Stopped signing off during dinner period, began broadcasting continuously from 5:30 p.m. until 11 p.m.

January 1, 1926 — Broadcast the Rose Bowl game between Alabama and the University of Washington. 'Bama won 20-19.

April 12, 1926 — Began broadcasting, from 6:45 a.m. until 8:30 a.m, a morning exercise program by Hugh Barrett Dobbs, who had been lured away from San Francisco.

KFI's popular morning show hosts Al Lohman and Roger Barkley were honored in 1985 with their own stars in the Hollywood Walk of Fame for 17 years of entertaining Los Angeles listeners.

An Editor Kidnapped

Reg Murphy, editor of *The Atlanta Constitution,* welcomed a stranger into his living room on the evening of February 20, 1974, and then left with him in an automobile a few minutes later. Murphy would not return home for more than 50 hours.

Earlier, the stranger had telephoned Murphy, said he wanted to give 300,000 gallons of fuel oil to some charities, and asked the *Constitution* editor to help choose them.

Murphy had made a few preliminary inquiries and found it was possible — though somewhat improbable — that the man could get a tax break on the deal. He then invited the individual to come by his house.

"I really had no choice but to go with him," Murphy would say later, "for newspapermen have to lead open lives and be available to anonymous or strange people."

Early into the trip, Murphy realized he was not going to a lawyer's office to select charities for a fuel oil distribution. The driver asked him if he had ever heard of the American Revolutionary Army. Murphy said he hadn't.

Now his captor, the man said, "Mr. Murphy, you have just been kidnapped. We're going to straighten out this damn country. We're going to stop these lying, leftist, liberal news media."

"A nickel-plated gun lay in the elbow crook of his right arm," Murphy recalled. "He cocked it with his left thumb. I could see two cylinders on either side. I assumed that was the death weapon. He made me tape my eyes, and I assumed that might be the last time I would see."

Reg Murphy was overwhelmed by tiredness while writing a column in 1974 on his kidnapping.

Murphy endured 49 hours of terror with a captor who hated "lying, leftist, liberal news media."

Calling himself "Colonel One," the kidnapper stopped the car, tied Murphy's hands and feet together behind his back, blindfolded him and locked him in the trunk.

Over the next two days, Murphy spent most of his time bound and blindfolded in the trunk as the "colonel" drove from place to place. At one point, the kidnapper stopped and telephoned Jim Minter, *Constitution* managing editor, and put Murphy on the line to say he had been kidnapped.

At a stop in a private home, the "colonel" spoke with a female accomplice. The kidnapper then telephoned Murphy's lawyer, who wasn't in, and dictated a $700,000 ransom demand to a secretary. The kidnapper said he wanted the money in small bills.

He then sent a 900-word taped message from Murphy to an office complex mail drop, saying in the recording that he would be telephoning Atlanta residents at random with instructions on delivering the ransom.

Calls were made to three such people, who in turn called Minter with the information. One told him the location of the drop point. Another said he was to come in an open Jeep and must be dressed only in a short-sleeved shirt, pants and tennis shoes.

To prove that Murphy was alive and well, Colonel One allowed him to talk to Minter for a few seconds. Bill Fields, executive editor of *The Atlanta Journal and Constitution*, then went on television and radio to assure the kidnapper that the money was on the way.

Shivering, Minter drove off in a yellow Jeep that cold February evening to the designated drop point, where he was to unload two suitcases filled with the ransom money. Although Georgia 400 was supposed to be blocked off, he noticed what appeared to be an old farmer parked on the side of the road with the hood of his car raised.

"As I approached the drop point," Minter said, "I saw a man on a nearby hill chasing two horses. He had a bridle in one of his hands. The FBI had told the kidnappers there would be absolutely no air surveillance, but, just as I dropped off the suitcases, a twin-engine airplane swooped down, and flew right over my head at an altitude of less than 500 feet.

"I saw a car behind me stop at the drop point. I drove real slow to see if someone picked up the suitcases, but the pickup apparently happened after I turned off on the road to Alpharetta.

"I found out later that the 'farmer' parked beside the road, the man chasing the horses and the people in the airplane were FBI agents. I was also told that they had high-powered rifles trained on the drop area. What I didn't know was that the FBI had already identified the kidnappers through a tip from Miami."

Minter drove to a drug store and telephoned his wife and FBI agents at the *Constitution.* Before returning to the newspaper, he stopped at a discount store, where he bought a coat, cap and a pair of gloves for $17.

The "colonel" telephoned the *Constitution* and said, "We will release Reg Murphy around nine o'clock somewhere in Atlanta."

Still blindfolded, the *Constitution* editor was released at a motel parking lot. His captor had given him 30 cents in change and a $100 bill, saying, "I'll send you a $3,000 certified check for your assistance."

Murphy's 49 hours of terror were over. He thanked everyone who had helped in his release, and especially Jack Tarver, Atlanta Newspapers president, who had agreed to the ransom and then raised the money.

Within six hours after Murphy was set free, the FBI, acting on a tip, arrested the "colonel," William Williams, 33, and his wife, Betty Ruth, 26, at their residence in Lilburn, Georgia. According to an FBI agent, the ransom money was scattered all over the house.

The U.S. attorney's office in Atlanta said it had no reason to believe that more than two people were involved in the abduction.

Showing a macabre sense of humor, some newsroom wags said, "We know Murphy's worth $700,000. I wonder what they would pay for me?"

FBI agents counted the recovered ransom money.

Last Flight

After a lengthy illness, James M. Cox Jr. died October 27, 1974, in Miami's St. Francis Hospital. He was 71. Under his 17-year stewardship, the company grew and prospered, becoming truly national in scope.

His tenure saw the acquisition of television stations in Pennsylvania, California and North Carolina, the beginning and development of cable television, entrance into the exciting and expanding auto auction business, purchase of Palm Beach Newspapers, the creation of Cox Broadcasting Corporation as a public company and the organization of Cox Enterprises, Inc., the private company under which Cox operates today.

James M. Cox Jr. was born on July 27, 1903.

His widow, Betty Gage Cox, said one of her husband's greatest gifts was finding and supporting talented people. "He had this uncanny ability for picking the right man for the right job," an associate said.

Jack Tarver, retired president of Atlanta Newspapers as well as Cox Enterprises, said, "He was not always breathing down your neck. He was one of the best newspaper operators I have ever known, because when he called you on the phone, he got right down to the heart of things and didn't ask a lot of damn-fool questions that had nothing to do with the business at hand."

"I will always remember the last time I felt I had to debate a point with him," recalled Jim Fain, who became editor of the *Dayton Daily News* in 1953. "I knew he wasn't feeling well, and I hated having to do it but thought it necessary. He listened thoughtfully as always, his eyes probing, occasionally asking a question for clarification.

"Finally, he sighed with some resignation and said, 'I think I'll have to go along with you. My God, I've gone along with you for a long time.'

"'I know, Boss,' I said, 'and I know it ain't easy. But if it helps, I sure thank you.' God, do I thank him."

Reg Murphy, editor of *The Atlanta Constitution*, wrote: "He allowed his editors to speak to what they thought was the best interests of the community. He never would have thought of embarrassing them by explaining that many of his views were more conservative than their own.

"That is a very special human trait which many will not understand. It took a great deal of restraint and respect for others to allow his properties to be entirely free and public-spirited, rather than exercise his own prerogatives at every step of the way.

"Jim Cox did leave his editors free, and he did believe emphatically in a vigorous, community-minded communications industry. We all are indebted to him for his will to make it work."

The governors of three states where the Cox organization did much of its business paid him tribute. Ohio's John J. Gilligan called Cox "a giant in American journalism," while Jimmy Carter of Georgia said, "I deeply regret the death of a figure of great stature and influence in American journalism."

In Florida, Reuben Askew said, "Mr. Cox was one of the great men of journalism of our time. Here in Florida that independence is exemplified by the *Miami News* and the Palm Beach newspapers that carry on in the finest traditions of journalism and in the high standards that Jim Cox expected."

He had a strong interest in education. In 1960, he headed a $20 million national development fund for Wittenberg University at Springfield, Ohio, which later awarded him an honorary doctorate. His financial contributions helped create Wright State University near Dayton.

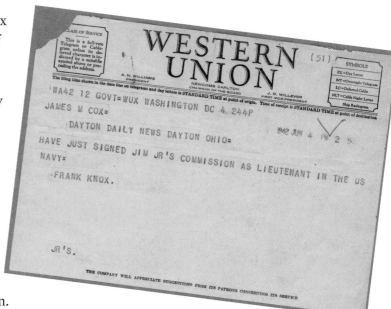

Cox maintained the family interest in the University of Miami in Florida, for which his father had signed the articles of incorporation in 1926. He later served on the board of trustees, and continued family gifts to the school. The university's $6 million science center bears his name.

An aviation enthusiast, Jim Cox received a pilot's license as a young man, and served in the U.S. Navy's air arm in World War II.

With funeral services and burial scheduled in Dayton, his body was placed on a couch aboard the company's Gulfstream jet in Miami and covered with an American flag. His Navy lieutenant commander's hat rested on his chest.

When the plane reached cruising altitude, Betty Cox said, "This is Jim's last flight. I know he would want all of you to have a drink. The bar is open."

"We had a drink and light lunch, and reminisced about the boss," Fain recalled. "It was all very nice."

A coffin and a hearse waited at the Dayton airport. Cox was laid to rest next to his father in the city's Woodland cemetery.

James M. Cox Jr. (in 1972), died on October 24, 1974.

The New CEO: Garner Anthony

Following the death of James M. Cox Jr., Garner Anthony of Honolulu and a long-time director of both Cox Enterprises and Cox Broadcasting was chosen to lead the company. The husband of Barbara Cox Anthony, he began serving on several Cox boards in 1962.

A nationally ranked tennis player, he was a college standout earlier at William and Mary, and played on the national tour in 1951, facing most of the top stars of that era. Following action as a Marine officer in the Korean War, he received a law degree from Vanderbilt University.

His father, J. Garner Anthony, who went to Hawaii on his honeymoon and liked it so much that he stayed, also was a lawyer. He served as Attorney General of the Hawaiian Territory during World War II.

Garner Anthony succeeded his brother-in-law as chairman.

"Having good people in place was helpful to me," Anthony said. "Jim Cox was very, very bright, but I don't think a lot of people appreciated that. If you could convince him that whatever it was made sense, he would go the last mile to back you up. That created a big sense of loyalty with the people who worked under him.

"He was a fiscal conservative and left the company with an extremely solid balance sheet.

"Barbie was always the one who was closest to Jim, and when somebody in the business wanted to present something that Jim was wavering about, they often would come to Barbie and try to convince her it was a worthwhile project. If she backed it, then Jim would go along.

"Jim was very sick the last two years of his life, and during that period I would go see him in Miami and talk about the business. From those meetings, I would get a sense of what he wanted to do. I would then go back to Atlanta and sit down with Jack Tarver and Leonard Reinsch and tell them Jim's thoughts.

"We really didn't have any centralized budgeting until Carl Gross started it in 1968. Before that, each operation was run like an independent fiefdom. I think, to a certain degree, that some of the people who were in charge of some of those different fiefdoms resented any kind of central intrusion.

"There were some things that were good about the independent operations, but there also were some things that weren't so good. For instance, it didn't make any sense at all for individual papers to be buying newsprint. By centralizing its purchasing and buying in bulk, we got a lot better price.

"After I became chairman, we immediately started looking to see what was out there that could be acquired. We had a substantial net worth that would support a lot of borrowing. Fear of debt had been ingrained in the organization, so it was a matter of our people understanding how the proper use of debt could bring growth."

The Nine-Bar cattle ranch near Houston was one of the first acquisitions under Anthony. The company bought the 3,200-acre property in January 1975, from Gus Wortham, founder and chief executive officer of American General Life Insurance Company, for less than $10 million.

The ranch was in Houston's growth path. Those who may have looked askance at the company's purchase of a Texas cattle ranch stopped doing so when the land was sold in 1984 to the Friendswood Corporation, builders and developers, for $56 million.

Mr. Anthony (R) and Ben Love, a director, at an annual meeting of Cox Broadcasting Corporation in the 1970s. Mr. Love — retired chairman and CEO of Texas Bancshares, Inc., Houston — is a director of Cox Enterprises.

In September 1975, Cox Broadcasting Corporation reached an agreement in principle to acquire radio station KOST(FM), Los Angeles, from the McLendon Pacific Corporation for $2.2 million in cash and notes. The transaction was completed on May 12, 1976.

Cox Broadcasting president Cliff Kirtland announced the station would operate from new modern facilities recently built for KFI, the 50,000-watt clear-channel AM radio station in Los Angeles, which Cox Broadcasting bought in 1973.

"We're pleased we'll have a companion FM radio facility to serve the vast audience in the Los Angeles metropolitan area," Kirtland said. "All Cox Broadcasting stations are characterized by high standards of public service, and we can assure Los Angeles listeners that KOST(FM) will continue in that tradition."

The year 1975 also saw the auto auctions division reach its manifest destiny with the acquisition of its first West Coast auction in Fresno, California. Darryll Ceccoli, chief operating officer of Manheim Auctions, said, "We bought Fresno, which had a good track record, to get a toehold in California and build experience with the state's way of doing business in regard to licensing, title documents, ownership certificates and methods of payment by West Coast auto dealers.

"Fresno was a good spot to do this. The auction was in a rural setting and sold mostly older cars. There weren't too many auto auctions in the West at that time. The biggest was the Los Angeles Dealers Auction or LADA, which was run by Harold Henry, a legendary figure in the business. Years later, Manheim acquired LADA.

"Using the experience gained at Fresno, we opened an auction at Anaheim, which quickly became one of our major operations."

The Heart of Texas

Eleven years after Cox entered Texas, the *Austin American-Statesman* made history with a 232-page, 2-1/2 pound supplement commemorating the 150th anniversary of the Republic of Texas.

Garner Anthony's aggressive acquisition program took Cox Newspapers west of the Mississippi in 1975. Striking deep in the heart of Texas, the company bought dailies in Waco, Port Arthur, Lufkin and Austin, the state capital.

Harlon Fentress, chairman emeritus of Newspapers, Inc., announced on October 18, 1975, that an agreement in principle had been reached with Cox Enterprises, Inc. for the purchase of the *Austin American-Statesman, Waco Tribune-Herald, Port Arthur News* and *Lufkin News.*

After hearing the papers might be for sale, Bob Sherman, executive vice president of Cox Enterprises, telephoned Pat Taggart, an old fishing buddy who ran the Fentress papers, and confirmed the report.

Sherman; Jack Tarver, CEI president; and Carl Gross, chief financial officer, soon were on their way to Waco, Texas, where Newspapers, Inc. was headquartered. After a meeting with Taggart, Cox was invited to make a bid for the properties.

Returning to Atlanta, Gross began putting together numbers. According to Gross, "Garner authorized us to bid what we thought it would take to make the deal. We were back in Waco several days later, and this time we met with Taggart and Mr. Fentress.

"We told them we liked very much what we had seen, and were prepared to make a proposal. We said that we hoped we could reach an agreement that day. After Tarver laid out our offer, they came back and told us what they were looking for, which was somewhat higher than what we had proposed.

"Finally, we agreed on their figure, and they approved our proposal to pay so much money up front, and spread the balance of the purchase price over the next 10 years.

"'Can we get this down in writing?' I asked, and Fentress said, 'Sure, why don't you walk outside and my secretary will type up whatever you want.'

"I felt we needed a memorandum of understanding, so when I told her I wanted to dictate a letter, she said, 'I don't take dictation, but if you'll talk real slow, I'll get it.'

"I took a pencil, jotted down a little outline to give me a guide, and dictated the memo to her, slowly. She typed it out, and it was perfect. She might not have taken dictation, but she sure knew how to type.

"I showed it to Tarver, Sherman, Taggart and Mr. Fentress, and they said, 'That's it. That's what we agreed to, so let's sign it,' which they did."

The memorandum of understanding was turned over to Richard Braunstein of Dow, Lohnes & Albertson in Washington, D.C., and he began preparing the final agreement, which normally takes several weeks."

On Sunday evening, December 7, 1975, Harlon Fentress was returning home from church when his car slammed into the back of a parked truck. He died in the early hours of December 9 at a Waco hospital. He was 74.

Sherman said he was concerned that Fentress' family members might change their minds and set aside the preliminary agreement. He and Gross flew to Waco the next day.

"We went to the Fentress home to express our sympathy," Sherman said, "and Mrs. Fentress met us at the door.

"'Well,' she said, 'I guess you're wondering whether or not you have a deal.'

"'No, not really, Mrs. Fentress,' I replied.

"She assured us there would not be any problems with the transaction, adding, 'My husband's word was his bond.'"

The closing took place on January 7, 1976. Anthony expressed gratification at the completion of the transaction, saying:

"These are newspapers with long histories of service to their readers and their communities. They are located in growing markets, including the capital city of one of the nation's most progressive states. We look forward to carrying on the fine Fentress tradition of journalistic excellence in Texas."

Responding for the Fentress family, Taggart said, "Our relationship with the executives of Cox Enterprises during the past several weeks has been pleasant and productive. I am confident that the steady growth and improvement of our newspapers in Waco, Austin, Port Arthur and Lufkin will continue under their leadership to the further benefit of our readers and advertisers."

On a subsequent trip to Waco, Gross said he experienced "the most embarrassing moment" of his life, explaining: "I was at the Waco office when Mrs. Fentress came up, put her arms around me, and said, 'Mr. Gross, will you promise me that there will be no liquor ads in the newspaper?'

"'Mrs. Fentress, I wish I could do that,' I said, 'but times are changing and other people don't feel that way, so I can't make that promise.'"

Sherman said she made the same request of him, saying, "As long as we've owned the Waco paper, it has never carried an advertisement for any alcoholic beverage."

"'Well, Mrs. Fentress,' I said, 'we really can't refuse them.' I sweated for a while after we ran the first one, but she never called. She was a grand lady."

Bob Sherman died after a long illness on September 19, 1998, at the age of 88.

Randy Preddy, business manager of Dayton Newspapers, Inc., succeeded Lynwood Armstrong as publisher of the *Waco Tribune-Herald*.

The combined paid circulation of Austin, Waco, Port Arthur and Lufkin amounted to 187,450 daily and 203,697 Sunday.

In 1973, Jim Fain, who had been editor of the *Dayton Daily News* for 20 years, took on a second job — editor of the troubled *Miami News*. Flying constantly between Dayton and Miami, he served in this "floating editor" capacity, as he called it, until January 1976, when he was named the first Cox publisher of the *Austin American-Statesman*.

A pair of managing editors, Arnold Rosenfeld in Dayton and Howard Kleinberg in Miami, were promoted to editor of their respective papers. Editor & Publisher magazine ran a little story, with the headline, "Two Editors Replace Fain."

Lee Hills of Knight-Ridder sent Fain a note, asking, "Are you sure two's enough?"

The Waco *(Texas)* Tribune-Herald *in September 1993 was named the winner of the Associated Press Managing Editors' (APME) national public service award for its series, "The Sinful Messiah," which reported the questionable activities of Branch Davidian leader David Koresh.*

The articles were written by reporters Mark England and Darlene McCormick, who accepted the award on behalf of the Tribune-Herald *at the APME's annual meeting in Minneapolis.*

Bob Ritter, APME president and editor of the Gannett News Service, said that of all the candidates for the annual award, the Tribune-Herald *series was by far the strongest example of public service. "Overall," he said, "we felt it was a high-quality piece of journalism that shed light on what was and continues to be an important story in the country."*

The first installment of the seven-part series ran in the Tribune-Herald *on February 27, 1993, the day before a shoot-out between cult members and agents of the Federal Bureau of Alcohol, Tobacco and Firearms. After an eight-week standoff, Koresh and most of his followers died in a fire they apparently set themselves as Federal Bureau of Investigation agents closed in on the Branch Davidian compound.*

The APME is an association of news executives from the more than 1,500 member newspapers of the Associated Press.

Pulitzer at Lufkin

The *Lufkin* (Texas) *News*, at that time the smallest Cox newspaper, won the 1977 Pulitzer gold medal for meritorious public service for its investigation of the recruitment and death of Lynn (Bubba) McClure, a 20-year-old Lufkin resident who died in March 1976, of injuries received in a Marine training exercise.

Editor Joe Murray and reporter Ken Herman were cited for their work on a series of hard-hitting stories, supported by editorials, that ultimately changed the Marine Corps.

The Pulitzer gold medal is considered the top prize in American journalism. It is awarded by the president of Columbia University on recommendation of the Pulitzer Prize board for work done the previous year. It has been called the Pulitzer of Pulitzers.

On Saturday, March 13, 1976, the following item moved on the United Press International news wire:

HOUSTON (UPI)—PVT. LYNN MCCLURE, 20, A MARINE RECRUIT FROM LUFKIN, HAS DIED AT THE VETERAN'S HOSPITAL FROM HEAD INJURIES HE SUFFERED LAST DECEMBER DURING A TRAINING EXERCISE AT THE MARINE CORPS RECRUIT DEPOT IN SAN DIEGO. A MARINE SPOKESMAN SAID THE INJURY OCCURRED DECEMBER 6 AS MCCLURE AND OTHER MARINES WERE TAKING PART IN A CLOSE COMBAT CLASS USING PUGIL STICKS TO SIMULATE BAYONETS.

On Monday morning, Murray came to work to find a man he knew from the community standing in the newsroom.

"Well, I walked right by him," Murray related, "and said, 'How y'all doin'?' and I went into my office. He followed me in and sat down and started telling me this story.

"The man talking to me was Lynn McClure's great-uncle. Lynn McClure had dropped out of high school when he was in the tenth grade. Had he stayed in school, he probably would have been put in special education for people with learning disabilities.

"The kid had been unable to hold down even the most menial job. In addition, he had been in trouble with the law from time to time, though mainly it was just misdemeanor scrapes.

"What his great uncle was telling me, though, was that somehow — the family couldn't understand how — he managed to join the Marine Corps. And somehow — the family couldn't understand why or how — he had managed to get himself killed.

"The Marines were saying it was just one of those things. It was a tragic accident, but there wasn't anything that anyone could have done to make it any different.

"Lynn McClure had gone off, joined the Marines, and, as the posters say, had become one of those 'few good men.' And he came home in a box. And the family wanted to know why. And they had questions. And they had no way of getting answers. They didn't have any power or influence, and they didn't have anybody to turn to — except their newspaper.

"I was sympathizing, and I was shaking my head, and I was telling him how sad it was. And at the same time, I probably was wondering, 'Well, I wonder how long he's going to take because, after all, I have other things to do.'

"But he made this statement, and it made all the difference in the world. He said, 'They beat that boy's brains out — literally.'

"When he said that, he made a cold chill go down my spine. It makes a cold chill go down my spine today, because we found out they did beat that boy's brains out — literally."

Murray assigned one-third of his reporting staff to cover the story. One-third was one reporter and his name was Ken Herman, who was 21 years old at the time and had been working for the *Lufkin News* for six months.

Herman, who grew up in Brooklyn and Miami, was a bulldog reporter. Murray said, "He had already proven that he had the perseverance to get on a story and stay on it until he got it."

Herman said after he was graduated from Florida Atlantic University, he wrote about 125 letters of application to newspapers, but the only one that offered him a job was the *Lufkin News.*

The day after Murray's talk with McClure's great uncle, Herman covered the young Marine's funeral, reporting that friends of the family recalled that McClure's difficulties began as early as elementary school, where he showed evidence of learning disabilities.

"Even the young man's abilities to meet the physical requirements apparently were borderline," he wrote. "He is described as being hardly five-feet, six inches tall, the minimum height for a Marine. He weighed perhaps 125 pounds."

Over the next nine months it was revealed:

McClure was improperly recruited. He attempted to join the Marines in Lufkin, but failed the written test badly. He was declared "mentally unqualified." Two months later, he took the exam a second time in Austin and received a passing grade. Although it was never proven, it was obvious that someone took the test for him or gave him the answers in advance.

Certain Marines lied in an attempted cover-up, claiming that before accepting McClure, who had a police record and had spent some time in a mental hospital, they had checked his background with the Lufkin and Angelina county law enforcement personnel. Their reports even included fictitious names of people they said they had called.

Six weeks after McClure's death the Marine sergeant who tested and recruited him was abruptly transferred to Okinawa.

The Lufkin Marine was sent to San Diego for training, and after trying to go AWOL, he was placed in a "motivational platoon," a punishment unit for problem recruits. Platoon "training" included crawling through a long ditch full of mud with buckets of water, breaking big rocks into small rocks with a sledgehammer, and jousts with pugil sticks, which are rifle-length poles padded at both ends. They were used to simulate bayonet fighting.

On December 5, 1975, McClure, wearing protective gear, which included a football helmet and a mask, was forced to fight seven other men in a pugil stick bout. A drill instructor was present, but no officer, as required by the Marines.

Eyewitnesses said McClure basically refused to fight. Goaded by the drill instructor, the other recruits pounded the Lufkin Marine from all directions. He tried to flee, finally curling up in the dirt and screaming, "God, make them stop. Oh, God, help me. Oh, God, why is this happening to me?"

When McClure was finally knocked unconscious, the drill instructor had other recruits pour a five-gallon bucket of water on him to revive him, but he never never regained consciousness. He was in a coma until the day he died.

The Associated Press, the *Washington Post* and the *New York Times* picked up on the story. In the wake of congressional investigations and hearings and inquiries by President Gerald Ford, there were trials and courts martial.

Out of all of this came changes in Marine Corps recruiting and training practices. Among the many changes, motivational platoons were disbanded; 84 Marines were appointed as company executive officers to increase supervision levels and double the officer supervision at the lowest unit levels; a brigadier general

was assigned to each training depot to enhance leadership and supervision; and psychiatric evaluations were ordered for all drill instructor students.

"Before it was over," Murray said, "no less than the Commandant of the Marine Corps would say that 1976 was a year of change for the U.S. Marines, because of Lynn McClure. And because of that, the Marine Corps was getting well. So, I guess, in the best sense, that was what it was about, finding something wrong and doing something to change it."

Joe's and Ken's 1976 investigative reporting woke up Washington and changed Marine Corps training standards.

Madame Ambassador

The White House announced April 8, 1977, that newly elected President Jimmy Carter had picked Anne Cox Chambers to be the United States ambassador to Belgium.

Mrs. Chambers, chairman of Atlanta Newspapers and a director of Cox Broadcasting Corporation, has a home across the street from the Georgia governor's mansion, where Carter lived from 1970 to 1974. She had been a Carter admirer since the South Georgia peanut farmer was a state senator.

Belgium was an important ambassadorship, particularly since the North Atlantic Treaty Organization (NATO) was headquartered at Brussels.

"It was the only place where we had three American ambassadors," Mrs. Chambers said. "I was the ambassador to King Baudouin. There also was an ambassador to NATO and another to the European Community organization, also headquartered in Brussels.

"Before I left for Belgium, Secretary of State Dean Rusk, a fellow Georgian, came to see me, and he said, 'You're the ranking ambassador and don't let those other two forget it.'

"Just representing the president of the United States in another country is quite overwhelming. It was thrilling to attend a reception at another embassy and have someone announce, 'The ambassador of the United States.'

"On Memorial Day weekend, I visited all the American cemeteries. One day, I was on my way to Bastogne, which had figured so prominently in the Battle of the Bulge in World War II. The American flag and my ambassadorial flag were flying from the front of the car.

"There were some small boys playing soccer in front of a house. They seemed too young to have even known about the war, but, when they saw the American flag, they flashed the 'V' for victory sign.

"It was wonderful to be an ambassador in a country that loves the United States so much. People would tell me, 'You saved our country twice.' I went to a doctor once for some minor thing, and, as I was preparing to leave, I asked, 'How much do I owe you?'

"'Nothing,' he said. 'I feel this is something I can do to repay what your country did for us.' There were incidents like this over and over."

Mrs. Chambers said someone asked her one time what she thought her father's reaction would have been to her being appointed an ambassador.

"I laughed," she said, "and answered, 'I think he would have been as surprised as I was.'"

As ambassador to Belgium, Anne Cox Chambers participated in the opening reception for a U.S. food exhibit in Brussels in 1977.

Pushing West

Cox Newspapers moved into Arizona in 1977 with the purchase of the *Mesa Tribune*, 15 miles east of Phoenix. Other acquisitions in what became known as the East Valley quickly followed.

The Arizona Pennysaver, a free shopping publication, was bought before the year was out. The *Tempe Daily News*, serving the community that is home to Arizona State University, was acquired in 1980, and the *Chandler Arizonan* in 1983.

The East Valley was one of the fastest growing areas in the metropolitan area. The concept was to make the Cox newspapers the newspapers of choice for East Valley residents, which in turn would attract advertising dollars.

The East Valley took on a separate identity, with an East Valley Chamber of Commerce, East Valley service clubs and so on. A central production plant was built in Mesa, and the Mesa, Tempe and Chandler papers were printed there.

In 1978, Cox made another newspaper acquisition in Texas, buying the *Longview Morning Journal* and the afternoon *Daily News*. Also included in the purchase was the Lens Publishing Company, publisher of the *Longview Shopper* and *Community News*.

The *Daily News* was founded in 1871 by James Hogg, who later became governor of Texas. The Longview papers had won numerous journalism awards over the years. In the year of the Cox purchase, the *Morning Journal* and *Daily News* received 11 Associated Press, seven United Press International and nine state awards.

Cox Chairman Garner Anthony said: "We pledge to carry on the fine tradition of newspaper excellence as practiced by Mrs. Margaret Estes and her late husband, Colonel Carl Estes, pioneer of Texas journalism. We are looking forward to knowing and working with the many fine people who produce the Longview newspapers."

Tom Meredith, publisher of *The Lufkin Daily News*, became the first Cox publisher of the Longview newspapers. Joe Murray succeeded Meredith in Lufkin.

In April 1979, Cox Enterprises bought its first property in Colorado — *The Daily Sentinel* in Grand Junction, the largest Colorado city on the western slope of the

Chairman Garner Anthony (L) and Arizona Gov. Bruce Babbitt (now Secretary of the Interior) were at the *Mesa Tribune* a few years after Cox acquired the paper in 1977.

As publisher, Jim Kennedy explained the remodeled plant and new press of *The (Grand Junction) Daily Sentinel* to Colorado Gov. (R) and Mrs. Richard D. Lamme. When Gov. Lamme finished speaking at the ceremony, he immediately was given a newspaper showing him speaking. At Kennedy's right is Chuck Glover, president of the Cox newspaper company.

Rocky Mountains. Also acquired was the *Delta County Independent*, a twice-weekly newspaper published in the town of Delta, 40 miles southeast of Grand Junction.

Jim Kennedy, grandson of the company's founder, was named publisher of the paper. He had been executive vice president and general manager of Atlanta Newspapers. Kennedy had joined the company in 1972 as a production assistant in Atlanta. He later worked at various positions, including reporter, copy editor, advertising salesman and business manager.

At the time of the purchase, the region was booming. Exxon and Union Oil were digging shale out of the mountains and extracting oil from it. It was said there was more oil locked in the shale of the mountains around Grand Junction than in all the states of the Persian Gulf.

Oil was extracted, but the cost of producing it was prohibitive. It was a dark day when Exxon announced it was pulling out. The boom became a bust, and the region was plunged into despair.

What followed became *The Daily Sentinel*'s finest hour. With Kennedy leading the charge, the newspaper became the rock of the community, elevating spirit, seeking help from the state government in Denver and, most of all, taking a leadership role in bringing new business and industry to the city.

Grand Junction again believed in itself. The shale oil mines are quiet, but the oil is still there, waiting for a technology that will make it economical to extract.

Bumper Years for Auto Auctions

In 1972, after four years of Cox ownership, Manheim Auctions — the world's largest auto auction company — sold a record 213,000 cars. Eight years later, the number had climbed to 263,624, and by 1986 that figure had more than doubled to 549,323.

This eye-popping growth came about through expansion of existing sites, start-ups and acquisitions. It is a business where Manheim collects money from both the buyer and the seller, but never owns a single car they sell.

Cox entered the auto auction business in December 1968. In those days, Manheim was a division of Cox Broadcasting Corporation. On March 3, 1969, the company bought the Kansas City Automobile Auction Company for approximately $1 million in cash, giving Manheim a strategic location for the wholesaling of used cars in the Midwest.

Also acquired in 1969 was an auto auction at Lakeland, Florida. Leonard Reinsch, president of Cox Broadcasting, noted that Lakeland is located between Tampa and Orlando, which was near the site selected for the construction of Disney World.

In May 1970, construction was completed on the Atlanta Auto Auction, a sprawling modern complex near the Atlanta airport. The new facility included three auction lanes — now 12 lanes — a registration area, executive and business offices, and a cafeteria.

An electronic closed-circuit television system was installed throughout the complex, which also featured a paved parking lot and display area that would accommodate 1,000 cars.

Acquisition of High Point Auto Auction and High Point Recon Center at High Point, North Carolina, for $1.6 million cash and notes was announced July 1, 1970. The Recon Center does not do engine work or other major repairs, but reconditions cars from an "appearance" standpoint.

Manheim acquired its ninth auto auction on August 18, 1971, when it bought Butler Auto Auction of Gibsonia, Pennsylvania, which is near Pittsburgh. The purchase also included reconditioning facilities.

The Metropolitan Milwaukee Auto Auction came into the Manheim fold in January 1972. Reinsch commented, "The Milwaukee auction is presently registering 400 cars a week. We are confident this highly industrialized area of the country will continue the growth which has characterized it in the past."

Jacob Ruhl, one of the five founders of Manheim Auctions, announced September 27, 1974, that he would retire as president of the division at the end of

Jake Ruhl was the first president of Cox's new auction business, after he and his partners sold their three auctions to the company in 1968.

the year. Warren Young, executive vice president, was named to succeed him.

In an interview, Young said, "I want employees who are bright and have common sense. Experience with automobiles, accounting and banking or auctioning helps too. A financial person with good people skills is a real find."

In 1975, Warren Young succeeded Ruhl as president and accelerated acquisitions.

Young had joined the company in 1965 when Manheim bought out his employer, National Auto Dealers Exchange at Bordentown, New Jersey.

Florida Auto Auctions in booming Orlando was acquired in 1974, and Fresno Auto Dealers Auction came aboard a year later. It was Manheim's first California auction. Cliff Kirtland, who succeeded Leonard Reinsch as president of Cox Broadcasting, said,

"With the company's 12 other auctions all in the eastern part of the United States, we hoped for some time to expand toward the West. We're particularly pleased to move into a flourishing area of California, and expect the Fresno acquisition to be the first step in an expansion program on the Pacific seaboard."

That expectation came to pass in 1976 when Manheim bought land at Anaheim and built the California Auto Dealers Exchange (CADE). Southeast of Los Angeles, Anaheim was already home to Disneyland, an American League baseball team — the California Angels — and Knotts Berry Farm.

CADE would later buy 10 acres of adjacent strawberry fields for expansion. By 1982, the

Prestigious brands, such as Rolls Royce, roll through at a Manheim "Exotic Highline" sale.

auction was averaging 1,400 cars per sale.

Establishing a presence in New England, Manheim started the American Auto Auction at Walpole, Massachusetts, in 1981. The company made two major acquisitions in 1983 — buying its first auto auction outside the United States at Toronto, Canada, and the Southwest Auto Auction at Chandler, Arizona, just east of Phoenix.

Ten-gallon hats and cowboy boots were the fashion at the Big H Auction in

Houston, which Manheim purchased for $75,000 in 1984. Only the Big H wasn't really that big. Sitting on leased land, it had several run-down buildings and low sales. At the first auction under Cox ownership, only 157 cars were registered and 53 sold.

The company immediately made moves that would permit the Big H to live up to its name. Forty-nine acres were purchased in a new suburban office park, a 29,000-square-foot building was erected and more than 2,700 parking spaces were created.

At its grand opening sale on November 18, 1986, the Big H, now billing itself as the

"The Best Little Auction House in Texas," sold 1,143 vehicles.

In 1984, Manheim held its first "Exotic Highline" sale in Atlanta, where the auction lanes were filled with cars bearing the names Ferrari, Jaguar, Rolls Royce, Porsche, Maserati and Lamborghini. Exotic Highline is a registered trademark owned by Manheim.

Don Kessler, Manheim's security chief, said, "The high dollar value of Exotic Highline units requires the auction to pay particular attention to its lot security and serial number verification procedures. During an Exotic Highline sale, we might have $12 million worth of cars on the lot. We hire extra security guards, and dealers are screened carefully."

Exotic Highline sales are held at a select group of Manheim auctions about once every quarter.

Manheim entered the Rocky Mountain West in 1985, buying the Colorado Auto Auction at Denver, which became the company's 17th auction. Denver and Colorado's growth rate in the 1970s and early 1980s had been twice the national rate.

In December 1986, Manheim bought the Imperial Auto Auction at Lakeland, Florida, which put the company into its first night-sale auction. Imperial had been selling cars at night for years, and at the time of the Manheim acquisition was the second largest night sale auction in the country.

Young said, "Imperial helps us serve a segment of the market — older model vehicles — we are not currently reaching in the busy central Florida area through our successful Lakeland Auto Auction and Florida Auto Auction of Orlando."

Lakeland Auto Auction already had acres of cars on sale day in the early '70s when Disney World was created nearby, luring even more people to the lively Florida area.

The Environment: Saving Trees

By 1976, Cox Newspapers found itself managing two crucial needs. The first was to ensure a steady supply of newsprint. The second was to find ways to save trees. Next to payroll, newsprint is the highest cost factor in the company, as well as in the newspaper industry.

In 1997, when Cox began its newsprint recycling program, it was using no recycled paper. By 1998, 45 percent was recycled.

Cox Enterprises of Atlanta, Miami-based Knight-Ridder and Media General of Richmond, Virginia, formed a partnership in 1976 to build a plant at Dublin, Georgia, that would manufacture newsprint from waste paper.

The partners created the Southeast Paper Manufacturing Company. Media General held the rights to a de-inking process that made recycling possible. Ron Wilson, who had worked for Cox in the 1960s at a newsprint mill at Augusta, Georgia, was chosen to manage the new $125 million facility.

Ground was broken at Dublin in September 1977, and Southeast began making paper in June 1979. The newsprint machine was state of the art, running a 330-inch-

Southeast Paper could produce enough newsprint annually to fill 24,000 tractor-trailers after expansion doubled capacity in 1989.

In 1986, some creative minds at *The* (Grand Junction) *Daily Sentinel* enabled schools to turn recycled copies of the *Sentinel* into cash to buy more papers and other reading material for classroom use.

wide sheet at 3,000 feet per minute. It had a production capacity of 215,000 tons a year.

"Originally," Wilson said, "the manufacturing process was to be one-third mechanical pulp made from wood chips and two-thirds recycled paper, mostly old newspapers. But during construction, the federal government put in a special investment tax credit, which said that if a recycling mill did not exceed 10 percent in wood pulp, the company would qualify for the credit. So we changed our process and limited pulp to a maximum of 10 percent. It saved the owners a great deal of money."

Cox started buying 45,000 tons of Southeast newsprint a year and, together, the other two partners purchased another 45,000 tons. The balance of the plant's capacity was sold to more than 100 other customers.

Carl Gross, senior vice president and chief administrative officer of Cox, who was later named president of Cox Newsprint Supply, a newly created division, explained: "Cox buys newsprint from a dozen or so suppliers, not just Southeast Paper. You see, we don't want to depend too much on any one mill. If there was a fire, or if the plant shut down for some reason, we'd have a problem."

As for recycling, he said, "Church groups, Boy Scout troops and schools like to use newspaper recycling as fund raisers. I also believe that more and more communities are going to require people to segregate newspapers, glass and cans from the rest of their garbage. If these things all were recycled, it would decrease by half the amount of trash that has to be disposed of in landfills."

A second newsprint machine was installed at the Southeast plant in 1989 at a cost of $392 million. It puts out a 364-inch sheet at 4,500 feet per minute and has an annual production capacity of 505,000 tons.

Cox and General Electric

Publicly traded Cox Broadcasting Corporation almost became part of the giant General Electric Company in the early 1980s, but it was not to be.

The two companies announced February 21, 1979, the signing of a definitive agreement for combining Cox Broadcasting properties with GE's radio, television and cable businesses.

The announcement said the transaction probably would not close until well after September 30, 1979, because of the need to receive government approvals, particularly from the Federal Communications Commission.

The agreement provided for a tax-free exchange of 1.3 shares of GE common stock for each share of Cox common. The parties also agreed that if the deal closed after September 30, holders of Cox common stock would receive not less than $68 nor more than $75 in GE common for each Cox share owned.

There was an agreement for slightly less money if the transaction was completed prior to September 30, 1979, but that quickly became moot.

The minimum value of GE stock traded for Cox common would be about $461 million and the maximum about $508 million. Using the closing price of GE common stock on February 20, 1979, approximately 9.66 million shares of GE common stock worth about $461.47 million would be exchanged for all the outstanding Cox shares.

The actual number of shares to be issued would be determined by the average closing prices of GE stock during a 20-day trading period immediately prior to the date set for closing the transaction.

"It was a complicated deal and it took forever and a day to get the necessary approvals through the FCC," said Garner Anthony, chairman of Cox Broadcasting's executive committee.

The Washington Post
BUSINESS & FINANCE

FRIDAY, OCTOBER 6, 1978   F1

GE and Cox Broadcasting Planning Merger

By Jack Egan
Washington Post Staff Writer

NEW YORK—General Electric Co. and Atlanta-based Cox Broadcasting Corp. announced yesterday that the two companies are entering into negotiations "of a definitive agreement for combining Cox Broadcasting with General Electric's radio-and-television broadcasting and cable-television business."

Because both companies have substantial broadcasting properties, the merger—if completed—would require the sale of three VHF TV stations, at least one AM radio station, and five FM stations to meet Federal Communications Commission ownership limitations rules.

The announcement that GE, the world's largest diversified industrial company and Cox, one of the country's most profitable and highly regarded broadcasting companies may merge came as a complete surprise to Wall Street analysts who follow the two firms. The stock deal would be approximately $450 million and reportedly would be the biggest broadcast deal in history.

There was meanwhile some speculation that a third company might come in and make a tender bid for Cox.

The rationale behind the proposed GE-Cox merger appeared to be two-fold:

• To eliminate the media cross-ownership problems for the Cox family which holds nearly half the shares of Cox Broadcasting, and also separately owns all of Cox Enterprises, which has newspapers in a number of cities, including Atlanta and Dayton where there also are key Cox Broadcasting properties.

Garner Anthony, chairman of Cox Broadcasting's executive committee, said a major factor behind the combination under consideration is "the increasing regulatory pressure on

— GENERAL ◉ ELECTRIC —
COX
Broadcasting Corporation

common ownership of different media in the same market area."

• To combine the extensive cable television operations of both GE and Cox and apply GE's financing muscle to take advantage of the fast-growing but capital-intensive cable business. GE now operates 12 cable systems

with a total of 170,000 subscribers. Cox Broadcasting through its cable subsidiary operates 44 cable systems with a total of 550,000 subscribers.

With a total of 720,000 subscribers, that would form the second largest cable television company after Tele-Prompter.

"We've looked positively at the cable business ever since the early 1960s," said Cox Broadcasting President Clifford Kirtland Jr., "and we think it's the next major evolution for entertainment in the home."

He said the two companies first approached each other a month ago and "it was as close to a mutual get-together as you can have. There was a recognition on our part that we needed to do something to relieve the cross-ownership pressure. And there was a recognition at GE that they would like to expand in broadcasting and cable."

GE Chairman Reginald Jones, prior

to addressing a special shareholders meeting for the company's 100th birthday celebration, noted that "General Electric has been a pioneer in radio and television broadcasting."

GE has had a long history in telecommunications, being responsible for some of the key technical developments that made radio possible. It owned some of the earliest broadcast properties. And, at the urging of the U.S. government, GE and American Telephone & Telegraph in the early 1920s took over the American Marconi Co. and formed the Radio Corporation of America.

But for GE, broadcasting has not been as important over the years as it has been for arch electronics rival Westinghouse, which has a very strong and profitable broadcasting division.

If the negotiations are successful

See MERGE, F3, Col. 2

The Atlanta Journal

Vol. 96, No. 158 ★ P.O. Box 4689 "COVERS DIXIE LIKE THE DEW" Atlanta, Ga. 30302, Thursday Evening, October 5, 1978

Blue Streak FINAL EDITION Latest Stock Quotations

112 Pages, 5 Sections ★★★★ Price May Be Higher Outside Rated Trading Zone 15 Cents

Cox Broadcasting Sale Planned

WSB-TV and Radio Included in $467 Million Merger With General Electric

By PAUL TROOP
Journal Business Writer

Cox Broadcasting Corp. of Atlanta and the General Electric Co. announced Thursday that their directors have started negotiations leading to the merger of Cox Broadcasting with GE's broadcasting and cable television business.

Under the preliminary terms announced in a joint statement, Cox shareholders would receive about 8.8 million GE shares currently valued at about $467 million.

Cox Broadcasting owns WSB-AM-FM-TV and a cable TV system in Atlanta, broadcast properties in eight other U.S. cities and cable systems in 43 other locations. It also operates a movie production company, a chain of auto auctions and trade magazines. It was created in 1964 from the broadcast properties owned by the late Gov. James M. Cox of Ohio and included stations in Atlanta and Dayton, Ohio. The Cox family also owns the major daily newspapers in those two cities, The Atlanta Journal and Atlanta Constitution, Dayton Herald-Journal and Dayton News.

Although separate corporations, the Cox family's involvement as directors and major stockholders in both the newspaper and radio and television companies in these cities has been the target of criticism before the Federal Communications Commission.

Garner Anthony, chairman of Cox Broadcasting's executive committee, said in a statement that a major factor in the director's decision on the merger was "the increasing regulatory pressure on common ownership of different media in the same market area."

He added that Barbara Cox Anthony and Anne Cox Chambers, the daughters of the late Gov. Cox and the principal shareholders in the broadcasting company, favor the merger with GE.

Jondell Johnson, executive director of the Atlanta NAACP, said Thursday the move will have no effect on a 1975 challenge to WSB's broadcasting license filed by the group with the FCC. The NAACP charges WSB with discrimination in employment and promotions and maintaining a communications monopoly in Atlanta.

"I will assume the FCC will not approve this transaction, because this type of transfer . . . is prohibited by FCC rules," she said.

Commenting on the joint announcement, GE Chairman Reginald H. Jones said, "General Electric has been a pioneer in radio and television broadcasting. We welcome this opportunity for GE to extend its broadcasting services by building upon Cox Broadcasting's fine record of entertainment and public service through the electronic media."

The directors of both firms authorized negotiations for a tax-free exchange of 1.3 shares of GE common stock for each of the 6.7 million Cox common shares that are projected to be outstanding at

See COX, Page 6-A

As time dragged by, the value of Cox Broadcasting stock increased significantly. Once the transaction finally was approved, the figures proposed in 1979 were no longer realistic. Cable values in particular had gone through the roof.

After the parties failed to reach agreement on new figures, Cox Broadcasting announced April 25, 1980:

"The proposed merger of Cox Broadcasting Corporation and General Electric's radio, television and cable television businesses has been abandoned since it does not appear possible to satisfy all the terms and conditions of the merger agreement."

Within weeks after the deal collapsed, Cox Broadcasting stock, traded on the New York Stock Exchange, increased in share value well above what Cox initially was willing to sell it for, and what GE had proposed paying for it.

At the "White Columns" holiday luncheon, a corporate chorus, to the tune of "Rudolph the Red-Nosed Reindeer," sang to WSB TV and radio employees:

Then one clear October day,
GE came to say...
"Cox, with your stars so bright,
Can we buy you out tonight?"
OH! How you hurt our feelings
As you shouted out with glee,
"Please take the Corporation,
but leave us all alone, GE!!!!!"

A New Name, a New Home

In September 1982, Cox Broadcasting Corporation changed its name to Cox Communications, Inc. to better reflect its position in both broadcasting and the growing cable television industry.

At the annual meeting of Cox Communications on March 21, 1983, Cliff Kirtland announced he would step down as chairman and chief executive officer, effective June 1, but would continue as a director and be involved in company affairs until the end of the year.

The board elected William A. Schwartz, who had been president and chief operating officer, to president and chief executive officer. Kirtland told the directors, "I can assure you that with Bill Schwartz in place . . . along with Bob Wright, executive vice president of the company and president of Cox Cable, and other members of top management, the company has strong leadership to take it to new levels of accomplishment."

Schwartz told Cox Communications shareholders: "Our position in expanding businesses, as well as the actions we've taken to strengthen our capabilities for a vigorous growth environment, resulted in record revenues and earnings in 1982.

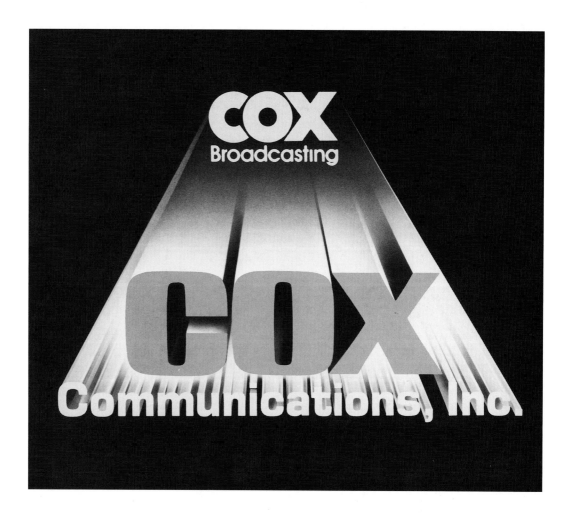

For the current year, we expect to extend Cox's 19-year unbroken record of sales and earnings increases."

Schwartz started his career with Cox in 1973 as vice president of operations for TeleRep, Inc., the company's national television sales representation firm. From 1974 to 1979 he was general manager of Cox-owned KTVU(TV), San Francisco-Oakland.

In June 1983, Cox Communications employees began moving into a new home — a just-constructed five-story building at 1400 Lake Hearn Drive in Atlanta, containing 293,000 square feet, of which Cox Communications initially occupied 220,000.

"The new building will allow us to bring the management of our three operating divisions — broadcasting, cable and auto auctions — together with our corporate staff for the first time," Schwartz said. "We anticipate this will greatly improve communications and the productivity of our Atlanta-based employees.

"The rapid growth of Cox Cable Communications has made the need for more office space vital. Cox Cable is now scattered in seven locations in northern Atlanta between the Perimeter Mall and Roswell Road. Since 75 percent of the estimated 630 Cox employees moving into the new building work for Cox Cable, it was important that the new facility be located in the general area of our existing cable division locations. WSB radio and television will remain at White Columns at 1601 Peachtree Street."

Cox entered into an arrangement for construction of the building with Lake Hearn Associates, a joint venture of the Holder Construction Company and the Mutual Life Insurance Company of New York. Cox owns the land, but holds a long-term lease on the building from a financial institution.

In 1983, headquarters of publicly traded Cox Communications, Inc. moved to 1400 Lake Hearn Drive in Atlanta, from the WSB TV and Radio building. After the 1985 merger of CCI into Cox Enterprises, Inc., the building became the headquarters of the combined company.

A Great Sportswriting Tradition: Si Burick and Furman Bisher

Whether the Cox newspapers shrewdly developed a great sportswriting tradition, or whether they have been singularly fortunate, their pages have been graced with great tellers of sports tales, writers who have seen sports in context and whose words have enhanced a sense of community and involvement.

Whether it was Ritter Collett in Dayton, Dave Campbell in Waco, Morris McLemore in Miami, Jim Minter, Dave Kindred and Lewis Grizzard in Atlanta, Tom Archdeacon in Miami and then Dayton, Ben Garlikov and Hal McCoy in Dayton, or Leo Suarez in Miami and Palm Beach, Cox sportswriters and columnists created a mature culture of fine reporting and attention to the human equation in sports.

Two sportswriters exemplify that tradition: the late Si Burick of Dayton and Furman Bisher of Atlanta. Their careers have spanned a total of 108 years of professional sportswriting.

Burick, *Dayton Daily News* sports editor, used to say, "I haven't had a promotion in more than 50 years." He was right, but his stature in the business grew a hundredfold.

Son of an East Dayton rabbi, Burick's first job at the newspaper was as an office boy in the editorial department. It was 1926 and he was 16 years old. One of his tasks was to deliver the latest edition of the paper to Governor Cox.

"It surprised, even shocked me, that this man would engage a kid in conversation," Burick later wrote, "asking about family and ethnic background or talking sports."

Burick's first writing assignment was covering sports at Stivers High School, his alma mater. The pay was two dollars a week. After he became a summer regular on the sports staff in 1927, Governor Cox would greet him as "doctor" after learning that he had spent a year as a pre-med student at the University of Dayton.

As he was about to return to college, he was offered double his weekly salary — from $15 to $30 — to stay one year. He took the offering, figuring he could take night courses at the University of Dayton, and save a little money to help him through medical school. Then, he was invited to stay one more year.

In November 1928, sports editor Carl Finke resigned to go into private business and Burick was offered his job.

Just like that, the 19-year-old kid without journalism-class training was asked to become sports editor. The boy grabbed it, even though he wasn't prepared for such responsibility. Or aggrandizement.

What made it so dramatic to the awed kid was that, in the early years, he was one of only a few representing a paper and a town our size to make trips regularly to the "big event," where the action is.

Governor Cox, an avid sports fan, wanted Burick covering the World Series, National Football League championship games, the major college football bowls, the Kentucky

Derby, the Indianapolis 500 and heavyweight championship fights. This he did and much more, including the Olympic Games at Rome, Munich, Mexico City, Montreal and Los Angeles.

His talent brought him offers from New York, Chicago and other big cities, but he chose to stay in Dayton, writing more than 13,000 columns.

He was fond of telling *Daily News* managing editors that they were part of that "long gray line of managing editors that have served me so well."

Actually, I gave him that line when I was a young managing editor in 1959, but he used it on all who came after.

Burick was honored many times by his peers, being selected Ohio's Sports Writer of the Year 19 times in 21 years by the National Sportscasters and Sportswriters Association of America. In 1972, he was president of the Football Writers Association.

The honor of which he was most proud came in 1983 when he was inducted into the writers section of the Baseball Hall of Fame in Cooperstown, N.Y. He was the first writer ever selected from a city without a major league team. Speaking of his choice of careers, Burick said, "In one way, it was a boon to humanity. I would have made a terrible doctor."

He was a terrible punster, saying things like, "Wouldn't you really rather have a Burick?" When Jim Fain was editor in Dayton, he said Burick gave him one of the best put-downs he had ever received.

Fain would write tongue-in-cheek columns about baseball being a boring sport that took so long to play that pitchers occasionally would fall asleep on the mound.

In one of his columns, Burick responded: "As Mae West always said, 'I like a man who takes his time.'"

Governor Cox loved Burick, but he could become exasperated at the stacks of newspapers, magazines and clippings piled on his sports editor's desk. One time, when the editorial department was housed in the old building, the governor came through and pushed everything on Burick's desk to the floor.

Burick was full of stories about the governor, and told them all with great affection. One of his favorites was about the governor and the 1940 World Series between the Cincinnati Reds and the Detroit Tigers.

The Reds had just won the seventh and final game to become baseball's world champions. It was their first legitimate World Series title of the century, because even though they had won the 1919 series, it was tainted by opposing Chicago White Sox players throwing some of the games.

"After the last out," Burick said, "the Reds were jumping up and down, hugging and

Si Burick was named sports editor of the *Dayton Daily News* in 1928 and kept the position for nearly 60 years.

slapping the backs of anyone they could find. I was watching Warren Giles, the Reds' general manager. He had tears streaming down his face.

"It was his ultimate moment. Then, this short man came up to him, and started punching a finger in his stomach, and said, 'Giles, you need a new shortstop.'

"It was Governor Cox."

On November 22, 1953, Burick's 25th anniversary as sports editor, Governor Cox wrote a lengthy tribute to Burick, which ran in the Sunday paper.

It said, in part, "Si was born with a nose for news and he can sense easily what there is in the sports activities that will claim human interest. Some columnists grow to be cynics, but not Si. He can follow a baseball or football team which runs into a slump, but he is charitable and cheerful about it.

". . . Si has been a patron of every movement for the entertainment, improvement and uplifting of the young generation in the great Miami Valley. He was one of the leaders in the project that brought the high school stadium to Dayton. . . .

". . . I have been his publisher since the day he, as a sprawling kid, walked into the *News* office. I have taken a deep interest in his work because I liked him, and also because I am tremendously interested in sports, particularly baseball. Our relationship has been close, and in the 25 years there has never been an unpleasant word between us. This is my tribute — I confess inadequately done — as publisher to the kid who grew up under my eye and notice in the lapse of a quarter of a century."

Si attended his last Ohio State-Michigan football game a month later, sitting with legendary Buckeye coach Woody Hayes.

After a long illness, Burick died in Dayton on December 10, 1987. David Easterly, then president of Cox Newspapers, said: "Si was a gentle and quiet man of extraordinary talent. A great many of us who grew up in the Cox organization had the benefit of his wisdom and counsel.

Furman Bisher, named sports editor of *The Atlanta Constitution* in 1950 and of the *Journal* in 1957, is approaching 50 years with the Cox newspapers.

Being a young reporter in Dayton during the Si Burick era was a little like being a rookie on the 1927 Yankees and sharing a dugout with Babe Ruth."

Furman Bisher drove to Atlanta from Charlotte in February 1950, to talk about a job with *Atlanta Journal* president George Biggers. At the time, Bisher was writing a sports column for the *Charlotte News.*

Over dinner at the downtown Capital City Club, Biggers asked Bisher to write for the Atlanta afternoon paper's op-ed page. About a month after his visit to Atlanta, Bisher got a call from Jack Tarver, associate editor of the morning *Atlanta Constitution*, who asked, "How would you like to be sports editor of the *Constitution?*"

Bisher was confused until a few days later, when it was announced that former Ohio Governor James M. Cox had bought the morning paper and would merge production facilities with the *Journal.*

"I said to Biggers, 'That's what you had in mind for me all along, wasn't it?'" Bisher recalled. "That rascal knew what was going to happen. So, on April 15, 1950, I became sports editor of the *Constitution.*

"About noon that day, my wife and I were unpacking our things in our new apartment. I had come from a newspaper that had one deadline, which was midnight. I thought I would go down to the paper and write my column in the afternoon. About 2 p.m., some woman, looking frantic, showed up at my door, and said, 'You're Furman Bisher, aren't you?'

"After I assured her that I was indeed Furman Bisher, she said, 'You've got to get downtown. You've got a column to write!'

"'Well, I've got plenty of time,' I replied.

"'No, you don't,' she said. 'You have a 6 p.m. deadline.'

"The woman, whom I quickly learned was named Rita Van Pelt, drove me to the newspaper. Of course, I didn't have an office, so they put me in Ralph McGill's office, where I sat down at his typewriter and wrote my first column. It ran on Sunday, April 16, 1950, and it has been running ever since.

"I didn't have a typewriter, so McGill said, 'Take this one, because I've got another one.' And, you know, I'm still using McGill's old typewriter. It's a 1948 Royal and it's a good one."

Early that spring, the new *Constitution* sports editor covered his first Masters golf tournament and his first Kentucky Derby. His trip to the Derby was memorable. He picked the horse, Middleground, to win, and Ed Danforth, sports editor of the *Journal*, chose another entry.

When Middleground came home first, the *Constitution* trumpeted, "Our Man Bisher Picked the Winner!"

"It was an emotional charge for me," Bisher said, "watching my horse come down the stretch to win the big race. When asked why I had picked Middleground, I said, 'His name sounded like some farm I grew up on in North Carolina.'

"One day, I was called by Tarver and told to cover the Ohio State-Michigan football game. I had no idea why they wanted me to cover it. I knew he didn't like to fly, so I thought that might have been the reason. I made arrangements to fly to Columbus, Ohio, which in those days meant changing planes a couple of times.

"Ohio State won the game when a guy named Jack Gibbs intercepted a pass and ran it back for a touchdown. I was sitting there in the press box and feeling good, when I lifted my field glasses and looked across the way, where I saw George Biggers sitting in a box with the president of Ohio State University.

"I said to myself, 'Now, I know why he wanted me here.' I could just hear him saying to the president, 'Yes, I have my man Bisher here covering the game.'

"He was great. God, I loved that man. He was a Kentuckian who had once been a sportswriter in Louisville, and that's why he sent me to cover the Derby. He was one of the strongest influences in my life. My friendship with George was one of the most heart warming things that has ever happened to me."

It was Biggers who put Bisher on WSB-TV with a Sunday college football show called "Football Review." Bisher moderated the program for 20 years. In 1952, he covered Georgia Tech's football team, which won the national championship. He was presented with a football signed by the players, who told him, "We were the team that made you, so we're making you a member of our team."

In February 1957, Bisher became sports editor of the *Journal*. In those days, the *Journal* had a far larger circulation than the *Constitution* so Bisher began writing for a wider audience.

He started out in the sportswriting business with a love for baseball, but has become somewhat disenchanted with the sport for what he believes to be selfish actions on the part of both the owners and players.

"I lived in a little country town," he said, "where we were proud of our baseball team. I always dreamed of covering a major league team, and riding with the players on the train. I thought about hearing the whistle blowing in the night. It was all quite romantic. Unfortunately, I never got to do that because I was always the damned sports editor who had to stay home and watch the shop."

Bisher believes baseball has forgotten the common, everyday fan. In his opinion, baseball today is about television money, greedy owners, corporate luxury suites, overpriced concessions and pampered and overpaid players.

"Television really controls the game," he said. "It's because of all the mercenary factors that determine when games will be played and televised that I find myself writing my column at an hour of the night when most elderly gentlemen should be in bed. I still like baseball, but not so much at the major league level. I like going to Macon or Chattanooga and sitting in the stands. It reminds me of how it used to be to go to the ballpark, where you could buy a hot dog, peanuts and a soft drink for a couple of bucks.

"In the old days, many major league players had jobs in the off-season to make ends meet. They were making a little more money than the sportswriters, but not a whole lot. We were friends with the athletes, and used to pal around with them, but we don't do that anymore. Not only is it bad form, but they don't care to be around us, and, frankly, I don't care to be around most of them.

"Fortunately, golfers and race horses perform in the daylight. Those are two of my favorite things. I'm friends with some of the tournament golfers and like to see them win. One of my close friends is Sam Huff, who came out of West Virginia to star for the National Football League's New York Giants, and get himself elected to the NFL's Hall of Fame.

"Sam and I have raised horses together. In fact, we have one now, named

'Middleburg Light.' He has been to the track, but he hasn't run yet. We had a couple of good ones. A horse named 'Marco Island' made some money for us."

Bisher's most emotional moment at a sporting event? "The one I remember most," he said, "was the semi-final hockey game between the United States and Russia at the 1980 Winter Olympics at Lake Placid, New York. The Russians were professionals, while the American team was made up of college kids.

"You're not supposed to cheer in the press box, but, when the United States won, the emotion just swept over everyone. There were a lot of ruddy-faced, old sportswriters standing and cheering, with tears running down their faces. And I'll have to confess, I was one of them."

Bisher said two of the most amenable groups to deal with are stock car drivers and female professional golfers. He noted, "Most of the NASCAR (National Association of Stock Car Automobile Racers) have come up by their own bootstraps and women golfers want the publicity, and need all the help they can get for their tour.

"Many of the stock car drivers came from little towns all over North Carolina. They were not college guys and some of them learned to drive fast by running moonshine. I saw the very first NASCAR race. Staged by Bill France and a fellow named Al Hawkins, it was run at Charlotte in June 1949.

"It was pretty rustic stuff. They were running on dirt and when I got home that night, red clay had penetrated my underwear. The race apparently was won by a driver named Glen Dunaway, but when the officials checked under his car's hood, they found an illegal carburetor. Dunaway was disqualified and the win was awarded to a fellow named Jim Roper, who never won another race in his life."

In recent years, Bisher has hosted a weekend for some of his old sportswriting friends. About a dozen or so get together, including people like Blackie Sherrod of Dallas, Jim Murray of Los Angeles and Dan Cook of San Antonio.

"We chew over old times, drink a little hooch, and the guys that can't smoke cigars at home light them up. Last year, they presented me with a beautiful crystal plaque, mounted on a large base. It had all their names engraved on it, along with some names from the past. The message was: 'In tribute and admiration for one who has spent nearly half a century with his newspaper.'

"To me, that was better than the Pulitzer Prize, because they don't give Pulitzers with heart."

How does Bisher want to be remembered? "I would like for people to think that I was a pretty darned good newspaperman, and a fair one."

There was a sportswriter at the Dayton Daily News *named Lefty McFadden, but Governor Cox always called him "Flanagan." An avid sports fan, the Governor often would call the sports department and ask for Flanagan. The answerer of the telephone would tip off Lefty as to who was on the line by calling out, "Flanagan, it's for you." McFadden would grab the phone and say, "This is Flanagan, Governor."*

Broadcasting Icons

For five decades, Lou Emm and Don Wayne were the premier radio and television voices in Ohio's Miami Valley. They came to WHIO-AM, Dayton, a year apart, Emm in 1941 and Wayne in 1942.

Before coming to Dayton, Emm made $17 a week working as an announcer at WLOK, Lima, Ohio, where his boss was Hugh Downs, who, with Barbara Walters, co-anchors ABC's "20/20."

Wayne made his broadcasting debut at WISH-AM, Indianapolis, where he changed his name from Wesley Wayne Bouslog. He started at WHIO radio as a play-by-play announcer of high school football and basketball games, supplementing his weekly salary of $32.50 by playing drums at a local nightclub. He didn't know it at the time, but he would find his future in television.

Emm was 18 when he was hired by WHIO to read the news and play dance music. After two years in the Army during World War II, he returned to the station, where he became known for his relaxed style and friendly banter with his listeners.

He hosted such shows as "Hello for Dough" and "Breakfast in Bedlam," and originated "Conversation Piece," a talk show that was later taken over by Phil Donahue. But he found his niche as the voice of morning drive-time, where he ruled in the ratings.

When he began his career, there were no ratings in radio. "Radio was a lot more creative then," he said. "A lot of what we did was ad-libbing. Back then, if you showed up for work and did your job, you kept your job."

Teen-agers who had listened to Emm while driving to high school were doing the same thing as parents, and even grandparents. He was content to stay with one station, explaining, "Most times you have to give up being on the air to take a promotion. Luckily, I didn't have to. I think they realized I would be unhappy without it.

"Besides, I love this town. Where else can I live five minutes from work and 10 minutes from the golf course? I've always enjoyed being with the people because they are the ones who have allowed me to have a career in radio all these years. I think the secret to surviving in this business is to be yourself. I was never very good at doing impressions, so I've been content to be me, and I guess that has gone over well with my listeners."

Emm observed his 50th year with WHIO radio in October 1991, and retired in August 1992.

Wayne and WHIO television pretty much started together. Only weeks after

Lou Emm promoted a scrap rubber and metal drive by interviewing an owner of a filling station that was used as a collection point in World War II.

WHIO-TV went on the air, Wayne was asked to replace a newscaster who had lost his job because he insisted going on camera with a cigar stuck in his mouth.

"There I was," he recalled, "with an old 16 millimeter Bell & Howell film camera and some sloppy editing equipment. I had to shoot, write, edit and deliver the news."

And deliver the news he did, for the next 38 years. In 1969, he was one of seven news anchors chosen to report public reaction to the first U.S. moon landing for Walter Cronkite's "CBS Evening News." Wayne modeled his crisp, concise broadcasting style after Cronkite and Edward R. Murrow.

Stan Mouse, Wayne's long-time boss at WHIO, said, "Don sounded like Cronkite. If you shut your eyes, you could tell they had the same kind of pace or rhythm. Once in an interview, Cronkite said, 'When I go around the country I run into people who will say, "You know, you sound just like a newscaster in Dayton, Ohio."'"

By the late 1970s, WHIO-TV had a higher Nielsen rating than any other CBS affiliate in the nation, with a 43 percent share of the evening news audience. Wayne, by now a Dayton institution, was getting job offers from places like Los Angeles, San Francisco and Chicago.

"Fortunately, I was always able to talk him into staying," Stan Mouse remembers.

"Don was a giant in the business and knew people like Cronkite, Chet Huntley and David Brinkley on a first-name basis."

As the years passed, Wayne became affectionately known as Pappy to his colleagues, and when "happy talk" became the vogue, Mouse recalls, "Don bought a joke book, ending his newscasts with a humorous quip." "Sometimes I'd get in a bit of trouble because some of those jokes had double meanings," Wayne said.

He delivered his last newscast in April 1988, two days before his 66th birthday. Dan Rather came to his retirement party.

Lou Emm, 74, and Don Wayne, 75, died just five weeks apart in 1997, Emm in late April and Wayne in early June.

"It was a sad time," Mouse said.

Emm (L) had been with WHIO 51 years when he retired in 1991. He died in 1997, five weeks before broadcasting icon Don Wayne.

In 1943, spiffy Don Wayne (C) reported on a captured Japanese submarine.

Wayne (R) retired from WHIO in 1988 with 38 years of service.

The Art of the TV Newscast: John Pruitt and Monica Kaufman

Monica Kaufman's changing hairstyles are such a trademark that WSB-TV once ran a lighthearted promotion, "Best On-Hair Coverage."

The human and technical art of the television newscast changes daily. Success, however, relies finally on a simple equation: Total team effort and an everything-counts drive for success. And success can be measured.

Cox TV stations have prided themselves on outstanding rating performances for its news programs. WHIO, Channel 7, in Dayton, for instance, has maintained one of the highest-rated newscasts in a major market, consistently holding the top spot at all prime news hours: 5 p.m., 6 p.m. and 11 p.m.

In recent years, Cox has held the top spot in every market in which its TV affiliates broadcast.

Nick Trigony, president of Cox Broadcasting, puts it this way:

"The bottom line for any local affiliate is being the local leader in news. We have concentrated on being the local leader in news, and that has accounted for our success."

Monica Kaufman and John Pruitt, respected news anchors of Cox's WSB-TV, Channel 2, in Atlanta, represent what Trigony had in mind: Experience, maturity, viewer trust, a dedication to get the news on the air and get it right.

When Kaufman arrived at WSB-TV from Louisville on August 25, 1975, Pruitt, who had been at the station since 1964, except for two years of Army duty, was anchoring the 6 p.m. and 11 p.m. news.

His first memories of his future co-anchor? "She was young, innocent and demure, but she was not shy by any means. It was obvious that she was someone of great warmth and vibrancy, and a very good communicator wanting to learn. And it quickly became apparent that she was going to be a big hit."

Kaufman, who had worked as a reporter for the *Louisville Times* for four years, was once told by a Kentucky TV station that she would never make it in television. Despite those discouraging words, she landed a job as a reporter and weekend anchor at WHAS(TV), Louisville.

After almost two years at WHAS(TV), Kaufman sent a job inquiry and a tape to an Atlanta television station, only to be told that she needed to "stay in Louisville a little bit longer." Three months later, she went to work at WSB-TV in Atlanta, Cox's first television station.

For Kaufman, it was not an easy time. After she

became co-anchor with Pruitt, first at six o'clock, and later on the 11 p.m. news, some of the station's audience reacted angrily to her presence.

"People did not want a black or a woman on the six o'clock news," she recalled, "and I was both. The letters we received were unbelievable. But I must tell you, John Pruitt and Don Elliot Heald, the station manager who hired me, were the most supportive and protective two men I had ever seen. We used to call him 'Daddy Heald' because he was so wonderful."

The University of Louisville graduate worked hard at gaining acceptance in Atlanta. "I immediately started doing what I had done in Louisville," she said. "I started going to the schools and making talks. I spoke to all the service clubs — Lions, Rotary, Civitan — and did work for the Butler Street Y.

"I was speaking every day when I first got here. I was building bridges, and, after that, the criticism started wearing down. That was my bread and butter, reporting and public speaking. As long as people feel they can touch you and know you, they'll watch you.

"But I wouldn't have been able to do even those things without Don Elliot Heald and others taking the heat from the public and saying, 'Give her a chance! We hired her and we're going to stick with her.' They did for me what no one else would do."

Her most embarrassing moment on television happened at the Louisville television station. "I thank God today that it happened in Louisville and not Atlanta," she said, explaining, "I was working as a weekend anchor with a weatherman who was frequently inebriated. You know, in those days a lot of people would drink and work.

"This guy was not even a meteorologist; he just read the weather report. Anyway, there was a break for a commercial about Dove detergent, featuring Dolly Parton and Porter Wagoner, and this weatherman was making some really obscene remarks about Dolly Parton's anatomy. So I uttered a four-letter expletive, followed by 'shut up.'

"I didn't know it, but my microphone was open! Someone from the control booth told me, 'They just heard you say that.' Everybody in southern Indiana and Louisville, Kentucky, just heard me say that.

"So, I immediately came back on and apologized, saying, 'Profanity on the air is not the policy of WHAS(TV). I am very sorry.'

"As soon as I went off the air, I walked into the newsroom still shaking, when someone told me my mother was on the telephone. I picked up the receiver and my mother said: 'Monica Rosie Lee Jones Kaufman (which is my entire name), why would you put something in your mouth that you wouldn't hold in your hand,' and hung up the phone.

"A second call was from the news director, who was laughing his head off. 'Everybody has made that kind of stupid mistake,' he said. 'You were right to apologize. Now you've learned your lesson; never say anything around a microphone that you wouldn't want your mother to hear.'"

Pruitt came to Atlanta fresh out of Davidson College, and applied for a job at *The Atlanta Journal*, but no one wanted to hire and train him because he

Co-anchor John Pruitt just changes his ties.

was going in the Army as a commissioned officer in eight months. The newspaper didn't have a spot for him, but he ended up talking with a man named Bob Harrell, who took an interest in him. Harrell sent young Pruitt to see Ray Moore, WSB-TV's news director at the time.

"I interviewed with Ray," Pruitt said, "and one of the first things he asked me was, 'Have you read "War and Peace?"' After I told him I had, he said, 'Well, I didn't like it very much. Did you?'

"'Actually, I liked it very much,' I answered, but that didn't seem to bother him. Ray and I hit it off and he hired me for $1.25 an hour, which came out to $50 a week. I was doing menial jobs around the newsroom, filing film and that sort of thing.

"In the summer of 1964, the South was in turmoil as the civil rights movement was unfolding. On July 4, there was a big segregationist rally at the Lakewood Fairgrounds in Atlanta. Dave Riggs, one of our top reporter-photographers, was assigned to the story. Back in those days reporters shot their own film.

"Ray Moore said, 'Go with Dave and help him carry his gear.' So we went to Lakewood and they had a bunch of segregationist speakers there, including Ross Barnett, the governor of Mississippi. Dave set up his tripod and began filming the

"Monica Kaufman: Close-ups" is a favorite of viewers, awards judges and Monica, who has asked Oprah Winfrey everything her viewers ever wanted to ask.

event. The speakers were on a flatbed truck in the middle of the stadium and the crowd was in bleacher seats.

"Four young, black students from Atlanta University were there, protesting against the rally and its speakers. The crowd, now stoked to a fever pitch, suddenly turned on these four little demonstrators, and began beating them. And they weren't beating them with their fists. They were hitting them with metal folding chairs.

"Dave said, 'John, here's a camera; I've set it for you; here's the button to push; go see what you can get for me.'

"I was able to get close enough to shoot this horrible video of these young people being beaten. I thought they were being killed. Somehow, I got the pictures and the cops came and quieted the thing down.

"And that night, on the 'NBC Nightly News,' the first TV film I ever shot in my life went coast to coast. I said to myself, 'I think I've found a career.'

"So I finished my eight months with Channel 2, and went off to Korea for a couple of years, where I served in the infantry. I missed Vietnam because I got my orders to Korea before the big buildup began in Southeast Asia.

"I came back to WSB in 1967, and went to work as a reporter/cameraman. I got a break when Ray Moore had me doing five-minute local news cut-ins on NBC's morning 'Today' show. I did that for several years, and then was promoted to weekend news anchor. Back in those days, if you were an anchor, you also produced, wrote, edited and ran the assignment desk. Five years later, I moved to the 6 p.m. and 11 p.m. newscasts. We started calling ourselves 'Action News' in 1974.

He and Kaufman were Atlanta television's top-rated news team in 1978, when Pruitt suddenly left Channel 2 for WXIA(TV), Channel 11, where he became the anchor for the station's 6 p.m. and 11 p.m. news shows. He said he made the change because of a combination of factors, one being that a new news director pulled him from the 11 p.m. newscast, and put him on at noon and 6 p.m.

"I didn't feel these and other changes in the newsroom were beneficial to my career, so I left," Pruitt said. "After I was taken off the 11 p.m. newscast and before I went to Channel 11, I felt validated and redeemed when the ratings book for February 1978 showed that for the first time in history WSB fell to number two behind WAGA(TV), Channel 5, on the 11 p.m. news."

Pruitt put in 16 uninterrupted years at Channel 11 before Greg Stone, vice president and general manager of WSB-TV, brought him back to Channel 2 in 1994, where he again teamed up with Kaufman. Because he had a non-compete contract at Channel 11, he had to wait six months before he could go on the air at WSB-TV.

"I've been through 16 news directors in my long career. Depending on the strength of the station and upper management, a news director can wreak havoc or make beneficial changes. In a place like Channel 2, because of the upper management and the fact that this is the home of Cox, there is an underlying stability that, I think, mitigates against those rash decisions that can disrupt things and cause the viewers distress."

Pruitt's most embarrassing experience on television happened early in his career on WSB-TV. He explained: "I was working on the 11 o'clock news and it was before we had TelePrompTers, so I had memorized the first couple of sentences of the evening's lead story. It went something like this: 'Five prisoners broke out of the Jackson County

Public Works Camp today. They were armed with homemade knives and ice picks.'

"So I had memorized those two lines, and when the camera's red light came on, I looked straight into it, and got the show off to a dynamite beginning, saying, 'Good evening, this is John Pruitt. Five prisoners broke out of the Jackson County Public Works Camp today. They were armed with homemade knives and TOOTHPICKS!'

"Because I was so intent on my opening delivery, I didn't realize what I had said. I knew something terribly wrong had happened because the people off camera were on the floor, rolling with laughter. I don't know how you live that one down."

During Pruitt's long absence from Channel 2, he and Kaufman were collegial, but didn't maintain close contact because they were competitors. However, they were always friends.

Monica has been seen all over the community, including at the mike singing the national anthem for a 1985 Atlanta Falcons professional football game.

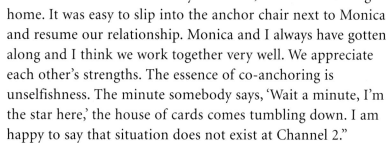

"When I came back to Channel 2 after that 16-year hiatus, it was like coming home. It was easy to slip into the anchor chair next to Monica and resume our relationship. Monica and I always have gotten along and I think we work together very well. We appreciate each other's strengths. The essence of co-anchoring is unselfishness. The minute somebody says, 'Wait a minute, I'm the star here,' the house of cards comes tumbling down. I am happy to say that situation does not exist at Channel 2."

Kaufman was delighted when Pruitt returned to WSB-TV as her co-anchor. She laughed and said, "I kept saying to John, 'You gotta come back,' and when he did our numbers went right through the roof.

"I think one of the reasons our newscasts are on top in the ratings is that people know if a big story breaks, we're going to go all guns to cover it. Also, on a day-to-day basis, we're going to work very hard to get people what they want. And I believe our viewers like stability, too. Even though John was gone for a very long time, I think many of our viewers forgot that he left."

One of the big stories that Kaufman and Pruitt reported was the 1996 bombing in Olympic Park in downtown Atlanta. Pruitt said with great pride, "Beginning at 1 in the morning, Monica and I were on the air for five hours without a break. You knew that people were hanging on your every word because they wanted all the information you could give them.

"And it's up to you to do that, and do it accurately, even though what you have may be limited. The unfolding of the story as you talk conveys something of the enormity of the event. At those times, you're sorely challenged. If the viewers see somebody stumbling around, they will switch to another channel."

Kaufman and Pruitt agree that their real bosses are their viewers. "It's always important to remember who you are working for," said Kaufman. "Even though WSB is my parent company, my boss is the viewer.

"Funny things have happened to me in 23 years," Kaufman said.

"I think the one thing viewers would change about me, and the one thing news directors would love to change about me, has to do with my hair. They would say, 'Monica, don't change your hair so much!'

"In an earlier contract of mine there was a clause saying I could not change my hair without the express consent of the news director. It's not in my contract now. I think all the changes in my hairstyle have become a promotional tool for the station. From time to time, I wear wigs, and sometimes I've had braids. To me, hair is an accessory. It's the same as changing my earrings.

"At the 1997 Southern Regional Emmy Awards, the station ran a page in the program featuring photos of my different hairdos, accompanied by a caption that said, 'Best On-Hair Coverage.' Viewers also called when I started wearing glasses. I had worn contacts for years, but my eyes dried out. Everybody wanted to tell me what glasses to wear and how to wear them. That problem ended two years ago when I had laser surgery. Now I have 20-20 vision."

In 1986, Channel 2 began a show called "Monica Kaufman: Close-ups," which has become the new anchor's favorite thing she does at the station. The show, which has won a wall full of awards, appears four times a year, and features Kaufman interviewing celebrities.

Her favorite interview? "That's hard to say," she said, "because how do you compare an Oprah Winfrey to a Paul Newman? It's hard to pick one or two. The joy of doing them is that you get to ask celebrities everything you and your viewers ever wanted to ask. And when you have done your research, they will open up and tell you anything."

Kaufman continues to be deeply involved in the Atlanta metropolitan community. She will do upwards of 70 speeches in 1998. Ten years ago, she was the first black person and second woman to serve as chairman of the Metropolitan United Way.

Kaufman and Pruitt have been honored with numerous awards. Her recognitions include 20 local and regional Emmys, the Distinguished Service to Broadcasting Award (1989), Woman of Achievement Award from the Metropolitan Atlanta YWCA (1992), the Friends of Children Award from the Georgia Chapter of the American Academy of Pediatrics (1992) and two national awards from American Women in Radio and Television for her 1994 series, "Hot Flash! The Truth about Menopause."

His awards include two local Emmy Awards, five Associated Press awards, three Sigma Delta awards, the United Press International Award for best documentary for the Carter presidential campaign, the Green Eyeshade Award for News Coverage (1977) and the Georgia Winner Award for Community Service (1994).

Cox television stations WSB-TV, Atlanta, and WHIO-TV, Dayton, in 1989 won the broadcasting industry's most prestigious award for local programming — the IRIS — given by the National Association of Television and Program Executives.

WHIO-TV was recognized for its live six-hour broadcast of the 1988 Dayton International Air Show. WSB-TV received its IRIS for "Monica Kaufman: Close-ups," which featured the station's news anchor interviewing celebrities.

Bombeck and Donahue

Phil Donahue and Erma Bombeck, two Cox alumni who found nationwide fame and fortune, both arrived in Dayton, Ohio, in their early 20s, and ended up living in the same suburban neighborhood.

In his autobiography, "My Own Story," Donahue wrote: "Centerville is where I became a homeowner for the first time. . . . Although I didn't realize it then, I had chosen a home across the street from a woman who would become a national celebrity. Her name was Erma Bombeck.

"Erma and I had three things in common. We were both Catholics, we both had Early American furniture and we both lived in the same kind of house."

A Notre Dame graduate from Cleveland, Donahue started with Cox as radio and television newsman at WHIO. He was a fine reporter and broadcaster, and many felt he would end up as a network television news anchor.

"At Wit's End" columns Erma wrote for the Dayton paper spread through syndication to 900 papers with 30 million readers.

"Oh, he could have been a network anchor all right," said Stan Mouse, who ran WHIO radio and television for years. "He was one of the best. When it came to getting a story, he had the same bulldog tenacity as Geraldo, but without the abrasiveness. He knew how to chase a story down. Phil was a nice guy, and smart as hell.

"Of course once he got into syndication with his own show, he was making so much money that he couldn't afford to go to the network. We had him on a radio show called 'Conversation Piece,' which could have given him the idea for the television talk show that later became his life.

"He used to come to me and say, 'You know, I like being on the air, but I really want to be in sales because, you guys, you're all red carpet. You just go out and float around, entertaining people. I want to be in sales.'

"I said, 'Well, number one, you won't make it, and number two, you're too good on the air to go into sales.' But he wanted to give it a try, so he left us to go to a local company that specialized in sales incentive programs, but that didn't last. He soon returned to local television with Channel 2, one of our competitors, and began his talk show."

In 1973, Donahue moved his show to Chicago. He later said, "The decision to move our act to a bigger town followed six years of trying to encourage program guests to come to Dayton. The growth of our show had stalled at about 38 cities, and it became clear that Donahue in Dayton had gone about as far as it was going to go."

Fresh out of the University of Dayton, Erma Bombeck stayed in her hometown, hiring on at the morning *Dayton Journal Herald* in 1949, where she had been a copy girl five years earlier. It was there that she met her future husband, Bill, who was a sportswriter. He later became a high school teacher.

I first met Erma in June 1949. I also had just graduated from college. Like many cub reporters, we both wrote obituaries. She later moved to the Modern Living section, where she wrote and shepherded the women's pages through the composing room.

Erma quit her job in 1953, after her first child was adopted. Later, she had two other children.

I was managing editor of the *Daily News*, when Erma telephoned me in 1964. She told me she had been writing some columns at home, and asked if I would look at them.

"Sure, come on by," I told her. I was looking for a full-time writer, but Erma wanted to free-lance because of her young children. After reading her columns, I said, 'Erma, these aren't for us. Why don't you take them to the *Kettering-Oakwood Times?*'" (a suburban newspaper south of Dayton that published three times a week).

She did just that and they paid her three dollars a column, which she later said was about what they were worth. In 1965, Glenn Thompson, editor of the *Journal Herald*, offered her $50 to write two columns a week. She called her column "At Wit's End," and it was filled with wonderful and funny stories about motherhood, kids and life in suburbia.

Within three weeks, the Newsday Newspaper Syndicate picked up one of her columns, and it was reprinted in 38 newspapers. Five years later, she was in 500 papers. She topped out with 900 papers and 30 million readers. Erma went on to write more than a dozen books, most of them best sellers, and appear on the cover of *Time* magazine.

Phil was sure he wanted to go into sales at WHIO-TV in Dayton but was told he was too good on air.

Someone once wrote that I was haunted by my decision not to hire Erma, but that really wasn't so. I was pleased for her. I invited her to my retirement party in June 1989.

She sent her regrets, writing:

"Dear Chuck: We started together in the city room of the *Dayton Journal Herald.* By all odds, I should be joining you in retirement, but I am the sole support of weekly shipments of Retin-A to my house.

"I wish I could be in Atlanta to watch you grope for words and try to look humble, but I can't. Enjoy the leisure. I have five or six more adjectives to use up and, when they go, I'll join you. I'm cheap!"

Erma, who had been ill for some time, died April 22, 1996, in a San Francisco hospital following kidney transplant surgery. She was buried in Dayton.

The Bizarre Deal for Yuma

Between January and April 1984, Cox Enterprises bought 50 percent of the *Yuma Daily Sun* from the Don Soldwedel family. The owners of the other 50 percent had sold their interests to the Donrey Media Group, headquartered at Fort Smith, Arkansas.

Cox named Soldwedel's son, Joe, editor of the paper. Don Reynolds, president and chairman of Donrey, did not like Joe and wanted him removed. He said so in a meeting attended by Garner Anthony, CEI chairman; myself and Fred Smith, Donrey's executive vice president.

When the meeting, which had become argumentative, ended in an impasse, Garner asked Reynolds, "Have you given any thought to selling your half of the paper to us?"

"Have you thought about selling your half to me?" Reynolds responded. It was left at that, and there was no further discussion between Cox and Donrey until May 1984.

Garner and this writer were sitting in a Montreal hotel ballroom, where Lee Iacocca of Chrysler was about to address the annual meeting of the American Newspaper Publishers Association, when Garner spotted Reynolds and Smith at a nearby table.

"I think you ought to go over there," he told me, "and ask your friend, Fred Smith, if Mr. Reynolds is prepared to talk about Yuma."

I walked back to the table, knelt beside Fred and whispered Garner's message. Seconds after I returned to my seat, Fred looked at me and nodded. Both he and Reynolds got up and headed for an exit. Garner and I followed. This happened just as Iacocca was being introduced. I often wondered if he thought we were walking out on his speech.

The four of us — Reynolds, Smith, Garner and myself — gathered in a hallway outside the ballroom. I could hear the crowd inside loudly applauding Iacocca.

It was agreed that both parties would write down a number on a piece of paper, and the one with the larger number would become the sole owner of the *Yuma Daily Sun*.

Garner and I walked about 40 feet down the hall, and after a brief talk, he wrote down a figure and asked, "What do you think?"

"I don't know, Garner," I said. "I would add $250,000," which he did.

After Smith signaled that he and Reynolds were ready, Garner and I walked back to meet them. We exchanged pieces of paper. Appearing somewhat shaken, Reynolds said, "Congratulations. You have just bought a newspaper."

"Congratulations, Mr. Reynolds," I answered. "You have just made a lot of money."

On July 3, 1984, Richard Tatum, vice president and treasurer of Cox Enterprises, and I delivered a check for $15,500,000 to Smith at Donrey's western headquarters in Las Vegas. The night before, as Tatum and I walked through a hotel gambling casino, I said, jokingly, "Richard, what do you say to our putting the whole check on red or black at the roulette wheel?"

Before you could say "$15.5 million," we determined that was not a good idea, so we decided to try our luck with $100 of our own money, just to see what would happen. We put the $100 on red. The tiny ball bounced into the black.

A Whole New Company

The 1985 merger of publicly traded Cox Communications into Cox Enterprises to create one of the largest privately held media companies in the nation was the realization of a dream for CEI Chairman Garner Anthony.

"It had been on my mind for some time," he said. "It is one of the achievements I am most proud of during the time I led the company. Being private gave us much more flexibility in our operations."

On April 8, 1985, Cox Enterprises announced a tender offer of $75 a share, or a total of $1.2 billion, for the 54.6 percent of Cox Communications stock not owned by the Cox family and CEI. On the last full day of trading before the announcement, the stock was listed on the New York Stock Exchange at $62.25 a share.

At the time of the offer, several Cox trusts owned 40.2 percent of the 28.2 million Cox Communications common shares of stock. Other members of the Cox family, officers and directors of both companies, and other business associates owned an additional 5.2 percent of the stock.

Anthony, also the chairman of the executive committee at Cox Communications, said the combined companies would have revenues in excess of $1.3 billion. "It would rank very favorably with most media companies in terms of revenues and earnings," he said.

Cox Enterprises announced May 2 that it had entered into a $1.5 billion definitive loan agreement with a consortium of 15 banks to finance the acquisition of Cox Communications. The banking group was headed by the Texas Commerce Bank of Houston.

Five days later, CEI reported that it had agreed to settle four class-action lawsuits filed in Fulton County Superior Court by Cox

The 1985 merger of publicly traded Cox Communications into Cox Enterprises doubled the size of either previous company and formed a totally private organization.

Communications shareholders on grounds that the $75 per share offer was "grossly inadequate." It was announced at the same time that Cox Enterprises had agreed to extend its tender offer deadline from midnight, May 9, to midnight, May 17.

As of May 21, CEI owned 95 percent of Cox Communications stock, more than enough to effect the merger. The company made one last extension of its offer to 5 p.m., May 24, "to give the remaining shareholders some additional time to tender."

When it was over, CEI had bought 16,883,417 shares of Cox Communications for $1,266,256,275, which amounted to 97 percent of the shares.

On September 3, 1985, Anthony, chairman and chief executive officer of the merged companies, announced that Bill Schwartz, former chairman of Cox Communications, would become president, chief operating officer and a director of CEI. John Dillon was named vice president and chief financial officer.

Anthony later said, "If the merger had not taken place, I think the value of what the family has would be 60 percent less. I believe you can document that."

Asked if there were differences in cultures when the two companies merged, he replied: "There were and still are differences — and there is nothing wrong with that. Broadcasters are different from auto auction people and auto auction people are different from newspaper people and so forth.

"That is one of the strengths of this company. We're not looking for conformity or uniformity. One of the challenges of upper management is to bring all those diverse elements together and to capitalize on their strengths.

"Hopefully, people in this company know there is no 'pet' division. We have to look aggressively at expansion in all our divisions, and will continue to do so. One thing that has happened in the last few years is that media properties have gotten so expensive. Sometimes it doesn't make good business sense to overreach, but we certainly will be alert to any opportunities that are out there."

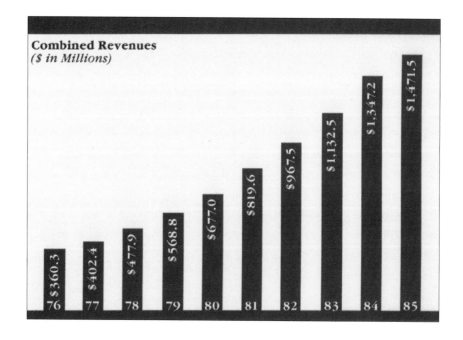

Combined Revenues
($ in Millions)

76	$360.3
77	$402.4
78	$477.9
79	$568.8
80	$677.0
81	$819.6
82	$967.5
83	$1,132.5
84	$1,347.2
85	$1,471.5

Getting to Be Number One

When Kevin O'Brien became general manager of KTVU(TV), San Francisco-Oakland, in April 1986, the station had fallen on bad times. But to O'Brien, this was nothing new.

"With Metromedia I was like the roving ambassador for taking over poorly run assets," he laughed. "I went on missions to Cincinnati, Kansas City, Minneapolis, Washington and New York."

O'Brien worked for Metromedia for 20 years, but when it was sold to Rupert Murdoch, he decided to go elsewhere. He spoke with Al Masini, who ran TeleRep, the Cox-owned company that places national advertising with independent television stations.

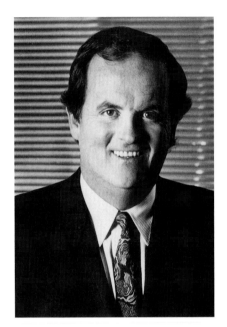

Kevin O'Brien, (general manager since 1986), who led KTVU to the top in Bay Area TV news.

"Al called Bill Schwartz and told him I was available. Bill then called me and we pretty much made a deal. But before I was hired, I met with Garner Anthony in New York City, where I was running a Metromedia station. I think he wanted to see whether I had two heads or not. We had a nice, hour-long chat. I was impressed with Garner. He had a certain magnetism about him.

"Anyway, I signed on with Cox to run its three independent television stations — KTVU, KDNL, St. Louis, and WKBD, Detroit, from my base in Oakland. St. Louis and Detroit were later sold.

"I will tell anyone who will listen that joining Cox Enterprises was the best thing that ever happened to me. The company is very well run. It's very efficient and decentralized appropriately. Cox is also very caring about its employees.

"When I arrived at KTVU, the station was in bad shape. It had fallen behind the three big network affiliates. I think that Channel 44, the UHF station, was making more money than we were. On the other hand, I was working at what was generally accepted around the industry as the finest broadcasting facility in the country. It was only four years old. That kind of facility with good equipment and a great signal gave me something to build on."

Since KTVU already had a good infrastructure for news, O'Brien made increasing sales his first priority. "We needed to make more money, so we could spend more money," he said. "We didn't do a housecleaning, but we expanded staff, hiring people for both programming and news. Early on, I started a 10 p.m. newscast that has become very successful.

"I think the biggest reason the station's been so successful is because, when I really needed something, the company never said, 'No.' When I needed money for capital or for the news operation, the company supported me."

Greg Stone, leader of two number one stations: WSOC-TV (general manager, 1982-1990), and WSB-TV (1990-present).

KTVU also received a sales and audience boost when the station became affiliated with the Fox Network. From the time Cox bought KTVU in 1969, it had been an independent. The first Fox show went on the air in 1987. "I think," O'Brien said, "the fact that Fox became so incredibly successful was one of the real secrets of the success of the station, especially in the early 1990s."

Under O'Brien's leadership, KTVU has become the Bay Area's top news station. It also telecasts the games of the San Francisco Giants and the 49ers, making the station a broadcasting powerhouse.

Operating as the number one news station in San Francisco-Oakland, the nation's fifth largest market, KTVU entered 1998 as Cox's most profitable television property. It also enjoyed the distinction of being the largest Fox affiliate in the world that was not owned by the network.

Besides being vice president and general manager of KTVU, O'Brien is executive vice president, independent group/Fox. In that role he has the responsibility for KFOX(TV), El Paso; KAME(TV), Reno; KRXI(TV), Reno and WAXN(TV), Charlotte. Although KAME and WAXN are not owned by Cox, the company manages them under a contract with their owners.

Greg Stone, vice president and general manager of WSB-TV, Atlanta, also knows what it's like to take a television station to the number one position in its market. He went to work for Cox in 1963 as a newsman for WSOC radio in Charlotte, and later became a salesman at WSOC television.

After 10 years with TeleRep, he was named general sales manager for WSOC-TV in 1980, and soon thereafter became general manager. "When I came back to Charlotte, the station was not only number two, it was number two by a significant margin.

"WBTV, one of the premier CBS affiliates in America, was the dominant station. It took a while, but, because of the dedication of a lot of people, we managed to knock them out of their number one position.

"Because WSOC-TV had been the second station for so long, the staff just didn't believe they could ever get on top, but I was too young and too dumb to believe that we couldn't do it. After a while, I got the staff to believe it too.

"One of the first things we did was strengthen our news operation, because that's where you win or lose. We did the usual things in off-air commitments and community affairs, but in terms of on-the-air, it's the news product that is everything.

"Our leading newsman was Bill Walker, who anchored the 6 o'clock and 11 o'clock news. He is still at WSOC-TV and doing well. It reached the point that whenever people in Charlotte thought of television news people, they thought of Bill Walker.

"And so, if you win in news, you're going to win, period. Once we did that, everything else followed. We also worked very hard on the sales side. Realistically, sales should follow the ratings. The revenue share follows the rating share.

"So little by little and inch by inch we continued to make gains, and in 1989 we overtook WBTV. It was the like 'The Little Engine That Could.'"

When Stone was asked by Nick Trigony, president of Cox Enterprises' broadcasting division, in 1990 if he would be interested in coming to Atlanta and running WSB television, he admitted becoming somewhat emotional.

"I'll never forget my answer, and it came from the heart," he said. I told Nick, 'My goodness, anybody in this industry would be honored to have the opportunity to run WSB.' That's the way I felt about it then, and I feel even more that way now.

"WSB has always been a wonderful television station, with a great history. What a wonderful time, not only for me, but certainly for our whole staff, to be involved in the operation of this station during its 50th anniversary, and during the company's 100th anniversary.

"I'm proud that we have maintained our leading position in the Atlanta market, and I

WSB-TV produced "The Boy King," timed for the first federal holiday, in 1986, honoring Dr. Martin Luther King Jr. The program was syndicated nationwide and earned a Peabody Award. Mary Childes (shown with cast members) was the local programming producer.

Andy Fisher, Cox Broadcasting executive vice president, has guided Cox's network-affiliated TV stations to increased audiences and revenues.

Helping their markets weather storms helps stations stay number one in news. In 1995, James Ford, WFTV Brevard County (FL) bureau chief, covered Hurricane Erin at 2:30 a.m. when the storm peaked.

also am pleased to say that our margin has widened. I tell our people that even though we are number one, we need to act like we're number two.

"You have to work at it very hard. The other people come to work every morning just like we do, and they come to work to beat us. And you have to remember that. There is a great challenge in not becoming complacent yourself and not allowing your people to become complacent about our leadership position. If you start taking it for granted, you won't have it long.

"We are blessed with good people, but it is the total team that counts, not just one personality. Seldom does the move of a single anchorperson from one station to another in the same market make much difference at all in the ratings once the sampling settles down.

"Right now, here at WSB, we are programming more news than anybody in the market. We do the traditional newscasts, but we do them bigger and longer and, hopefully, better."

From Monday through Friday, WSB-TV does two hours of news in the early morning and two hours in the early evening, plus the traditional 30 minutes at noon and 11 p.m. On Saturday, the station devotes five and one-half hours to news programming, and five on Sunday.

WSB-TV also does five-minute local news inserts on CNN Headline News. "I'm pretty confident," Stone said, "that before long we'll be doing the 10 p.m. news on another station in the market through some kind of joint revenue-sharing venture where we would provide the product and they would provide the time period. Of my staff of 200, close to half are news people.

"Leading this station into the future and keeping it on top is a wonderful challenge. If I had to pick one thing that I feel best about it is the relationships that I have had with the people I work with. To me, that is what it is all about.

"I was fortunate to have brought a couple of people into the company within the last few years who have been chosen to be general managers of Cox television stations. Lee Armstrong, who was our director of programming and public service here, is now running WHIO-TV in Dayton. She replaced John Woodin, former WSB-TV news director, who was chosen to become vice president and general manager of KIRO(TV), Seattle, after we acquired that station in 1997.

"Now we have this wonderful new building going up next door. Our new quarters — the studio space,

the concept of the building — are being built for the future. Even though we will not occupy some of the additional space when we move in, it will be there for future growth and expansion. It is the first all-digital television facility built from ground up in America.

"But what I preach to our people is that the new building is great, and it's on time, and it's on budget, and it will be a wonderful new working environment for everybody, but it is still brick and mortar and it is still wires and equipment. What is infinitely more important than the building itself is the quality of the people we put in it."

John Swanson, vice president of engineering for Cox Broadcasting, said the building cost $32 million and the equipment $12 million. WSB staffers began moving into the building in May 1998. The dedication was in the fall of 1998.

When the company bought WFTV(TV), Orlando, in 1985, the station had been the news leader in its market for seven years in a row. After some slippage in the late 1980s early 1990s, it has regained its top position.

WPXI(TV), Pittsburgh, fought a long, uphill battle to gain news primacy in its market. Once a poor third among the city's television stations, WPXI decided to focus more on hard and local news. It was the first in the country to air a Saturday morning newscast from 8 a.m. to 12:30 p.m., and the first in its market to broadcast the early evening news at 5 p.m.

Research director Rosanne Eppich said, "Our station is strong, but right now there is no dominant station in the market. Our goal is to not only maintain our number one news ranking, but to widen the gap."

The gradual destruction of Atlanta landmark "White Columns" marked the end of an era, but the impressive new home of WSB TV and Radio is a thrust to the future.

Cox Chairman and CEO Jim Kennedy pushed the button in 1998 signing on WSB-TV's new digital channel. HDTV is in its infancy, but only 2,400 Atlantans owned televisions when Gov. Cox put the south's first TV station on the air 50 years ago.

The turnaround at WPXI is recognized in the industry as one of the most dramatic in the nation.

WHIO(TV), Dayton, has been number one in its market by a wide margin for decades. KIRO(TV), Seattle, bought by Cox in 1997, is viewed as a station with great growth potential.

Trigony credits Andy Fisher, executive vice president-television affiliates, for developing market strategies that propelled Cox's network affiliates into higher market positions, both in audience and revenues.

"I can't say enough good things about what Andy did with our television stations," Trigony said, "because he created enormous bottom-line profits for the company. We also instituted a lot of research in television that had come from Cox Radio. Andy jumped all over that and, with his research and news expertise, the television stations started to get better immediately."

At the invitation of the Japanese, Ray Boylan, chief meteorologist at WSOC(TV), Charlotte, traveled to Tokyo in March 1997 to assist Japan in preparing for "Japanese Weather World '97," an international conference of broadcasting meteorologists.

Boylan, a winner of four consecutive local Emmy Awards from 1990 to 1993 for his weather reporting at WSOC(TV), delivered one of the keynote addresses. He predicted: "The phenomenal changes we've seen in technology, science and international relations in the last 20 years, as remarkable as those have been, are only a drop in the bucket compared to the changes we'll experience in the next 50 years.

"We gnash our teeth if 10 people are killed in a hurricane on the East Coast, but a cyclone in the Indian Ocean, which is basically the same as a hurricane, will wipe out 100,000 people in one afternoon, mostly due to lack of information and preparation."

Boylan, who in his military career flew with the Navy's "Hurricane Hunters," said he and his staff take a no-nonsense approach to meteorology, noting, "We have fun with it, but we don't fool around with it. Our forte is severe weather, and our efforts have been rewarded by our audience's patronage. When severe weather occurs, people in the Charlotte area turn to WSOC(TV)."

A Move into Mickey World

Cox in September 1985 paid $185 million in cash for WFTV(TV), Orlando, the top television station in one of the hottest markets of the country.

WFTV(TV), an ABC affiliate, has long been a leading station in Orlando — the second fastest growing market in the nation. Channel 9 has a tradition of local news excellence and leadership.

A Central Florida magazine article published at the time quoted Bruce Northcott, news consultant and a senior vice president of Frank N. Magid and Associates, as saying: "Orlando is probably the most upbeat, lively market that exists in coverage and audience anywhere. The news presentation is younger and more vibrant."

General sales manager Bruce Baker said, "This is the only market in Florida where the population thrust is off the coast. Other stations lose a lot of their signal out over the water. We have an unlimited land base and a real opportunity for growth. I expect to see advertising dollars pulled out of other markets and into Orlando."

WFTV is near Walt Disney World, but its news leadership isn't fantasy.

Baker is now vice president and general manager at WSOC(TV) in Charlotte.

The arrival of Walt Disney World in Central Florida in the early 1970s touched off a boom in the tourist industry. New hotels, motels, entertainment centers and convention facilities rose from former citrus groves.

When WFTV(TV), then WLOF(TV), went on the air in 1958, its logo was a cat with nine lives. Cat with nine lives? Channel 9? Get it? One staffer described 1958 as a year when "hula hoops were popular, a general was president and the King of Rock and Roll was in the Army." The call letters became WFTV five years later.

In 1958, the station was prepared to serve an audience of 167,000 residents. By the time of WFTV's 30th anniversary in 1988, the number of potential viewers exceeded four million.

The task of serving this massive audience was about to be made easier for staffers, who were operating out of a converted warehouse that had been the station's home since the beginning. To everyone's delight, ground was broken in early 1988 for a 67,000-square-foot, state-of-the-art facility with two studios.

Since station management wanted to maintain a presence downtown, the company bought a four-acre lot, dotted with oak trees, near the central business district. The new location also assured a direct line-of-sight microwave link to WFTV's transmission tower 20 miles east of the city.

The new studio/broadcast facility solved expansion needs, enabled WFTV to keep pace with the growth and progress in Central Florida and helped maintain its leadership position. It was the only station within the city limits.

WFTV's new two-story home was dedicated in the spring of 1989.

New owner Cox moved WFTV out of a converted warehouse and into a new state-of-the-art building in 1989.

PART THREE

Into the Future

Changing the Guard

Garner Anthony announced in early 1987 that he would step down at the end of the year as chairman and chief executive officer of Cox Enterprises. He said his successor would be executive vice president Jim Kennedy, grandson of former Ohio Governor James M. Cox, the company's founder.

When Bill Schwartz resigned as president in May 1987, Kennedy moved up to president and chief operating officer of Cox Enterprises, a position he would hold until Anthony departed.

Garner Anthony's years as chairman were marked by growth, expansion and the realization of his goal to operate one unified, private company.

Speaking of Kennedy, Anthony said, "Jim comes to the job with considerable operational experience in a variety of positions in this company. He brings his experience, the enthusiasm of his age, a fresh and positive outlook, and a deep commitment to the company and its employees.

"In turn, he is blessed with not only a strong company from an economic point of view, but, more importantly, from an employee point of view. He also is lucky to have the board of directors that he does. All this should bode well for the future."

Anthony's association with the company spanned 25 years. He became chairman and chief executive following the death of James M. Cox Jr. in October 1974. The merger of Cox Communications into Cox Enterprises in 1985 was the realization of a long-term goal to operate one unified private company.

During the Anthony years, a dozen newspapers were acquired and the broadcasting division grew from 14 to 19 outlets. Cox Cable changed from a rural to an urban company with multiple channel offerings of basic and premium services. With 24 systems and 1.4 million customers, Cox became one of the largest cable operators in the country.

Manheim Auctions grew from nine to 20 auctions, including operations in Toronto, Canada, and Atlanta.

The 1987 annual report printed these comments:

"Garner's contributions to Cox were many, but to single out a few, I would cite his strong business discipline and his sense of purpose — to be good at whatever you do. These are especially important characteristics to a family-owned business, and explain why Cox prospered under Garner's leadership while other family-owned businesses went by the boards. Also, his style was to delegate authority to the key people around him and he always backed them."

—Carl Gross, former senior vice president and administrative officer, president, Cox Newsprint Supply

"I worked closely with Garner for 10 eventful and exciting years. He possesses all the qualities of leadership — courage, determination and powerful ability to motivate. Sometimes tough, but always fair, Garner also is compassionate and generous. I always felt he led a team that would follow him down the mouth of a cannon. It was a decade of challenge, change and growth, a time I will never forget."

—Chuck Glover, editor-in-chief, Cox Newspapers

"Garner's contributions to the stability and outstanding growth of our company are certainly well-documented. His tough business decisions and long-range planning kept Cox ahead of its peers. Perhaps Garner's most long-lasting decision was the timing and execution of bringing Cox Communications back into private ownership after being publicly traded for 23 years. I feel certain this will ensure for many years to come a stable atmosphere in which Cox employees can prosper and excel."

—Stan Mouse, president, Cox Broadcasting

"We owe a great debt to Garner Anthony," Kennedy said. "His wisdom guided this company through its major years of growth. He developed talent among our employees, inspired their loyalty and challenged them to exceed their best, year after year.

"The merger was a tremendous undertaking that went very smoothly. On the whole, it was a real success. Cox Communications, being a public company, was run a good deal differently from Cox Enterprises as a private company, and there were two, very separate and unique corporate cultures. We're seeing a lot of progress in bringing these companies together.

"Through the merger, we doubled in size. And with that merger came a $1.5 billion debt. Though our debt is substantial, we still are a very strong company. We will continue to look at acquisitions, concentrating on those that are of strategic importance to the businesses we are in and that will yield a good return.

"I want to get around as much as possible and to be accessible, but I don't want to be the focus of attention. One thing I am convinced of is that the heroes of the company are the people who are at our locations doing the job. The employees at our newspapers, radio and television stations, cable systems, auto auctions, and other businesses are the people who make this company what it is today. I will try never to forget that."

Anthony and his successor Jim Kennedy talked about the decisions that shaped Cox Enterprises, for a 1987 article in the company's employee publication, *FOCUS*.

New Generation, New Ideas

David Easterly, publisher of *The Atlanta Journal and Constitution*, moved into the president's chair at Cox Newspapers on May 13, 1986, replacing me, and touching off a wave of other executive changes.

President since January 1, 1977, I was named the newspaper group's first editor-in-chief, with responsibility for 21 daily papers and the Cox Washington bureau. I was less than four months from my 61st birthday, and Easterly was approaching 44.

"These moves will enhance our newspaper group by capitalizing on our strengths," said Garner Anthony, chairman and chief executive officer of Cox Enterprises, Inc. (CEI). I continued as a CEI director.

Easterly started to work for the company in February 1970, as a reporter for the *Dayton Daily News*. He became city editor, then moved to corporate management, serving Dayton Newspapers, Inc. He was named president of Dayton Newspapers, Inc. in 1977.

He came to Atlanta in 1981 as vice president of operations for Cox Newspapers, and was named publisher of the Atlanta newspapers in April 1984. Jay Smith, publisher of the *Austin American-Statesman*, filled Easterly's job at the *Journal-Constitution*. Like Glover and Easterly before him, he started with Cox in the editorial department of the *Dayton Daily News*, and had been president of Dayton Newspapers, Inc.

As CEI president and chief operating officer, David Easterly told company-wide human resources managers in 1998, "We need employees who know how to do business in a way that gives real value to the customer. We have to operate with honesty, quality, service. Our people have to make decisions with integrity and respect."

Roger Kintzel, who also had come through the Dayton pipeline to become president of Cox Arizona Publications, succeeded Smith in Austin. Kintzel had spent his 40th birthday in Dayton, where he was business manager, his 41st at the *Springfield News-Sun*, where he was publisher, his 42nd in Arizona and his 43rd in Austin. Some of their fellow workers called Glover, Easterly, Smith, Kintzel and others who had emigrated from Ohio the "Dayton Mafia."

Asked how he saw his role as president of Cox Newspapers, Easterly said in 1987, "I guess I'm a coach and a bit of a counselor. I certainly don't issue a lot of orders, and I think I take a lot more telephone calls than I place."

Tom Giuffrida, publisher of *The Palm Beach Post*, said of Easterly: "Corporate buzzwords and faddish management theories are completely foreign to David. He is down to earth, very smart and very supportive. Sometimes you know he thinks you are wrong, but he'll let you go ahead — and chalk it up to trust."

In November 1992, Easterly named Smith executive vice president of Cox

Newspapers, and moved him to Cox's headquarters. Dennis Berry, president of *The Atlanta Journal and Constitution*, replaced Smith as publisher of the papers.

In October 1994, Easterly was promoted to president and chief operating officer of Cox Enterprises, and Smith to president of Cox Newspapers.

Jim Kennedy, Cox chairman and chief executive officer, said in a personal note to employees:

"The promotion of David Easterly to president and chief operating officer demonstrates our commitment to push forward with an aggressive growth plan. We're determined to continue being leaders within our core businesses and to embrace new information and communication media.

"This means I'm concentrating more and more on strategic plans and new ventures — a positive demand on my time. It's also a tribute to the innovative people at Cox who step up with promising new ideas, and to the employees who enable us to pursue these opportunities and make the most of those we choose.

"We're fortunate to have strong management who can lead and support our plans. David Easterly is one of those, and I am confident of his leadership in keeping us focused on operational goals and objectives.

"David's promotion opens up an opportunity for Jay Smith as president of Cox Newspapers. This is the kind of bench strength we want within our company, and I am pleased we can count on Jay's experience and management ability as president of Cox Newspapers."

Bob O'Leary, CEI senior vice president and chief financial officer since 1996, previously held executive positions in Cox's cable company for 14 years.

Berry's move from publisher of *The Atlanta Journal-Constitution* to president of Manheim Auctions in October 1995 started another round of musical chairs. Kintzel replaced Berry in Atlanta, raising to five the number of Cox newspaper organizations for which he had worked. Succeeding Kintzel in Austin was Mike Laosa, a 20-year employee who began his career in the circulation department of the *Austin American-Statesman*.

Before returning to the paper as its publisher, Laosa served as circulation director of the *Mesa* (Arizona) *Tribune*, assistant circulation director at *The Palm Beach Post*, general manager and publisher of the *Port Arthur* (Texas) *News*, president and publisher of Cox Arizona Publications, and group vice president for Cox's community newspapers.

In 1992, Kennedy put forth a challenge to his managers: "Double the value of the company in the next five years!" The goal was achieved as 1997 came to a close, with gross revenues going from some $2.5 billion in 1993 to $5 billion in 1997.

Easterly helped Kennedy put the company into a growth mode. He was the strongest proponent for building Cox's services on the Internet. One of his first jobs as CEI president was to organize a professional business development office under the direction of Dean Eisner.

Simultaneously, he opened a second development office specifically commissioned to help chart CEI's future in the world of interactive media.

"What we do with on-line services could easily be as important as all of our other development taken together," Easterly said.

Jay Smith joined the Cox organization in 1971 as a reporter at the *Dayton Daily News* and, in 1994, succeeded David Easterly as president of Cox Newspapers.

The Telecommunications Act of 1996 broke down some barriers and opened up more opportunities and more competition.

Veteran business and technology analyst Bill Killen was named vice president of new media.

Asked about the future of Cox Interactive Media, Killen said, "We have some very believable projections from a number of supposedly knowledgeable sources that say that Internet usage will grow at a remarkable rate. We hope to build our local Internet businesses with enough interesting and useful content to capture much of that soaring audience.

"The Internet is a place where people buy and sell stuff; it is a place where news can be delivered; and it is a place where, instead of wading through pages and pages, you can push a button and call up all sorts of information — sometimes more information than you can possibly use. In the media business, it's all about audience. It's all about attracting enough eyeballs to deliver an appropriate audience to advertisers.

"The biggest single driver of the Internet today is E-mail," Easterly said. "It is as important as the mail that comes to my desk. It's not free, but it's reasonable. It permits me to receive and communicate information about the company more easily than anything else."

The Cox president said the company's 1993 investment in emerging Poland "was over the very top of our risk profile." Cox provided $5 million for new presses at the *Gazeta Wyborcza* newspaper in Warsaw.

"I am pleased to say that the risk was worth taking," he added. "The newspaper has done remarkably well, and the current value of our $5 million investment is well over $50 million."

Looking back over his 28-year career with Cox, Easterly, who celebrated his 56th birthday on June 26, 1998, said, "I could not have had a more challenging or rewarding career, nor can I imagine I would have had this kind of career anywhere else, because the company just kept giving me new opportunities. Some of it, of course, was probably dumb luck, you know, being at the right place at the right time. It's hard to beat that.

"Negotiating labor contracts in Dayton was one of the most difficult and most educational things I ever did. I believe that experience really taught me how to do business with people in difficult situations. Looking back, I would not have wanted to miss that experience."

Death in the Afternoon

A change in U.S. lifestyles resulted in declining circulation, and, in many cases, the demise of afternoon newspapers. Once a land of early-to-work factory workers, the nation shifted gradually to more service-oriented businesses in the 30 years following the end of World War II.

Many Americans who used to come home from work in mid-afternoon and pick up the afternoon paper were no longer doing so. CNN was running national and international news all day and TV's local evening news shows began airing in the late afternoon.

Confronted with falling circulation, it was only natural that advertisers would look elsewhere.

Morning newspapers, on the other hand, benefited from the changes, as readers grabbed these papers to find out what had happened in the world while they were sleeping, and advertisers simply followed the circulation.

It was no different at Cox, where, in the 1980s, three of its afternoon papers joined the morning field and a like number were relegated to sainted memory. The morning *Springfield* (Ohio) *Sun* and the afternoon *Daily News* became an all-day paper, known as the *News-Sun*, in May 1982. Three years later, all afternoon deliveries ceased. The conversion to an all-morning paper was complete.

Pretty much the same thing happened in Waco, Texas, where the *Waco Tribune-*

Morning readers and declining afternoon circulation led to combined, hyphenated names. *The Palm Beach Post* absorbed the *Evening News*.

Herald became morning only in August 1981. Then-Publisher Randy Preddy told his employees: "Many of you worked hard to make the all-day concept work in the Waco market. I am grateful for your efforts. For a time, we were able to stem the decline in afternoon circulation. But the ratio of new starts favored the morning edition four to one, and it became uneconomical to publish and deliver fewer and fewer afternoon editions with the rising cost of energy and other materials."

In Longview, Texas, the afternoon *Daily News*, which traced its history to 1871, printed its last edition on September 30, 1988. Three days later, the *Daily News* and the *Longview Morning Journal* became the *News-Journal*, a morning-only newspaper.

The last edition of the *Palm Beach Evening News* went to press on May 1, 1987, and was replaced by an afternoon edition of the much-larger *Palm Beach Post*. All circulation moved to the morning at the end of October 1987.

The situation in Dayton was more complicated, where on September 15, 1986, the morning *Dayton Journal Herald* was merged into the afternoon *Daily News*, the first Cox newspaper. For a time, the new all-day publication carried both mastheads.

With afternoon subscribers accounting for less than 60,000 of the paper's 185,000 daily circulation, management in September 1988 dropped the *Journal Herald* masthead and made the *Dayton Daily News* a morning publication, ending a 39-year run for the *Journal Herald*.

Publisher Brad Tillson said: "This is the final step in what has been a lengthy conversion process. The shift in readership from afternoon to morning is a national trend. This change guarantees that we will continue to publish the high-quality newspaper our readers have come to expect, while maintaining strong profitability and market position."

Sad news came on October 14, 1988, when Jim Kennedy, Cox Enterprises' chairman and chief executive officer, announced that the afternoon *Miami News* was for sale, and that, if no buyer was found, the newspaper would cease publication at the end of the year.

The newspaper had published under a joint operating agreement (JOA) with Knight-Ridder's *Miami Herald* since 1966. The 30-year agreement stipulated that the *Herald* would provide advertising, circulation, production and promotion services to the *News*, and that Cox would manage the editorial department.

Cox shared in the profits of the Miami Herald Publishing Company, and both Cox and Knight-Ridder have shared the ongoing losses of the *News*. David Easterly, then president of Cox Newspapers, said the net cost of publishing the *Miami News* was running about $9 million a year, and was expected to worsen over time.

"Quite simply," he said, "the *Miami News* — despite an outstanding editorial presentation — is not supported by advertisers or readers. Daily circulation has declined from 112,000 in 1966 to below 48,000 today, while Dade County households have grown by 80 percent in the same period. This means that the *Miami News* now serves fewer than 8 percent of Dade County households."

In 1986, Cox chairman Garner Anthony proposed extending the JOA with Knight-Ridder. Following a number of meetings, Knight-Ridder and Cox entered into an agreement in January 1987, under which Cox would continue to share in *Miami Herald* profits, but at a reduced rate, until 2021.

However, the new agreement required Cox to fund all losses from the operation of the *News*. Kennedy said he did not believe the losses could be reversed and, therefore, Cox determined to sell or close the newspaper.

He noted, "During the past 18 months, we examined a number of publishing scenarios which we hoped would keep the *News* alive, but we did not find any option that could reverse the steep decline in circulation and advertising.

"It is with a deep sense of sorrow and regret that we make this announcement. Published since 1896 and winner of five Pulitzer Prizes, the *Miami News* has a long and proud history as an outstanding, crusading newspaper. It has been home — and continues to be home — to a number of distinguished reporters and editors, and a vital voice in Miami's history."

With no buyers forthcoming, the *News* published its final edition on December 31, 1988. Of the 110 editorial staff members of the paper, 22 were placed in positions with other Cox newspapers. Ten joined *The Palm Beach Post*, including Pulitzer Prize-winning cartoonist Don Wright. Lou Salome, editor of the editorial page, transferred to Cox Newspapers' Washington bureau, and became the bureau's correspondent in Jerusalem.

Miami News publisher David Kraslow was named a vice president of Cox Newspapers, and Howard Kleinberg, the paper's editor, stayed with Cox as a columnist. Both Kraslow and Kleinberg took up offices at *The Palm Beach Post*'s Miami bureau.

Kraslow, 62, was chief of the Cox Washington bureau before becoming publisher of the *News* in 1977. Kleinberg, 56, went to work for the paper in 1950 as a sportswriter and became editor in 1976.

The movement away from afternoon newspapers continues today. According to the *Editor & Publisher Year Book*, 15 of 19 U.S. daily papers that closed in 1997 were afternoon publications. Another 32 afternoon newspapers switched to morning distribution.

Lewis Grizzard

Popular *Atlanta Journal-Constitution* columnist Lewis Grizzard used to say the happiest moment in his life was in 1977, when the wheels of his Delta flight lifted from a runway at Chicago's O'Hare Airport and carried him home to Georgia.

Grizzard came to work for the *Journal* as a sportswriter in 1968, with the reputation of a boy wonder. As a 19-year-old freshman at the University of Georgia in 1964–65, he was named sports editor of the *Athens Daily News*. He also was a summertime feature writer for the *Newnan Times-Herald*.

He left the university one credit short of graduation for the Atlanta job, but years later, the school awarded him a journalism degree. Living up to his boy wonder reputation, Grizzard became executive sports editor of *The Atlanta Journal* at age 21.

By 1975, he was an assistant city editor, and, some say, he was being groomed to become city editor. Be that as it may, Grizzard didn't like what he was doing and left the paper. After briefly free-lancing for *Sports Illustrated* and some other publications, he accepted a job in the sports department of the *Chicago Sun-Times*, where he quickly became executive sports editor.

But Grizzard was cold and miserable in Chicago, his southern blood unable to acclimate to the bitter Windy City winters. He would later say, "I left Atlanta . . . for Chicago, figuring what the hell, horizons are for stretching. I was homesick at the first stoplight in Cartersville. Horizons without a red clay motif are somebody else's horizons."

Meanwhile, his old friend and mentor, Jim Minter, had left his job as executive sports editor of *The Atlanta Journal* to become managing editor of *The Atlanta Constitution*. He and Grizzard spoke on the telephone from time to time, and, at one point, Minter offered Grizzard the job of Saturday editor of the combined edition of the *Journal and Constitution*. He came to Atlanta and accepted the job, but when he returned to Chicago, he was talked out of taking it.

"Later on," Minter said, "I was trying to find a columnist and I asked Lewis who he thought I might be able to hire. 'What about me?' he said. 'Why don't you hire me?'

"So, after he sent me five sample columns, I hired him and started running his columns in the sports pages. I thought he needed some time to get his feet wet in the column-writing business, and I knew he would be comfortable in sports.

"Before long, I switched him to the general news pages, where he started writing six times a week. I remember Jack Tarver (publisher of the *Journal-Constitution*) didn't want me to bring Lewis back because he had left us, but I did it anyway. Tarver grumbled a little, but that was all."

Minter had rescued Grizzard's career and Grizzard knew it. For the remainder of his life, he was fiercely loyal to the man he considered his mentor and champion. He later wrote a book about his venture "up north," titled, "If I Ever Get Back to Georgia, I'm Going to Nail My Feet to the Ground."

A son of the small town of Moreland, Georgia, Grizzard developed a cast of characters for his column, many based on people he grew up with in his hometown.

There was Kathy Sue Loudermilk, every adolescent boy's dream girl, and Wayman C. Wannamaker Jr., "my best friend and a great American."

He often wrote tenderly about his mother and all the things she told him to beware of in life. Some of his most moving columns were of his father, a decorated Army veteran of World War II and the Korean War who died in 1970 after years of heavy drinking. When Grizzard was six, his mother divorced his father. He was devastated when she died in 1989.

Minter, who went on to become executive editor of both the *Journal* and the *Constitution*, said, "One of Lewis' worries was that he could never measure up to his father as a man."

Grizzard wrote a book about his father — "My Father Was a Pistol and I'm a Son of a Gun." Of the 20 books he would write, he said that was his favorite.

His folksy, humorous columns quickly attracted an army of readers. When he published his first book, "Kathy Sue Loudermilk, I Love You," 7,500 copies were sold the first week.

Divorced three times, Grizzard from time to time would write bittersweet columns on love, marriage and divorce. His third wife, Kathy Taulman, later Kathy Schmook, responded with her own book, "How to Tame a Wild Bore and Other Facts of Life With Lewis: The Semi-True Confessions of the Third Mrs. Grizzard."

Popular *Atlanta Journal-Constitution* columnist Lewis Grizzard had become one of America's favorite humorists by the late 80s.

Grizzard infuriated some of his female fans when he wrote that women's activities should be limited to rubbing his back, hugging his neck, baking pies, frying chicken and washing his clothes. The *Washington Post* wrote: "He compares every woman to his mother, who spoiled him rotten."

But writing with his tongue in his cheek often was Grizzard's way of stirring up his readers. Minter said: "He was absolutely the best of anyone I know of at walking up to the edge of bad taste without being in bad taste.

"A lot of people at the newspaper didn't know how good Lewis was. He was not a one-dimensional person. He was probably the best overall newspaperman I've ever been around. He was a better newspaperman than columnist. He was the kind of person I wanted to work for me for two reasons. One, he was loyal, and, two, he was much smarter than me."

When Cox acquired the *Austin American-Statesman* in 1976, Grizzard was offered the editorship, but turned it down.

In January 1982, a dark cloud appeared over Grizzard's otherwise sunny life. Minter recalled: "He telephoned me at home one night and said he noticed his chest jumping at night when he was in bed. His heart was having to beat so hard to push the blood through."

His wife said his heart was beating so hard that it was shaking the bed. As a teenager, Grizzard had been told to forget military service because he had a heart murmur. So, at only 35, he underwent open-heart surgery. His damaged aortic valve was replaced by one from a pig.

Writing about the experience in his next book, "They Tore Out My Heart and Stomped That Sucker Flat," he said, "Every time I pass a barbecue joint, I get all choked up."

This book got its name from a quip Grizzard made before his final, unsuccessful heart operation in 1994.

His column, syndicated for some time, was now appearing in more than 435 newspapers, one-third of them outside the South. In 1985, he released his first comedy album and began making concert stage appearances.

But that same year, Grizzard had his second open-heart surgery, but that did not slow him down. He was on a roll. Several of his books appeared on the *New York Times* best-seller list and he was getting up to $25,000 an appearance for his stand-up act. He did guest spots on several television shows and was interviewed by CNN's Larry King. Some compared him to Will Rogers and Mark Twain.

But his heart continued to let him down. In 1993, his doctors replaced the pig tissue with a mechanical stainless steel valve. He received more than 30,000 letters, cards and packages from well wishers.

For a while, he was able to return to the golf course, but eventually became too sick even to attend the home football games of his beloved Georgia Bulldogs. In early March 1994, he was stricken at his home in Florida. Cox chairman Jim Kennedy sent the corporate jet to fly him back to Atlanta, where he entered Emory University Hospital for the last time.

After medication failed to reduce the size of a fungal infection or blood clot near his heart, Grizzard, 47, was told that his only hope was a risky operation, in which his chances of survival were less than 50 percent.

On March 16, two days before the surgery, he married Dedra Kyle, with whom he had a four-year relationship. In a tense moment before the operation, Grizzard was asked if he had any comment. "When's the next bus to Albuquerque?" he responded.

But Grizzard's luck had run out. He suffered massive brain damage when an obstruction closed off an artery. After life-support systems were removed, he was pronounced dead on March 20, 1994.

More than 800 people telephoned the *Journal-Constitution* over the next two days to talk about their favorite Grizzard column, and tributes came from his fans across the country, from the U.S. Virgin Islands to San Jose, California.

Cox in Washington

After more than 20 years of existing separately, the Washington news staffs of Cox Broadcasting and Cox Newspapers moved into shared quarters in July 1998, leasing 17,000 square feet of space near the U.S. Capitol.

The two bureau chiefs, Steve Gasque for broadcasting and Andy Alexander for the newspapers, both were promoted into their jobs in 1997. In January, Gasque replaced Andy Cassells, who retired after serving as bureau chief since 1974. On December 1, Alexander succeeded Andy Glass, who had been in the job for 20 years. Being named Andy is not a prerequisite for the job. Glass is now senior correspondent for Cox Newspapers.

Gasque came to the broadcasting bureau in 1987 as a satellite correspondent. After a stint at Cox-owned WSOC-TV, Charlotte, North Carolina, he returned to Washington as reporter/anchor for WSB-TV, Atlanta. Gasque holds numerous awards, including North Carolina Radio and Television Journalist of the Year, which he won in both 1990 and 1991.

Reacting to his new assignment, he said, "What a wonderful turn of events, and

Andy Alexander (L), newspapers bureau chief; Andy Glass (C), newspapers senior correspondent and Steve Gasque (R), broadcasting bureau chief, celebrated the 1998 opening of joint quarters near the U.S. Capitol.

what a wonderful opportunity. I've been reporting for nearly 18 years and I love telling people's stories to our viewers.

"Our bureau has changed in several important ways. At one point, everyone here was a white male. Now, we have a wonderfully diverse group — men and women from all sorts of cultural and racial backgrounds. It's a different kind of place.

"We hit the ground running every morning. Our first satellite feed goes to KTVU(TV), San Francisco-Oakland, at 9:40 a.m., followed by another one at 10:15 a.m. We feed the East Coast stations at noon and go back to the West at 3:30 p.m., and then there are the regular evening feeds at 4:55 p.m. and 5:55 p.m."

Twenty-something Tracey Mitchell came to work for Gasque in the spring of 1997. "This is a great group of people," she said. "This is the first place I've ever worked where I really felt everyone worked hard. Everyone has a really great attitude about their work.

"I love reporting, I truly do. It's wonderful having a boss like Steve, who is a reporter himself. Sometimes you have a news director who's never been in the field, who's never gone out on a story."

Tracey came out of school with a double major in journalism and economics and had offers from Prudential and the IRS. "And I just thought, 'God, I can't do economics,' she said, 'It's so boring.'"

Her days of being bored have ended. Describing herself as "extremely busy," she said, "I normally cover stories at the White House and Capitol Hill, and, sometimes, the Supreme Court. Today I did a story on needle exchanges, which is a big issue."

Her ambition: "I want to own a television station. I think I can still do reporting and go back to school and get my MBA, so I'll know how to run my television station. At a Cox station, I know I wouldn't have any problem being number one in my market."

Alexander, who had been Glass' deputy, came to Washington in 1976 as a reporter for the *Dayton Journal Herald*. A prize-winning newsman, Alexander has reported from more than 50 countries and covered armed conflicts in Vietnam, Angola, Iran and Iraq.

Cox Broadcasting opened its Washington news bureau in 1969. Among the early

Andy Cassells (C) participated in a historic interview in 1986 when bureau chiefs from five independent group broadcasters were invited to a meeting with President Ronald Reagan.

Joe Albright covered the Persian Gulf crisis for all Cox newspapers. Gen. Norman Schwarzkopf, the U.S. military commander in Saudi Arabia, drew a diagram illustrating the command structure of U.S. and Allied forces in the Gulf during Albright's exclusive interview.

Ken Bridgham edited breaking news stories in 1987 before they were sent by satellite to Cox TV stations.

staffers were radio reporters Hal Cessna and Ken Bridgham, who later became chief editor.

In 1974, Cox Newspapers created its own Washington bureau and named David Kraslow its chief. He had been Washington bureau chief for the *Los Angeles Times* and assistant managing editor for national and foreign news at the *Washington Star*.

For years, several Cox newspapers maintained regional reporters in Washington, who covered their state's congressional delegation, as well as other news of interest back home.

But with a full-fledged bureau, national staffers began filing stories to all Cox newspapers. Kraslow hired four national reporters and an office manager. Also housed in the bureau were five regional reporters representing Cox newspapers in Atlanta, Dayton, Palm Beach and Miami.

When Kraslow left Washington in August 1977 to become publisher of the *Miami News*, Glass replaced him. One of the first reporters hired by Kraslow, Glass had worked for the *Washington Post* and the *National Journal*.

Under Cassells and Glass, the two

Elliott Jaspin (L) and Larry Lipman, of the newspaper bureau, peer around just a few of the computer tapes used in the 1992–1994 analysis of more than 100 million Medicare payments to doctors. Dozens of reporters from the bureau and Cox newspapers participated in the comprehensive, first-of-its-kind computer-assisted research effort for Cox Newspapers.

bureaus not only worked independently, but competed in some markets.

For the broadcasters, on-the-air deadlines are only hours apart and most of the news reported is fast-breaking. They also have to think more in terms of time zones between Atlanta and San Francisco-Oakland, for example. Television reporters may prepare up to seven or eight versions of the same story for different Cox markets. Currently, the bureau is responsible for more than 2,000 live broadcasts a year.

The print reporters also cover fast-breaking news, but spend a good deal of time producing in-depth and investigative stories of national or international scope.

Dramatic changes in technology helped both bureaus to improve their service. In 1980, live satellite broadcasting began. Before that, television reports were shot on film and flown to local stations for their evening newscasts.

When the newspaper bureau opened, information was transmitted back and forth by one-way machines. Now, state-of-the-art communication systems exist in Washington and most Cox newspapers. A photo department was added in June 1984. The bureau also has foreign correspondents covering Europe, Russia, the Caribbean, Central America, Mexico and the Middle East. Early in 1998, Cox received approval from the Chinese government to open a bureau.

Cox Newspapers also has its own news service that is distributed daily and Sunday to its newspapers and to the *New York Times* syndicated wire service, which goes to some 650 clients worldwide. Between 30 and 45 Cox newspaper stories are moved daily on the *Times* wire.

Ben Sargent

Mike Peters

Mike Luckovich

From afar, Cox Pulitzer Prize-winning editorial cartoonists attack government, both entertaining and irritating readers. Ben Sargent, the *Austin-American Statesman*; Mike Peters, *Dayton Daily News*; Mike Luckovich, *The Atlanta Constitution*, and Don Wright, *The Palm Beach Post* (page 78)—all still with the company —account for five of six Cox Pulitzers for editorial cartooning.

Auto Auction Colossus

Manheim Auctions strengthened its position as the highest-volume auto auction company in the world on March 29, 1991, when it acquired 20 new auctions in a merger with the Ford Motor Credit Company and General Electric Capital Auto Resale Services (GECARS). Since that move, Cox has acquired 100 percent of Manheim stock.

The joint venture, in which Manheim had a controlling interest, increased the number of Manheim auctions to 46 and the number of employees to more than 7,000. GECARS, jointly owned by GE Capital in Stamford, Connecticut, and Ford Credit in Dearborn, Michigan, was formed in 1986 to build a nationwide chain of auction locations. Separately, Manheim and GECARS were among the top three auto auction companies in the industry.

Automotive News wrote that the merger created an auto auction "colossus," and melded assets estimated at $1.2 billion. Reporter Charles M. Thomas said: "The merger provides Manheim with a potentially huge pool of captive vehicles to draw from. GE Capital Fleet Service is the largest corporate fleet management company in North America with more than 450,000 cars, trucks and specialty vehicles on lease.

Manheim Auctions nearly doubled in size (shown on map) through the acquisition of GECARS auctions in 1991. "The World's Largest" has 80 locations in 1998.

ARIZONA:
◆ Arizona
◆ Southwest

CALIFORNIA:
◆ Anaheim
◆ Fresno
◆ Riverside
◆ Bay Cities
◆ LA Dealers
◆ Fontana

COLORADO:
◆ Colorado
◆ Denver

FLORIDA:
◆ Imperial
◆ Daytona
◆ Lakeland
◆ Orlando
◆ St. Pete
◆ Tampa Bay

GEORGIA:
◆ Bishop Bros.
◆ Atlanta
◆ CARS
◆ GA Dealers

ILLINOIS:
◆ Greater Chicago

MASSACHUSETTS:
◆ American

MINNESOTA:
◆ Minneapolis

MISSOURI:
◆ 166 Springfield
◆ Kansas City
◆ St. Louis

NORTH CAROLINA:
◆ High Point

NEW JERSEY:
◆ NADE

NEW YORK:
◆ Newburg

PENNSYLVANIA:
◆ Butler
◆ Manheim

OHIO:
◆ Ohio

OREGON:
◆ Portland

SOUTH CAROLINA:
◆ Clantons

TEXAS:
◆ Big H
◆ Dealers of Dallas
◆ Fort Worth
◆ Houston Hobby
◆ San Antonio

UTAH:
◆ Utah

VIRGINIA:
◆ Fredericksburg
◆ Harrisonburg

WASHINGTON:
◆ South Seattle

WISCONSIN:
◆ Metro Milwaukee

CANADA:
◆ Oshawa
◆ Toronto

Many of those vehicles are marketed through auctions. Ford Credit uses auctions to dispose of about 350,000 company vehicles."

In 1991, Manheim sold 1,805,000 cars, almost doubling 1990's sales of 925,996. The following year, 1992, saw sales go through two million, with 2,190,558 vehicles auctioned. Ford and General Electric later sold their minority positions to Manheim.

Manheim and the Chrysler Corporation took a step into the future on May 18, 1994, with the first satellite television auction in North America. In the first test of Auction Vision International, 92 percent of the 250 vehicles offered for sale were sold to more than 200 registered Chrysler dealers.

The auction signal was sent by fiber optic cable from an Orlando studio to the Chrysler Dealer Network headquarters in Detroit.

General Manager Greg Gehman (L) and Arthur Walters brought past and present together last year at Manheim Auto Auction in Pennsylvania. In 1945, Walters and his partners established Manheim, their first auction and the first cars-only auction in the industry.

From there, it went via satellite to Chrysler, Plymouth, Dodge and Jeep Eagle dealers in Arizona, California, Nevada, New Mexico and Utah.

In Auction Vision, the buyer viewed the vehicles on a satellite-linked television in his or her office. Bids were then placed over the telephone to a bidding agent, whom the buyer could see making a bid on his or her behalf. A split screen showed the auctioneer on the block, the vehicle being offered and the bidding agents. It was live and interactive.

Ralph Liniado, Manheim's senior vice president of corporate development, said, "By allowing the dealer to participate in the auction process from his or her office, we provided an alternative for today's busy automobile executive. The success of Auction Vision can be found in the numbers. The sale results look just like those of a traditional sale. The percent of vehicles sold and the prices were consistent with the overall market."

Manheim signed a joint-venture agreement in January 1994 with Independent Car Auctions of the United Kingdom to bring the satellite auction technology to North America.

"We worked successfully with Auction Vision International for about a year," Liniado said, "but in satellite technology you have to have a receiver to be able to get the signal. So, naturally, that limited the audience. While we were doing satellite auctions, it occurred to us that maybe there was a better way to do it, and that would be the Internet.

"So we went from the satellite platform to the Internet platform. In 1995, we came up with the idea of creating what's known as an ISP or Internet Service Provider. We created Manheim Online, our own Internet site, for which users pay a subscription charge of between $20 and $50 a month.

"We built an auto dealer Web site, or what's known as an electronic commerce site. It was one of the first successful electronic commerce, business-to-business sites on the Internet. In order to get business people, in this case auto dealers, to the Internet, we had to come up with compelling reasons to get them to do so.

"On the site we put pre-sale catalogs, post-sale market reports, and then invented something called the CyberLot, which was a venue created in cyberspace. We digitally imaged cars that were sitting at our auctions, and put them up on the Internet with pertinent information.

"Lexus was our first customer — Lexus Financial Services. We created a site within Manheim Online called LFS Direct. A Lexus dealer could get on the Internet, call up his cyberlot, and view a list of individual cars and their prices. He could bring to the screen images of the cars and, if he wanted to make a purchase, he could just click and buy over the Net. There is no bidding. It's like a bulletin board; you just click and buy.

"We learned in Auction Vision that you could not sell cars electronically unless they were priced appropriately, and that was at about the same price you would pay at an auction. In January 1997, Manheim Online was selected by PC Week magazine as one of the top 10 electronic commerce sites on the World Wide Web. Microsoft was number one and we were number five.

"As of July 1998, we had sold more than $150 million worth of cars on Manheim

AutoConnect, launched in 1998, is racing toward becoming the largest on-line inventory of vehicles in the world.

Online. We anticipate these CyberLot sales, as we call them, to approach the $200 million mark by the end of the year. To me, the real success of Manheim Online is that by using this means to extend your core business, you really get a chance to bond with your customer, and that results in incremental business and other business opportunities. For instance, right now we are building sites for two of the Big Three carmakers."

Liniado became acquainted with auto auctions in the United Kingdom when Manheim signed the joint venture with the U.K.'s Independent Car Auctions to bring its satellite technology to North America. Between July 1996 and March 1998, Manheim bought or gained controlling interest in 10 U.K. auctions. More than 100,000 cars were sold through those auctions in 1997. Liniado estimated the total will more than double in 1998.

What about the near future? Liniado responded: "In my area, which is Europe, I can see further expansion and development of the U.K. market. Also, we are on our way to the Continent. We're looking right now at France and Germany. When we make these investments on the Continent, we will also bring our electronic assets with us."

An auction "spaceman" has the earthly responsibility of painting automobiles for sellers who want to enhance the appearances of their vehicles.

Dennis Berry, publisher of *The Atlanta Journal & Constitution*, became president and chief executive officer of Manheim Auctions on October 27, 1995, and Darryll Ceccoli was named chief operating officer.

Berry went to work for the *Journal-Constitution* as a classified advertising account executive in 1966, later becoming advertising director of the newspapers. He served as executive vice president and general manager and president before becoming publisher in 1992.

Ceccoli came to Manheim in 1975 from the National Auto Dealers Exchange at Bordentown, New Jersey. He became Manheim president after Warren Young retired in 1991.

Cox Enterprises President David Easterly said of the executive realignment, "To accomplish our goals, it makes sense to have Dennis focus on strategic plans and additional opportunities, while Darryll concentrates on operational objectives."

On Thursday, October 12, 1995, Manheim kicked off a celebration of its 50th anniversary with a three-day party at its founding auction at Manheim, Pennsylvania. More than 3,000 customers from across the United States and Canada were in attendance. Some $100,000 in cash and prizes were awarded to winners of contests held throughout the year at each Manheim auction.

Taking part in the festivities were Art Walters, one of the four founders of the company, Fritz Cassel, the first general manager, and NASCAR race drivers Dale Earnhardt and Harry Gant. The next day, with 19 lanes running and 45 auctioneers on hand, Manheim Auto Auction sold a record 4,843 vehicles out of a consignment of 8,600.

Greg Gehman, the auction's general manager, said: "For one day the market was fantastic. We sold 56 percent of the cars at the sale, compared to 50 percent two weeks before and two weeks after. Our gross sales that day reached $72 million. It was a tremendous way to celebrate the company's 50th birthday."

A little-known division of the company is Manheim Auctions Government Services (MAGS), which conducts auctions for the General Services Administration, Postal Service, U.S. Marshals Service, Internal Revenue Service and numerous public utilities and related organizations.

In November 1995, MAGS was awarded a nationwide government contract to auction forfeited merchandise received from U.S. marshals, which includes such items as jewelry, fine art, precious metals, furs, antiques and collectibles. In the previous five years, MAGS had held U.S. Marshal Service sales for items confiscated east of the Mississippi River.

Extending its business into soft goods, Manheim acquired a majority interest in SCM Marketing of Winston-Salem, North Carolina, in May 1996. SCM specializes in custom-embroidered shirts, jackets and hats

Cars for sale get up-close and personal attention from prospective buyers.

for corporate accounts, which range from tool and tobacco companies to auto racing and rodeo teams. Major accounts include U.S. Tobacco Sales & Marketing, RJR Sports Marketing Enterprises, Channellocks, Detroit Gasket and A.J. Foyt Sports.

SCM also has strong ties to a number of NASCAR corporate sponsors, as well as licensing arrangements with several NASCAR race drivers. Caroline John, Manheim's senior vice president of marketing at the time, said, "This partnership is a natural for auctions since we purchase large quantities of soft goods as incentives to our customers."

Manheim has another association with NASCAR that came about when the company bought the Statesville, North Carolina, Auto Auction in July 1993. The previous owner was Larry Hedrick, who fielded a car in Winston Cup stock car racing, the sport's major league. The race team came with the deal. The 1998 season opened at Daytona Beach, Florida, with Manheim as an associate sponsor of Car Number 41, driven by Steve Grissom.

Manheim's purchase in July 1996 of the Greater Auction Group with its nine wholesale auctions raised to 61 the number of Manheim auction operations in the United States and Canada.

"Manheim and the Greater Auction Group are a natural fit," Berry said. "This acquisition provides Manheim with auctions in three new major markets: New Orleans, Las Vegas and Fort Lauderdale, as well as additional auctions in Orlando and Phoenix."

After purchasing auctions in Lafayette and Baton Rouge, Louisiana, in July 1997,

Manheim ended the year with 63 locations in North America. Vehicle sales for 1997 were a record 3,321,364, topping 1996 by more than 450,000. Fifty-seven percent of the cars came from fleets, banks, finance companies, leasing companies and manufacturers, and 43 percent came from dealers.

In September 1997, Manheim and the Dealer Services Group of Automatic Data Processing, Inc. (ADP) formed a partnership to build a consumer automotive information and advertising business on the Internet. Manheim holds a controlling interest in the venture.

With the brand name AutoConnect, the service was launched in May 1998. "Our goal," Berry said, "is to create the largest on-line inventory of vehicles in the world. Within the first year we hope to be serving at least 50 percent of the nation's 22,000 auto dealers."

AutoConnect offers free used car listings to both dealers and consumers. With dealer consent, Manheim will provide AutoConnect with listings and digital photographs of the millions of cars that pass through its auctions every year. ADP will do the same from the vehicle inventories of the more than 10,000 North American dealerships that use ADP software and computer systems to manage their businesses.

"Our revenues are coming from advertisers who want to reach this vast, special-interest audience," Berry said. "These are auto insurance, finance and warranty companies. We also collect a small transaction for business done on the Web site."

Victor (Chip) Perry, former vice president of corporate development for the Times-Mirror Company, is president and chief executive officer of AutoConnect. He said: "Our aim is to become the leading marketplace for car buyers and sellers by offering the widest choice of used cars and auto-related services available in any medium."

Millions of cars led to $1 billion in 1997 revenue for Manheim Auctions.

Commenting on his move from *The Atlanta Journal-Constitution* to Manheim Auctions, Berry said: "Newspapers are these huge, horizontal, enormously complex engines of journalism and commerce, whereas the auto auction business is focused.

Dennis Berry went from publisher to president, the first Manheim leader not reared in auctions.

We have one narrow area where we do business. By the time I walked in the door Warren Young and Darryll Ceccoli had already built a national franchise. It was a wonderful experience to come to work for a company with the team in place that made this happen.

"Another thing I really like about Manheim is that our general managers across the country are a great collection of entrepreneurs. They are making good decisions. What we try to do is stay out of the way of the good ones, and let them do their jobs; just let them grow the business. That's really a fundamental cultural icon at Manheim.

"I call Ralph Liniado 'Manheim's plow.' He's out there turning over the soil, and we come behind him planting seed and hoping we'll harvest something. He plowed the United Kingdom, found a guy to do business with, and we acquired his auctions. And now we are working across the channel, looking into France, Germany and Spain.

"Of course, we don't own a single vehicle that goes through our auction lanes. In effect, what we do is create the marketplace for used cars in this country. We are on track to double the size of the company in five years, and I started counting two years ago. We will continue to acquire 'good fit' auctions, implement modest fee increases, use the Internet to build new revenue streams, and develop the supercenter concept, where dealers can buy and sell vehicles and take advantage of such services as wholesale and retail finance, broker warranty and insurance.

"Like classified advertising, Manheim is another business that's based on millions of small transactions. Our folks are out there calling on dealers, doing a good job, making people happy and giving them good results. There was never a single day that Manheim felt like an alien environment to me."

Shane Ratliff, sponsored by Manheim's Greater Chicago Auto Auction, in March 1992 won the Auto Auctioneer's World Championship at Kansas City, Missouri, besting 54 other competitors from the United States and Canada.

To add frosting on the cake, Roy Stinnet, sponsored by Manheim's 166 Auto Auction, Springfield, Missouri, captured the world championship for ringmen. A ringman works the crowd, encouraging buyers and helping the auctioneer spot bids.

Auctioneers were judged on bid calling, product knowledge, clarity, crowd communication, appearance and overall ability. Ratliff took home a trophy and a check for $5,000. Stinnet, who also received a trophy and check for $1,500, said, "I competed with 23 of the best ringmen in the world."

Through Fire and Flood

Like letter carriers who will not be kept from their appointed rounds, or the Broadway stage where "the show must go on," Manheim will not be deterred from selling cars on Auction Day.

Listen to Darryll Ceccoli, Manheim's chief operating officer:

"On a Sunday, in the spring of 1992, a bolt of lightning struck the electrical wiring box at the Metro Milwaukee Auto Auction. In a matter of hours, the place burned to the ground, leaving only a concrete slab. Ray Kalair, the auction's general manager, called Manheim headquarters on Monday morning and broke the news.

"Not even thinking of canceling his regular Wednesday sale, he said he had already ordered tents and trailers to bring it off. The tents and trailers were set up, Wednesday came, and the auction proceeded. It was different, but Ray ran his auction very successfully under those circumstances until a new facility was ready for occupancy seven months later.

"Milwaukee, which had been a tiny operation, rose from its ashes to become in 1997 our sixth-ranked auction in sales volume.

"It would not be our last Sunday fire. On another Monday, I got a telephone call from the general manager of our American Auto Auction in Walpole, Massachusetts. A fire had broken out on Sunday night and destroyed much of the building. Several of us flew to Walpole, and found that a guard had fallen asleep with a burning cigarette in a vehicle storage area.

"Exploding gasoline tanks from 20 cars fueled the blaze, which took off a large section of the building's roof, wiping out all of the utilities. The next day, Tuesday, was sale day. We were determined we were going to have a sale despite hell, which we sure got in

Metro Milwaukee Auto Auction burned to the ground in 1992, but the regular Wednesday sale was held three days later.

the fire, or high water, which hit us when firemen dumped a half-million gallons of water on the inferno.

"When sale day came, we set up portable amplifiers for the auctioneers, and put our clerks on manual typewriters. Then, the local building inspector arrived, and told us to stop the auction. No power meant no circulating air fans to get rid of exhaust fumes. No cars could be driven through the auction lanes.

"'What if we push them?' I asked.

"After his face froze for a moment, he said, 'Well, I guess you've got me there.'

"Everybody pitched in — both dealers and employees. We pushed 600 cars through the lanes and sold about half of them. It was almost a normal sale.

"When the Midwest was hit by some of the worst floods in its history in 1993, our St. Louis auction was in harm's way. Knowing we had some lead time before the Mississippi River crested, we hired giant earth-moving equipment to dig up our auction lot and build an earthen dam around us to keep out the flood waters.

"The lot was a mess, but the dam held and we stayed in business. Afterward, we spent $400,000 constructing drains to keep us dry in the future.

Surrounded by the destruction shown below, Milwaukee staff set up business in tents and trailers, and pushed cars through the auction lanes to avoid exhaust fumes.

"Blizzards in the first three months of 1994 forced Manheim, Pennsylvania, our first auction, to close because of bad weather for only the second time in its 49-year history. With our vehicles buried under tons of snow, we missed two regular Friday auctions and a special auction for Ford.

"Manheim spent $500,000 plowing and removing snow in January alone, and lost $2 million worth of business in the first quarter. Amazingly, by year's end, Manheim beat its budget.

"The first week in February 1998 brought El Niño storms to northern California, dumping more water on the area than ever before in recorded weather history. The rains flooded our Bay Cities Auto Auction's sales lots, inundating nearly 2,000 vehicles.

"It was the worst flood in Manheim's history, but we never missed a sales day. However, we lost about 300 cars that had water up to their dashboards. Once that happens, there is not much you can do."

Broadcasting under New Rules

After 45 years of working for the company, Stan Mouse retired as president of Cox Broadcasting in February 1990. He started at WHIO-AM, Dayton, in 1945 as an announcer, but soon moved to sales and then to management. He served as president of the broadcasting operation twice — from 1977 to 1981, and from June 1987 to his retirement.

Nick Trigony, an old radio hand who had just finished a year as Cox Broadcasting's executive vice president, succeeded Mouse. In the fall of 1986, he came to Atlanta to manage Cox radio stations, a job he had performed in Houston for Viacom.

"I think Cox owned about 10 or 11 radio stations at that time," Trigony said. "The radio operation needed some work. The annual pre-tax bottom line was about $11 million and heading south.

Mr. Stanley G. Mouse

Publicity Director Radio Station WHIO, Dayton, Ohio.

Graduate of Kent State University. Writer, Director of Public Entertainment for past ten years, Editor of humor for the "DUTCHESS."

Member Alpha Psi Omega, Kappa Mu Kappa and Blue Key.

Lectures suitable for Commencements, School Assemblies, Noon-tide Clubs, special meetings or wherever people meet in groups.

For appearances write P. O. Box 32, Dayton View Station, Dayton 6, Ohio, or call Radio Station WHIO, ADams 2261.

STANLEY G. MOUSE

"We emphasized research, programming and marketing. We found out what listeners wanted, built a product around the needs of listeners and told them what we were doing. We knew that if we got in a commanding ratings position in the market, the sales would follow.

"Bringing in Bob Neil, who now heads Cox radio, from NewCity Communications was key in improving the operation. I'm really proud of radio, because we took it from a company that was not doing very well to what is arguably the country's premier radio company."

Neil joined Cox in November 1986 as station manager of WSB-AM-FM, Atlanta, "working," as he said, "pretty much on a day-to-day basis while helping Nick with programming projects." He also used his programming expertise to assist other Cox radio stations. In 1990, he took on additional responsibilities as radio regional vice president-east for Cox Broadcasting.

Under the leadership of Nick Trigony and then Michael Faherty, Cox radio's executive vice presidents, the company's stations were selected as "America's Most Admired Radio Group" by industry executives in both 1991 and 1992. It was in this time period that Mike Faherty became seriously ill.

With Faherty on medical leave, Neil was promoted to executive vice president, with responsibility for the company's 13 radio stations, eight FM and five AM. Faherty, who had joined Cox in 1981, died on February 13, 1993.

Stan Mouse (L) and Jim Rouse, who retired in 1997 as senior vice president of finance and administration after 24 years with Cox Broadcasting.

In October 1996, Cox Broadcasting remembered Faherty with the dedication of the Michael J. Faherty Broadcast Management Laboratory at the University of Georgia's Henry Grady School of Journalism and Mass Communications. The late Cox executive had served on the board of advisers of the school, and was board president from 1987–89.

In 1992, the federal government relaxed the rules governing the ownership of radio stations. The "duopoly" rule, as it was called, permitted a single company to own up to two AM and two FM stations in the same market. Previously, one operator could not own more than 14 radio stations. Under the new regulations, that number increased to 50.

By the time the Telecommunications Act of 1996 became federal law, Cox owned 23 radio stations. The act really opened the door for broadcasting companies, allowing, in most markets, single ownership of up to eight radio stations, with no more than five AM or FM.

Cox wasted little time in taking advantage of the relaxed rules, buying 20 radio stations within five months of the signing of the act. "We intend to be a major player in the exciting environment that surrounds radio since the recent telecommunications deregulation," Neil said.

On September 26, 1996, Cox Radio, Inc. became a public company, offering 30 percent of its stock for sale. The initial public offering of 7.5 million shares of Class

A common stock opened at $18.50 on the New York Stock Exchange under the symbol CXR. The public offering served to finance Cox's acquisition of NewCity Communications, Inc. and a number of other acquisitions.

Neil was named president and chief executive officer of the public company. As of June 30, 1998, it owned, operated or provided sales and marketing services for 59 stations (40 FM and 19 AM), pending some closings, placing Cox Radio among the top 10 percent of radio companies in revenues. Cox stations are clustered in 13 large and medium-sized markets. The company has reached the maximum of eight stations in the San Antonio market, and has seven in Orlando.

"I think radio is going through a real renaissance," Neil said, "where advertisers are appreciating what it can bring to the table in terms of targeting audiences. That's become a lot more important that it was maybe 10 or 15 years ago. Advertisers now are really trying to super-target very specific ages and sexes, and radio does that really well.

"As time goes on, I think radio is going to continue to grow, even beyond some of the other media. Given the additional radio stations we're allowed to own, we can really do a good job in serving customers' needs and helping them grow their business because of the size of the audience we bring to the table. Radio is really starting to win some renewed respect.

"We span the whole format spectrum pretty much. In San Antonio, for example, our formats include country, classic country, smooth jazz, oldies, adult-oriented rock, hot adult contemporary and adult standards. Seven of our 12 markets offer four or more formats, ranging from news/talk to hip-hop.

"About the only things we centralize in our multistation markets are accounting operations and those kinds of things. We're believers in decentralization. We believe the radio stations in the field should make a lot of the decisions that cover their day-to-day business activities.

Dick Ferguson, vice president and chief operating officer, Cox Radio, became a director after Radio's 1997 acquisition of NewCity Communications, where he had been president and CEO.

Directors attending the first Board meeting after Cox Radio, Inc. became a public company in 1996 were (L-R) David Easterly, president and chief operating officer, Cox Enterprises; Paul Hughes, president and chief operating officer, OG Holding Ltd.; Jim Kennedy, chairman and CEO, Cox Enterprises; Ernest Fears Jr., lecturer, Howard University; Nick Trigony, chairman of Cox Radio and president of Cox Broadcasting, and Bob Neil, president, Cox Radio.

Cox Radio President Bob Neil, Dusty and Annie as they appeared on the cover of Radio Ink magazine in 1998.

We don't have a big corporate staff. We just don't believe in that."

In Cox Radio's 1997 annual report, Neil told shareholders: "The success of our growth strategy is reflected in outstanding financial results. Revenues were $199.6 million, up 50.2 percent over 1996, and broadcast cash flow increased 70.1 percent to $69.8 million.

"More importantly, same-station results were up considerably. On a same-station basis, we increased revenues by 15 percent to $139.3 million and broadcast cash flow was up 33.7 percent to $51.9 million. The broadcast cash flow margin increased to 37.3 percent from 32 percent."

The Telecommunications Act of 1996 also liberalized the ownership of television stations, permitting a company to reach up to 35 percent of national households with its TV operations. It also extended TV station license terms from five to eight years.

"One of the best things I ever did was to put Andy Fisher in charge of our network-affiliated television stations," Trigony said. "Because of Andy's efforts, our affiliates are the finest group in the land.

"Television is not as volatile as radio, where you can lose your market position overnight to a new competitor, or put on a contest and see improvement overnight. TV stations are more like battleships; their positions erode more slowly and it takes longer to turn them around.

"All our television stations except KIRO(TV), Seattle, which we bought in 1997, are number one in news ratings, number one in revenues and have the highest margins of any stations in their markets. Two-thirds of the money we're generating in the Broadcasting Division comes from television.

"We own or operate 11 television stations. With Kevin O'Brien looking after our Fox and independent stations, and Andy in charge of our network affiliates, I tell Jim Kennedy and David Easterly, 'You can sleep well at night, because nothing bad is going to happen to our television stations as long as these guys are around.'

"Our bottom line has gone through the roof, but we did not achieve that without some travail. My first full year in this job, 1991, was the worst year in history for media advertising. Everyone suffered — television, radio and newspapers. It was horrendous.

"I had to go before the board of directors of Cox Enterprises every quarter and report bad news, saying, 'We didn't get stupid overnight; we're victims of outside influence; we need to stay focused so when the business comes back we can take advantage of it and make up the lost dollars.'

"And Jim Kennedy said to me, and I'll never forget it, 'Just do the best you can. Get our stations ready, so when the economy turns around we can take advantage of it.' He never told me to cut expenses or begin layoffs. Not one discouraging word. I knew then that we would be successful if we did the right thing because we had such great backing. And, as they say, the rest is history.

"One of things I've always believed in is managing from the bottom up, not the other way around. What Jim Kennedy has done throughout the company — and I've tried to mirror that in broadcasting — is to operate with that philosophy. If you are a sales manager at a station, you need to be a sales manager. The general manager can't be the sales manager, nor can he or she be the program or marketing manager.

Nick Trigony, President, Cox Broadcasting

"In my view, managing from the bottom up is the only way you can grow a really solid company. Also, you put good people in the pipeline, so when there are job openings, the promotions are almost automatic.

"There's another thing that I have strong feelings about, and that is you do not have to be a tyrant or a jerk to be a good manager or a good leader. You can be nice to people; you can have fun and you can have a sense of humor. You can have all those things, and still be very aggressive, very innovative, and do all the things you need to do to grow your bottom line.

"To be a good sales manager in this division, you need to be out on the street making calls, not just handling inventory. This has become a street business and you

A lineup of leaders casually broke ground in 1996 for WSB TV and Radio's new home: (L-R) David Easterly, CEI president &COO; Bob Neil, Radio president; Jim Kennedy, CEI chairman & CEO; Marc Morgan, Radio senior group vice president and head of the WSB Radio Group; Greg Stone, WSB-TV vice president & general manager; Nick Trigony, and Andy Fisher, Broadcasting executive vice president-television affiliates.

have to get out on the street to get it before your competitor does. It's not a business for ladies and gentlemen."

In November 1992, Trigony told Broadcasting magazine, "Challenge one is operating the different businesses of Cox on a day-to-day basis. The second challenge is looking at the future and where the business is going.

"I try to set an environment in which people feel free to make mistakes and feel free to grow. I set the atmosphere and motivate, but I don't run anything; the key to our success is management in the field."

More than five years later, he was still standing by that statement, saying, "We don't want our people to be afraid to fail. If you are afraid to fail, you are never going to do anything good, because if you don't try anything, you'll never be great. One of the great things about this company is that you're not penalized for taking risks."

One of the risks that went awry was the acquisition in March 1993 of Rysher Entertainment, a motion picture and television producer. Rysher's biggest screen hit was "Primal Fear," starring Richard Gere.

"The economics of the movie business was changing," Trigony said. "Suddenly, there was a glut of movies and the cost to produce a film, market it and pay the stars ran out of sight."

Cox cut its losses by shutting down the movie-producing side of Rysher in 1997. Rysher Television continues to produce programming.

"We were always in the programming business," Trigony said, "first with Al Masini at TeleRep and with Television Programming Enterprises (TPE), which was formed by Masini as part of TeleRep." TPE had several successes, among them "Solid Gold," "Star Search" and "Lifestyles of the Rich and Famous." "Entertainment Tonight," jointly owned by Cox and Paramount, continues to be popular.

All told, Cox owns three television representation companies that report to Trigony. Besides TeleRep, there are Harrington, Rider and Parsons, and Major Market Television. The three rep firms account for approximately 40 percent of the billings of national TV advertising in the United States. By itself, TeleRep, which is now run by Steve Herson, is the nation's largest TV sales rep firm, with offices in more than a dozen major markets.

"There is intense competitive pressure in this business," Trigony said. "By 9 a.m. every morning, I get ratings reports telling me how our TV stations did against the competition the previous day. Think about that."

Expanding Cable

Before Jim Robbins took over in September 1985, Cox Cable Communications (CCI) went through several top-management changes. CCI President Henry Harris left the company in 1979, and the position was vacant until Robert C. Wright was named to the job in January 1980.

Wright, an attorney, had been general manager of General Electric's Plastics Sales operations. In 1983, a few years after the proposed merger of Cox Broadcasting and General Electric fell through, Wright returned to the manufacturing giant, where he eventually was chosen to run the GE-owned National Broadcasting Company (NBC).

Wright's replacement was David Van Valkenburg. Four months into his new job, Van Valkenburg hired Robbins from Continental Cable, and asked him to watch over two New York City franchises — one managed by Cox in Queens and another partially owned on Staten Island.

"After about a year in New York, I came to Atlanta to take on more responsibility," Robbins said, "but then Van Valkenburg resigned, and I was asked by Bill Schwartz to step up to the presidency of Cox Cable.

"And I will tell you very simply that the 10 following years were really devoted to two things. First, there was building the credibility of the management team. I applied some of the things that were done at Continental, because that was a well-operated company.

"We also worked in the first five years to deliver the numbers we said we would. The next five years were really about expanding the business and management opportunities and increasing the value of the company.

"We started with a small investment in the Discovery Channel and added some other little investments along the way, so people would know that we were serious about growing the business. Now, we own, I believe, 24.6 percent of the Discovery Channel, which has a value between $1 billion and $1.5 billion. Not bad for an investment of roughly $42 million.

Cable Television: "Cox Comm" delivers its core business through one of the nation's highest-capacity and most reliable broadband networks.

Digital Television: The service greatly enhances customers' choices of programming networks through digital rather than traditional channels.

"We really like that channel, and, you know, I believe it is the kind of channel with which the Cox family likes to be identified. We get no dividend from Discovery because they continue to plow back all of the earnings into programming. What you get, however, is an annual increase in value from that re-investment."

"Ajit Dalvi (CCI senior vice president-programming and strategy) has kind of been the godfather of our investment in the Discovery Channel. He got the original call, brought it in, and has nurtured it along the way.

"The Teleport deal didn't originate with us. It was brought to us from Cox Enterprises by Bill Killen (vice president-new media) and John Dillon (former senior vice president), and it has paid off handsomely."

High-Speed Internet Access: Cox@Home delivers access to the Internet at speeds up to 100 times faster than traditional phone modems.

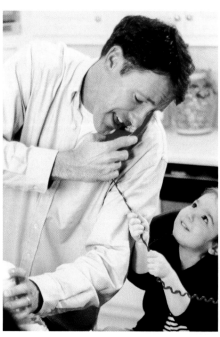

Local and Long-Distance Telephone: This highly reliable, competitively priced alternative delivers customers numerous advantages over traditional phone service.

Cox bought a 12.5 percent interest in Teleport Communications Group in November 1992. At the time, Teleport owned and operated fiber optic communication systems in 25 municipalities across the nation, a number that later grew to 60.

Fiber optic networks are used by communications-intensive businesses and long distance carriers for point-to-point digital communications links. Cox's original investment of $20 million later increased to $200 million and its percentage of ownership to 24.6.

Early in 1998, Cox and its partners — Tele-Communications, Inc. (TCI) and Comcast — accepted an offer to sell their interests in Teleport to AT&T for $11.6 billion. The deal, which analysts called "too rich to refuse," was in exchange for AT&T stock. For Cox, it was an elevenfold gain on its total investment. At mid-year 1998, Cox's AT&T shares were valued at $2.3 billion, with an annual dividend of roughly $40 million.

When Bruce Burnham joined Cox Cable in July 1975, he found it a "quiet place," with about 55 people working at corporate headquarters. "I was one of the first 'new' hires. You know, everybody had had the same secretary for years.

"That was when cable was really starting to come awake. HBO had been launched a year or two earlier. Bob Wright came along in 1980, which was about the time franchising really started. The whole world opened up almost overnight.

"It was wild. It was crazy. It was like a land

rush, because once a city awarded a cable franchise, it was gone, like a piece of land. You either got it the first time, or you never got it the rest of your life. From 1979 to 1983 or 1984, it was happening everywhere — from Fargo, North Dakota, to Miami, to whatever.

"Sometimes, you had to give away the store to get a franchise. We won our share, but nobody won most of them. When we got Tucson, there must have been bids from the top 10 companies in the industry. I remember in one case, a company offered to plant 10,000 trees in a particular city if it received the franchise.

"Almost all of this took place within a five-year period. I was talking to a lawyer about it and he told me that the last time something like this happened was when the rights to horse racing tracks were awarded, and that was done over a period of decades."

Burnham said that, in about 1984 or 1985, top management had determined that, of its 50 or so cable systems, almost all of the profits were coming from only about 30 percent of them. As vice president of market development, Burnham was given the job of selling off the small, marginal operations.

"By the time it was over," he said, "I had sold $350 million worth of cable systems. Cox Cable was the envy of the industry. Its average system size was larger than any company in the business. From a corporate viewpoint, we were looking at 20 entities rather than 50 or 60. It made a lot of sense."

Burnham became such an expert in brokering cable television franchises that on May 1, 1987, he left Cox Cable to make that his career.

Also, 1987 was a breakthrough year for cable television. For the first time, Nielsen statistics showed that a majority (50.5) percent of U.S. homes with television sets received their programs by way of cable. The National Cable Television Association said more than 44 million homes were served with cable, an increase of 4 million over 1986.

In an interview with Cable Marketing magazine, Robbins outlined two challenges facing the industry in 1988 — to maintain the customer growth momentum achieved in 1986 and to renew positive relationships with Washington and state political structures.

Speaking of rate deregulation, he said, "We have nothing to fear if we mind the store and

Commercial Services: Cox Fibernet, a competitive local exchange carrier, provides business customers a wide range of voice, video and data services.

Programming Networks: Cox Comm has investments in several leading programming networks, such as the Discovery Channel.

remain cognizant that we are a customer-driven industry with alternate methods of choice."

On December 7, 1993, Cox Cable Communications and Southwestern Bell announced they had signed a memorandum of understanding to form a $4.9 billion cable partnership. Under that memorandum, Southwestern Bell was to commit $1.6 billion in capital to the partnership and Cox was to contribute 21 cable systems.

However, on April 5, 1994, Southwestern Bell terminated its plans for the proposed partnership out of a concern that the federal government would "accelerate the imposition of cumbersome regulatory rules." Jim Kahan, Southwestern Bell senior vice president, said, "This in no way diminishes our respect for Cox Cable. Our due diligence confirmed that the Cox cable operations are extremely well managed and have excellent relationships with customers and regulators."

But Cox Cable remained intensely focused on growth, and only two months later was involved in the biggest deal in its history. On June 5, 1994, Cox Enterprises and the Times-Mirror Company signed definitive agreements to merge Times-Mirror's cable television units into Cox Cable.

The agreement called for Cox Cable to spin off into a publicly traded company on the New York Stock Exchange, where it would be called Cox Communications. Cox Enterprises would control 80 percent, Times-Mirror and other public shareholders 20 percent of the new company.

The multibillion dollar merger became official on February 1, 1995, and on that day Cox Communications stock traded at between $16 and $17 a share. The customer base increased from 1.9 to 3.2 million in 36 systems, a gain of almost 41 percent.

Cox Enterprises holds four of the seven seats on the company's board of directors. CEI chairman Jim Kennedy also is chairman of Cox Communications, and Robbins is president and chief executive officer. The other directors are David Easterly, Cox Enterprises president and chief operating officer; John Dillon, managing director of Cravey, Green & Whalen and former CEI senior vice president; Robert Erburu, retired chairman of the Times-Mirror Company; Janet Clarke, managing director, Global Database

Wireless Telecommunications: **The company has been a leader in developing Personal Communication Services (PCS), a wireless telephone technology.**

Education: **Every elementary and secondary school in communities served by "Cox Comm" long have benefited from free cable service.**

Marketing, Citibank and Andy Young, co-chairman of Good Works International LLC, and former Atlanta mayor, U.S. congressman and United Nations ambassador.

"This is a watershed event for our company," said Jimmy Hayes, Cox Communications chief financial officer. "It is the single best transaction we could have made."

Robbins agreed, saying: "We picked the company that was the best fit for Cox in geography, system size, culture, values and technology. Now we're strategically positioned to take advantage of the changing telecommunications environment."

The merger also fit nicely into Cox Communications' strategy of putting together systems in large operational units or clusters for a competitive advantage. After the transaction, Cox had more than 750,000 customers in Southern California and 584,000 in the Phoenix area, one of the largest and fastest growing television markets in the United States.

Currently, Cox Communications has nine large cluster markets, from which it receives 85 percent of its revenue. Each cluster has a vice president and general manager who report to one of three vice presidents for operations.

Cox serves Orange County, California, which is the only market in the United States, and potentially the world, to have a full-service cable network, providing residential telephone service, digital cable television and access to the high-speed Internet through one pipe.

Digital, which is the next generation of cable, gives the customers up to 12 channels in the same space that one analog transmission occupies. That means channel capacity can be added in a single band with digital television. It is a transmission that is totally free of distortion.

Also in 1994, Cox was one of only three companies nationwide — and the only cable television operator — to be awarded a "Pioneer's Preference" license for Personal Communications Services (PCS) by the Federal Communications Commission. Cox's license covers Southern California and Nevada, and was awarded for innovation in developing cable-based PCS. Later that year, Cox, TCI, Comcast Corporation and Sprint Corporation formed Sprint PCS, a partnership to acquire PCS licenses to provide 100 percent digital Personal Communication Services nationwide.

Marketing under the Sprint PCS brand name, Cox launched the nation's first cable-based Personal Communication Services in San Diego in 1996. Shortly thereafter, Cox PCS was ranked by J.D. Power and Associates as the wireless service provider with the "Highest Overall Customer Satisfaction" among wireless users in San Diego. Cox PCS was also awarded the Personal Communications Industry Association's 1997 Technology Award.

In just a few short years, the Sprint PCS partnership has brought 100 percent digital wireless service to more than 156 major metropolitan markets across the country. In January 1998, Sprint PCS reached a major milestone when it added its one millionth customer in record time.

Despite its huge local success in San Diego, Cox was unable to realize its initial concept of cable-based PCS on a national scale, and concluded that control of cable-based PCS no longer fit its principal strategy.

In June 1998, Sprint, TCI, Comcast and Cox announced an agreement under which Sprint would assume majority ownership and management control of Sprint PCS. A new common stock owned by the Sprint PCS partners and the public would be created.

When Cox digital TV was introduced in Aliso, California, in October 1997, it added nearly 100 video channels to Cox's cable television lineup in the Orange County market. Among the features were 25 new digital networks, additional premium services, enhanced pay-per-view and 40 CD-quality music channels. Customers also received an interactive program guide.

Robbins said: "Cox Digital TV delivers an explosion of new programming and advanced services that place enhanced levels of choice, convenience and control at our customers' fingertips. And Cox customers get the digital advantage from an experienced, trusted video provider without having to purchase a satellite dish or install an unsightly antenna. They also receive the award-winning service of a company that has been in the information and entertainment business for 100 years."

In addition to Orange County, residential telephone services have been launched in Omaha and New England. As of the end of 1997, Cox had regulatory approval to deliver phone service in nine markets nationwide, and had installed switching equipment in seven of those. By the year 2000, Cox Communications expects to be delivering full-service cable, which includes phones and high-speed data, to all nine of its clusters.

Cox Communications continues to buy and sell cable systems, shedding smaller, older ones, and looking at major acquisitions that will fit into the company's expanding clusters.

Another blockbuster cable deal was announced May 6, 1998. Cox Communications reported that it had reached a definitive agreement to buy an 80 percent stake in Prime South Diversified, Inc., the company that provides cable television to all of metropolitan Las Vegas.

Worth $1.3 billion, the transaction is expected to be completed by the end of 1998. It would add 319,000 new cable subscribers to Cox Communications, making the company the nation's fifth largest cable operator, with 3.8 million customers.

Prime South Diversified is owned by the Greenspun family of Las Vegas, which also owns the *Las Vegas Sun* newspaper and other media and publication assets. The patriarch of the family, the colorful Hank Greenspun, was a U.S. Army veteran who after World War II went to Las Vegas to set up a radio station.

Shortly after his arrival, he traveled to Mexico for six months, where he was a key figure in a covert operation that smuggled arms to the Israelis during their war of independence. His mission was so secret he couldn't even tell his wife where he was going.

In May 1950, with the help of a Las Vegas businessman, Greenspun bought the *Las Vegas Free Press* from the International Typographical Union and changed its name to the *Sun.*

He used its editorial pages to take on elected officials not to his liking and the FBI in general. He was an early opponent of Wisconsin Senator Joe McCarthy and fought the eccentric Howard Hughes. According to Joseph Yablonsky, an FBI agent at the time, "Hank could not get you elected, but he could definitely get you un-elected."

Greenspun died on July 22, 1989, at the age of 79. His son, Brian, a roommate of President Bill Clinton at Georgetown law school, took over the family business.

The Las Vegas system would become Cox Communications' 10th U.S. cluster and the industry's first mega-cluster. CCI already has 1.7 million customers in Southern California, Arizona and Nevada with 2.7 million homes passed.

Cox outbid Comcast, Charter Communications and Tele-Communications, Inc. for the Las Vegas system, which Robbins called "the most sought-after cable property in the country," adding: "This will allow us to maintain our vision as a single provider of advanced video, voice and data services, just as we're doing in existing Cox cluster markets throughout the United States."

Said Kennedy, "This was the last of the big clusters and a real gem. We really wanted it."

In addition to the cable system, Cox Communications will acquire Hospitality Network, Inc., the nation's largest provider of cable and interactive television services to hotels, casinos and resorts. The network serves 105,000 hotel rooms, including 77,000 in Las Vegas.

Some 20,000 additional hotel rooms are expected to be built in the city. The Las Vegas cable television system's annual growth rate has been between 5 and 6 percent, the fastest in the industry.

Cox Communications President and CEO Jim Robbins, shown with Bakersfield's Mary Gomez in 1988, led the cable division through transformation that, 10 years ago, already had enabled Cox systems to have local "ownership" and set customer service as their first goal.

Cox Communications strengthened its position in Arizona on June 1, 1998, when it reached an agreement to buy the Tucson cable system from Tele-Communications, Inc. for $250 million. The acquisition will give CCI another 117,000 customers.

"We were the original franchise holder in Tucson," Robbins said, "but we walked away from it in 1985 because city officials of that time were almost impossible to deal with.

"With a cable penetration of only 41 percent in Tucson, we have a real opportunity to grow there, particularly in the suburban areas. The average penetration in CCI markets is about 65 percent. We're looking at probably 285,000 homes passed by cable."

An announcement June 24, 1998, that AT&T planned to buy Tele-Communications, Inc., the nation's largest cable company, sent shock waves throughout the industry. But Robbins viewed the announcement as a clear confirmation of Cox Communications' in-place strategy of delivering voice, video services and other data in one efficient stop.

"It can only help the prospects for the entire cable industry," he said. "By the end of the year, we will be two-thirds complete with our upgrades. We have strong relations with our franchises and our customers, and our customers are confident of our ability to offer new services. Clearly, Cox has a leg up in this area versus the entire industry. I'm really proud of what we have done."

"We've worked for 10 years on the whole issue of customer service. We think that's a long-term strategic benefit. And we have sacrificed profit margin for this. In the past, Wall Street has beat us up over that issue.

"But we have said over and over that customer service is important for the long-term health of the business, and its ability to sell new services. I'll stand with lower margins than the other guys because they are trying to scorch the earth. And Wall Street now believes our theory. We enjoy the highest multiple of any of the public cable companies as a result."

Does Robbins feel threatened by the growing Internet? Not really. "The Internet is an opportunity for us," he said, "because our residential high-speed Internet service, Cox-at-Home, saves consumers so much time. It transmits data up to 100 times faster than a typical analog telephone modem, making access to the World Wide Web virtually instant."

Since Cox-at-Home debuted in Orange County in December 1996, it has been introduced into Cox markets at San Diego; Phoenix; Omaha; Hartford, Connecticut; and Hampton Roads, Virginia.

"We are enormously lucky in this company to have the management we have," Robbins said. "With the continuity of one family at the helm for 100 years, we have been incredibly stable. Secondly, the family has plowed almost everything back into the business. What more could we ask?"

Cox Communications had operating revenues of $1.61 billion in 1997, compared to $1.46 billion in 1996. Operating cash flow in 1997 was $609 million, up from $556 million in 1996. However, all of the cash over the last several years is being fully reinvested in system upgrades. Cox Communications ended 1997 with 3.3 million customers and more than 7,000 employees.

Sell-Offs, Swaps and Trades

With sales, purchases and trades, the geographical look of Cox Newspapers changed in the 1990s. The company bought its first newspapers in North Carolina on New Year's Day, 1996, with the acquisition of *The* (Greenville) *Daily Reflector* and 11 weekly publications.

Much like the history of Cox, *The Daily Reflector* had been owned by the Whichard family through four generations, dating back to 1882 — 16 years before young Jimmy Cox bought the *Dayton Daily News.*

The transaction came about because of two Daves — Dave Whichard, the third-generation owner, and Dave Easterly, president and chief operating officer of Cox Enterprises. The two had become friends through the Southern Newspapers Association and the Associated Press board of directors.

"I think Dave Whichard recognized the world was changing and he wanted his newspapers to be secure for the long run," said Jay Smith, president of Cox Newspapers. "His talks with David Easterly led quickly to our interest in making the acquisition.

"I have said several times that not only did we get a terrific 20,000-plus circulation newspaper and nine weeklies, but we also got a terrific publisher, who happens to be named Jordy Whichard, *The Daily Reflector*'s fourth Whichard generation publisher."

Greenville, one of the top-10 fastest growing markets in the country, is the home of East Carolina University and its more than 17,000 students.

Before 1996 was over, Cox would buy two more daily newspapers in North Carolina and end 20 years of newspapering in Arizona. All this came about after Smith had breakfast with top executives of Canadian-based Thomson Newspapers at the 1996 convention of the Newspaper Association of America in New Orleans.

Cox sold the The Orange Leader and Port Arthur News (both in Texas) in 1990, beginning an era of sell-offs, swaps and trades.

Smith sought the meeting so he could ask the Thomson people if they might be amenable to selling Cox their newspapers in Southwestern Ohio. Nothing developed from that, but Thomson's representatives subsequently came back to Smith, and said, "We'd like to talk to you about your Arizona newspapers. Are they for sale?"

"My immediate response was, 'No, we don't have anything for sale,' Smith said.

"'If we offered you a handsome price, would the Arizona papers be for sale?' was their next question.

"'Let's hear the handsome price,' I replied. We agreed to have another meeting."

On a cold and snowy Friday, Smith, accompanied by Brian Cooper, senior vice president of Cox Newspapers, and Buddy Solomon, controller, flew into Stamford, Connecticut, to try and hammer out a deal with Thomson.

Smith recalled: "Buddy shows up at the airport in just a suit. Brian's wearing a suit and a raincoat. I say, 'Guys, you know, we're going to run into some bad weather.'

"Sure enough, shortly after we got there, it started snowing like mad. As we're meeting with the Thomson people, we're looking nervously out the window at the worsening weather. Worrying about getting to the airport, I felt a need to push the issue, so I asked the Thomson representatives, 'What is it that you are willing to pay us?'

"They turned the tables, and said, 'What do you want?'

"After Brian, Buddy and I talked, we basically told them what it would take to

At $23 million, _The Palm Beach Post_'s new building, 1995, cost about the same as Cox had paid for the Palm Beach newspaper businesses in 1969.

close the deal. Their response was positive and we left the room, feeling we had an agreement in principle.

"We took a train to LaGuardia, only to learn that our flights had been snowed out. Of course, Buddy doesn't have any warm clothes and Brian, this whiz-bang financial guy, didn't bring any cash. I find out it's not snowing in Harrisburg, Pennsylvania, so we grab a train headed in that direction.

"I left the train in Philadelphia to visit with my daughter, and Buddy and Brian continued to Harrisburg, where they caught a flight to Atlanta Saturday morning. It was quite a trip and I felt confident we had accomplished our mission. It was one of those times when a sensible person, looking at the weather forecast, would have said, 'I shouldn't make this trip,' but given that the time is right to get something done, you say, 'To hell with your inconvenience,' and you make the trip."

Although it took another nine months to reach a final agreement, Cooper said the meeting in Stamford was the "magic moment" that energized the transaction.

The deal:

Thomson assumed ownership of Cox's five daily Tribune newspapers in Mesa, Tempe, Scottsdale, Chandler and Gilbert, Arizona, and the *Yuma Daily Sun*.

In turn, Cox received two Thomson dailies in North Carolina — *The* (Elizabeth City) *Daily Advance* and the *Rocky Mount Telegram* — as well as cash and other considerations. In addition, as a result of a separate newspaper trade between Thomson and Hollinger International, Cox picked up Hollinger's *Marshall* (Texas) *News Messenger*.

In December 1990, Cox sold two of its Texas newspapers — the *Port Arthur News* and *Orange Leader* — to the American Publishing Company, a division of Hollinger. A year earlier, Cox bought the Nacogdoches *Daily Sentinel* in East Texas.

"One of the worst days of my life was when I had to tell our people in Arizona that their newspapers had been sold," Smith said. "We were able to place some of the executives in other Cox locations. Sandy Schwartz, who was the publisher of the *Tribune* papers, is now general manager in Austin; Belinda Gaudet, who was general manager in Arizona, is publisher at *The Lufkin Daily News*; and Jeff Bruce, editor of the *Tribune* papers in Arizona, is editor of the first Cox paper, the *Dayton Daily News*.

"In addition to being publisher of the *Greenville Reflector*, Jordy Whichard watches over all our North Carolina properties. Through Jordy we were able to buy a direct mail company at Tarboro, North Carolina, in late 1997. He is a friend of a mother and son who started PAGAS Mailing Services some five years earlier.

"They talked to him about buying their company and he brought them to Cox. PAGAS each month serves 858,000 households of Eastern North Carolina with pre-printed advertising flyers. It is a perfect fit with our three dailies and 11 weeklies. Cox touches almost every household east of I-95 in North Carolina with either a daily newspaper, a weekly newspaper or direct mail."

In Dayton, Jay Smith worked as a reporter at the *Daily News* at the same time his wife, Susan, was promotion director of Dayton Newspapers, Inc. "In some ways, it was an awkward time for me," Smith said. "Here I was, a negotiator for the editorial labor union, being taken to the management Christmas party as my wife's guest.

"People who think newspapers are dying are dead wrong. We have some tremendously strong franchises in both big and small cities, where a talented group of journalists and advertising and circulation sales people work. They are people who know their communities, and serve them well.

"There is nothing that you pay 50 cents a day for or a couple of bucks on Sunday that brings with it more value than the newspaper. I think our future is only up. If it goes down, we have only ourselves to blame. There have been times, I think, when we thought we were smarter than we really were.

"I believe that if we maintain a positive and aggressive outlook, we'll be just fine. If we end up joining the naysayers and moan and groan and whine and bellyache, then we're in trouble. You don't win any games by walking onto the field and saying, 'We'll be lucky if we win today.' The only way you are going to win is to go out there and say, 'I wonder how badly we're going to beat them today.' And I believe our men and women have that attitude and that spirit.

"We know how to make money and, just as important, we know how to do good newspapering. I am proud of the fact that we have not forgotten that we are newspapermen and newspaperwomen who are equally skilled at being good businessmen and businesswomen. In my opinion, the two are inseparable.

"Also, most of our facilities are state of the art. *The Palm Beach Post* dedicated a new 150,000-square-foot office building in June 1995. Coincidentally, the building's cost of $23 million was about the same amount of money Cox paid for the Palm Beach newspaper properties in 1969.

"We're building a magnificent new $90 million satellite production and distribution plant for the *Dayton Daily News*. Once the building is finished in July 1999, there will not be a single press unit at the downtown facility."

In February 1996, Cox Newspapers repositioned the leadership of its Ohio publications to better serve the Miami Valley market of more than 1 million people. The *Dayton Daily News*, the *Springfield News-Sun* and Dayton's recently created electronic publishing units began operating as part of a new company, Cox Ohio Publishing.

Brad Tillson, who went to work for the *Daily News* as a reporter in 1971, was named president and chief operating officer of Cox Ohio Publishing. He retained his position of publisher of the *Daily News*. Doug Franklin, Dayton's general manager, added the title of executive vice president and chief operating officer of Cox Ohio.

Springfield publisher Charlie Rinehart moved to senior vice president and chief financial officer of Cox Ohio. Succeeding him as publisher was Bill Swaim, *News-Sun* vice president and general manager.

Smith said: "The creation of Cox Ohio Publishing will help accomplish a number of objectives. It will help Dayton and Springfield to continue to publish quality newspapers while moving into electronic publishing and niche products. It will help streamline resources to better serve customers and to respond to ever-increasing competition. And, it will result in increased revenues and cost savings."

Cathy Coffey, vice president of advertising for Cox Newspapers, said, "The last five years have seen the greatest growth of classified advertising in the history of the business. It's a combination of a healthy job market, a good automotive market and a booming real estate market.

"In 1990–1991 the advertising business tanked on the East Coast and a year or two

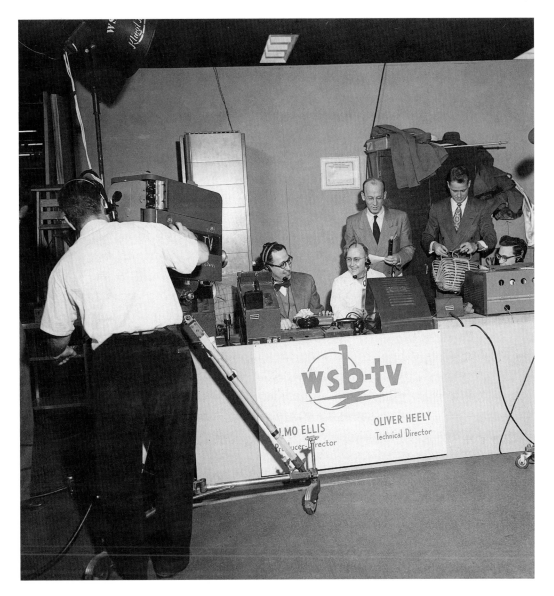

ELMO ELLIS
Producer-Director

OLIVER HEELY
Technical Director

wsb-tv

Born of a 1950 transit strike, "Rich's in Your Home" became a successful long-running WSB-TV series, originating daily from the downtown Atlanta store. Cox's strong relationship with the retailer has spanned the decades.

later on the West Coast. Everything that could sink, sank. After that monster retail recession, I'm pleased to say that business rebounded with a vengeance."

For years, retail advertising produced the most revenue for newspapers, but that has changed. For Cox Newspapers in 1997, classified as a percent of all advertising revenue was 40 percent. Retail was 38 percent, followed by retail supplement and national advertising.

Ferguson Rood, the man Coffey succeeded as vice president of advertising for Cox Newspapers in 1989, recalled that when he became ad director at Atlanta Newspapers in 1976, the advertising revenue breakdown was 50 percent retail, 30 percent classified, 18 percent national and 2 percent legal and other.

"Now, national advertising is almost nonexistent," Rood said. "Our big national advertisers used to be distillers, airlines, tobacco companies and automobile manufacturers. When I came to Atlanta, three of four retail advertisers dominated the amount of retail business we received, which in my view, put us in jeopardy. Too much of our business was in the hands of a few people.

"As advertising director, one of my first strategies was to go for small-space retail advertisers to broaden our account base. And that was higher-rate business. A lot of those small-space advertisers grew into bigger accounts and earned better rates.

"There are two things that I consider my legacy. One was that when I became ad director at *The Atlanta Journal-Constitution*, there were three women on the retail and national advertising display staff. When I moved to the corporate staff 10 years later, there were more than 50 women in display advertising and they were doing an outstanding job.

"The second thing was the introduction of a sales assistant program, which freed up the sales people to spend more time with customers, while the assistants did the paper-work back in the office. There was one sales assistant for every three sales persons."

Asked what makes Cox newspapers a more attractive buy for advertisers than its competitors, Coffey said: "There are several things, I believe, that make us unique. The first is that we're the kind of company that the very good people in the newspaper business want to work for, so we're able to attract the best talent at all of our papers. That's probably the single most important thing we've got going for us.

"Number two, we fundamentally believe in developing customer relationships that last, and we have done an extraordinary job with that at all levels within the company. Looking at the big picture, those are the two biggest differences. Another thing that has made a difference, I think, is that we recognized earlier than most newspaper companies the value of classified advertising and where it was heading.

"We were able to bring on top-notch classified talent to grow that business when the market hit rock bottom, so that when it came back, we were in a position to really take advantage of it.

"In 1997, Russel Stravitz, CEO of Rich's-Lazarus-Goldsmith's, our largest customer by a lot, held a thank-you luncheon for us. Jim Kennedy was there, along with David Easterly, Jay Smith, Nick Trigony and representatives from *The Atlanta Journal-Constitution, Dayton Daily News*, WSB, Atlanta; WHIO, Dayton; and WPXI, Pittsburgh.

"It is not very often that your largest customer hosts a thank-you party for you, and shares strategic issues, market by market, where you do business. It was very flattering, as well as an affirmation of how much we care for our customers, and how much they care for us."

Minor J. "Buddy" Ward, former president of The Atlanta Journal-Constitution, *died February 14, 1998, when his single-engine Piper Cherokee airplane crashed into a Florida citrus grove after hitting power lines.*

Ward, 63, retired from Cox Newspapers in 1990. He went to work for the Journal-Constitution *in 1953 as an apprentice printer, and rose through the ranks to become vice president of production and engineering in 1979.*

He was promoted to president of the newspapers in 1983, supervising everything but the news operations. Four years later, he became senior vice president-operations, for Cox Newspapers.

Cox Target Media

Bob Musselman saw his first auto trader publications in a convenience store in Mesa, Arizona, in the early 1980s. He bought an armload of the magazines, and took them to his motel room to read before going to bed.

There were separate publications for domestic cars, foreign cars and trucks, and one for everything else, ranging from motorcycles to recreational vehicles.

"They were great publications to read," said Musselman, a Dayton Newspapers executive at the time who was visiting Cox-owned papers in Mesa, Tempe and Chandler. "I got to talking with some of the store clerks about the magazines and they told me, 'Yeah, people stand in line, waiting for them to show up each week.'

"I said to myself, 'When it comes to selling motor vehicles, there's a real revolution going on here.' Historically, most people traded in their cars to dealers when they bought another one. But we had reached the point where, economically, it was worth your effort to sell the car yourself.

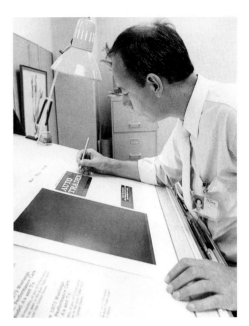

"Instead of the difference between a dealer trade-in and selling the car yourself being a couple of hundred dollars, it could be a thousand or more. From a price standpoint, newspapers couldn't compete. Back in those days, the people running the trader publications would come to your house, take a picture of your car, run an ad for as long as three weeks, and charge you all of twelve dollars."

As Musselman traveled the country, he began seeing more of the trader magazines — in Atlanta and in Florida, where he vacationed. Cox Newspapers had looked at some potential newspaper acquisitions at that time, but the asking prices were unbelievably high, in some instances as much as 10 or 11 times gross revenues.

"It was apparent to me," Musselman said, "that we were not going to buy any of those newspapers."

Meanwhile, Musselman, who had become president of Dayton Newspapers in 1983, moved to Atlanta in 1986 as senior group vice president of Cox Newspapers. He asked David Easterly, Cox Newspapers' president, if he could explore the feasibility of acquiring some of the auto trader publications.

Easterly, who also was intrigued with the potential of the special-purpose magazines, told him, "By all means, go ahead and check it out."

Musselman collected Auto Trader magazines from a dozen or so cities, but was unable to get information on who ran them. "I noticed all the publications carried the name Stuart Arnold, so I ran down Arnold's office in Clearwater, Florida, and called," Musselman said.

"His secretary wouldn't let me talk to him, asking, 'What do you want to talk to him about?' And when I said, 'I would just like to talk to him,' she wouldn't put me through. So, about the third time I called, I said, 'Tell Mr. Arnold I am interested in finding out if he wants to sell his company.'

Cox and Landmark were chief competitors for acquiring auto advertising books, so in 1991 they joined 50-50 in establishing Trader Publishing Company. Graphic artist Tom Hanlon (shown) prepared a cover for the popular Auto Trader.

"'Okay,' she said, 'I'll give him the message.' I got a phone call the next day from Lou Tarasi, who was his right-hand man. 'Come on down,' he said."

The transaction, completed on July 20, 1988, brought to Cox more than 50 publications. The magazines are published in 31 markets throughout the nation, and there are franchise operations in 24 other markets. Trader Publications also puts out several national distribution magazines that advertise antique cars, trucks, boats and airplanes.

Appointed president of Trader Publications on August 30, 1988, Musselman immediately started buying independent traders all over the United States, and within five months Cox owned the majority of the trader magazines in the country.

"There wasn't a whole lot of consolidating to be done, except in the composing room," Musselman said. "As part of the deal, we bought Arnold's 75,000-square-foot production and printing plant in Clearwater. Our Longview newspaper plant ultimately printed all the Texas magazines, and we built a facility in Los Angeles to print the Phoenix and California publications.

"Initially, everything was printed on standard newsprint stock, but we later went to a shiny cover, which gave us an opportunity to make more money, because we received a premium for advertising on the front, back and two inside cover pages.

"Unlike real estate and rental magazines, the automotive publications had circulation revenue. Early on, there were a lot of 50- and 75-cent books. We immediately took them to a dollar or more. When you raise circulation prices in the newspaper business, everyone knows it, but in the trader business hardly anyone notices because, for the most part, there are different advertisers and buyers each week."

In October 1989, Trader Publications bought a Clearwater neighbor, the Stuffit Company, a direct mailer of coupons and custom mailings, which operated primarily through franchises in 10 cities. Musselman called the acquisition "an extension of our present operation," explaining, "Our Trader publications are advertising-only publications. Entering the coupon and custom mailing market is an extension of that concept."

Trader Publications' chief competitor in the acquisition of automobile advertising books was Landmark Target Media of Norfolk, Virginia. By mid-1990, almost all of the trader-type magazines had sold out to either Cox or Landmark. "If you took our locations and laid them down on top of theirs, it would look like a map of the United States," Musselman said. "We were competing head-to-head in only three cities.

"When you looked at us, we were essentially across the South and up the West Coast, while Landmark covered the Midwest and East Coast. We had owned Trader Publications for only a year or two when other companies started offering us three times what we had in the operation. My view was, 'With all that money on the table, maybe we ought to take it.'

Landmark was among the suitors. On April 1, 1991, Cox announced that it had merged Trader Publications with Landmark Target Media. The new company was named Trader Publishing Company, with both Cox and Landmark owning 50 percent. With more than 200 titles published in 72 markets, it became a truly national company at its inception.

Norfolk was chosen as the headquarters, and Conrad Hall, former president of Landmark Target Media, became president of the Trader Publishing Company. Mitch Brooks, former general manager of the Cox Trader group, was named executive vice president.

Musselman, who remained as president of other Cox Target Media businesses such as Stuffit, Clipper and Main Street Advertising, became chairman of the new company's executive committee. A new six-man board included Cox executives Jim Kennedy, chairman and CEO of Cox Enterprises; David Easterly, president of Cox Newspapers and Musselman. Named to represent Landmark were Frank Batten, chairman and CEO; Dick Barry, vice chairman and Bill Diedrich, retired executive vice president.

On Friday the 13th in September 1991, Cox Newspapers announced the acquisition of Val-Pak Direct Marketing Systems, Inc. in Largo, Florida. Musselman, who had been wooing the direct mailer for three years, was named Val-Pak chairman and Bill Disbrow president. The direct mailer became part of Cox Target Media, of which Musselman was president and Disbrow vice president.

Val-Pak pioneered the concept of local cooperative direct mail, in which advertisements from many businesses are mailed in the same envelope to targeted households. At the time of the acquisition, mailings were going to 42 million households in the United States and 4 million in Canada. A group of 170 franchisees maintained local sales forces and performed local marketing throughout the country.

Val-Pak in 1997 mailed out 11 billion coupons in the familiar blue envelopes.

Musselman described Val-Pak as the "Coca-Cola of the direct mail business," adding, "One of the lessons we learned from all of our acquisitions was that you pay the price and go for the big guy, because with anything less than that, you're asking for trouble."

The coupon packages are mailed on an average of eight times a year, although some franchises mail as many as a dozen. Val-Pak, which is mostly mom-and-pop-type advertising, distributes its packages in zones of 10,000. In a market of 150,000 homes, for example, there would be 15 zones. An advertiser could buy one or all zones. Much Val-Pak advertising is placed by businesses such as dry cleaners, restaurants, pizza chains, hairdressers and service companies.

"Our circulation has grown to more than 52 million households in the U.S. and Canada," Musselman said. "In 1997, Val-Pak mailed out 11 billion coupons. We believe it is the largest desktop publishing operation in the world. We also are blessed with production equipment that is state-of-the-art.

"Operating three shifts, seven days a week, Val-Pak is one of the U.S. Post Office's best customers. They won't tell us where we rank, but I'll bet you we are in the top 20 in the country."

In early 1996, Cox added Carol Wright Promotions to Musselman's operation. Carol Wright, now called Cox Direct, distributes mostly-national coupons to some 25 million homes 10 times a year.

Cox Target Media operates in 350,000 square feet in Florida, which is the equivalent of seven football fields, and has another 110,000 square feet in Las Vegas.

After 25 eventful years with the Cox organization, Musselman retired at the end of 1997. He was replaced by his deputy, Bill Disbrow, who had joined Cox Enterprises in 1982 as a staff accountant.

Looking back, Musselman said, "You know, people talk about having a chance to hit a home run in their career, but, as far as I'm concerned, I was involved with two home runs, the first being Auto Trader, and the second Val-Pak."

Diversity

Cox Chairman Jim Kennedy has a long record of forthrightly supporting diversity in the workplace.

"Perhaps I approach the whole issue of diversity from a different perspective than other CEOs," he said. "I think the major reason for that is the environment in which I was born and raised.

"Growing up in paradise was terrific for a lot of reasons. One reason, which I didn't really appreciate at that time, was the people I grew up with in Hawaii. Some of my playmates looked like me, but most didn't. They were Polynesian, Asian, Filipino. I really thought that was the norm. I grew up in an environment that practiced diversity when we didn't know what diversity was.

"It seems to be pretty simple that if we are trying to serve a diverse marketplace, we had better have an employee base that reflects the diversity of the customers we are trying to serve. Developing and maintaining a diverse employee base is not only the right thing to do, it's the smart business thing to do.

"In this new century, change will happen faster than we have ever seen before. We will have to work harder and be smarter than ever before. Even in this world of instantaneous information and convenient service, our success will be rooted in the values established by my grandfather: commitment to customer and community service, respect for employees, and integrity. I look forward to what we will accomplish together in this new century of Cox Enterprises."

On August 15, 1995, Kennedy had posted on the bulletin boards of every entity of Cox Enterprises a "Commitment to Diversity" statement, which read:

COMMITMENT TO DIVERSITY

This company is committed to having a workforce that reflects the communities we serve. Also, we want to capitalize on the unique talents that come from a variety of people and perspectives.

A diverse workforce can more effectively serve all our customers, as well as enable us to be valuable citizens of our communities. And we are committed to competing for the best talent from a diverse pool.

We believe that a diverse workforce is a bottom-line business issue that leads to:

- increased creativity and innovation in problem solving
- closer customer and supplier relationships
- an enhanced company reputation
- attraction and retention of the best talent
- hence, increased productivity and profitability

Our managers are committed to valuing a diverse workforce and they demonstrate this by:

- creating an atmosphere in which employees can express themselves and take risks
- including a diversity of perspectives in decision-making
- demonstrating an inclusive leadership style
- confronting and eliminating intolerant behavior

Recruiting material in the mid-'90s emphasized that, at Cox Enterprises, "Our diversity is our strength."

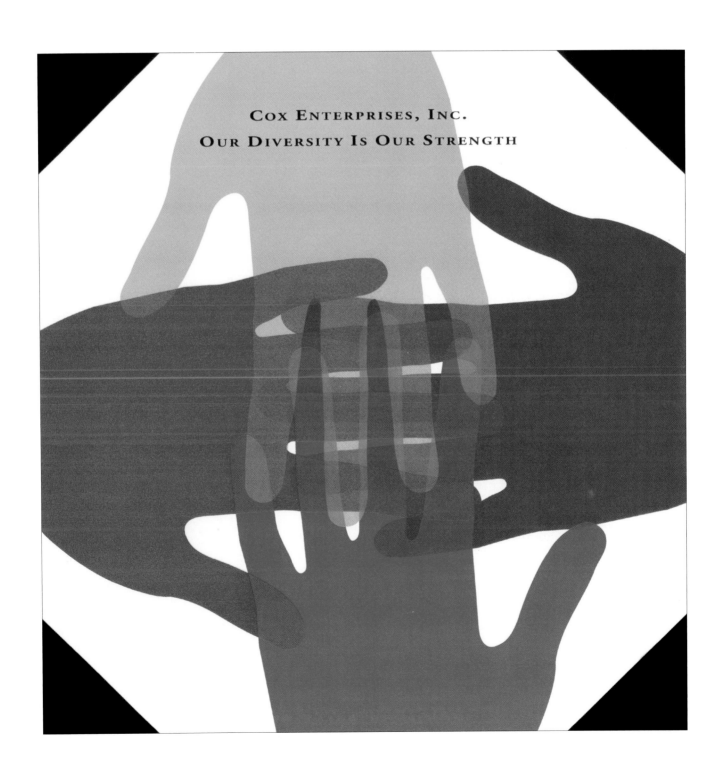

On April 20, 1998, with equal employment programs being challenged in the courts, Kennedy issued the following personal statement to Cox employees:

"A SPECIAL ANNOUNCEMENT

STATEMENT OF JIM KENNEDY
CHAIRMAN AND CEO OF COX ENTERPRISES, INC.

"A debate has been reopened by a decision of the U.S. Court of Appeals holding the Federal Communications Commission's (FCC's) Equal Employment Opportunity program requirements unconstitutional. I suspect that the debate will continue to rage as this important matter works its way through the judicial process. However, as far as Cox is concerned, making sure that the employees in our business reflect as much as is reasonably possible the diversity of the marketplaces that they serve is not debatable. It is simply good business and it is the right thing to do. At Cox we are able to understand and serve our customers and our communities best by ensuring such diversity. Whether or not the FCC's EEO rules survive constitutionally, Cox will continue actively to maintain and improve the diversity of its workforce."

Rosalynne V. Price succeeded Alexis Scott Reeves as Cox's manager of diversity in November 1997. She holds a Ph.D. from Georgia State University.

As manager of diversity, her principal concerns are with the recruitment, hiring, treatment and promotion of blacks, women, Asians, Hispanics and American Indians.

"However, diversity really means everybody," she said, "and we do some special recruiting to make sure everybody's included."

She has set four goals for 1998. The first is to re-establish contact with historically black colleges and universities in communities where there is a large minority population.

"I say 're-establish,' she said, "because, while we have been very good at giving grants and that sort of thing, we have not been seen as a place to find a job. We want our managers to establish a relationship with these schools so they can become a recruiting source for part-time work and management development.

"When it comes to the number of minority employees at our senior management level, it is not as good as we would like it to be."

"The second goal," Price said, "is to get a senior manager in each division to commit to one thing on a diversity agenda that will be accomplished in 1998. We want that commitment to be something that is really do-able.

"The third piece in 1998 involves putting together support information — the tools, if you will — to accomplish minority goals. This would be 'how to' information. Many times, it is not a matter of overt racism, or that people don't want to hire minorities, but it is that some people don't know how to do it."

Her fourth goal is to get either current employees or new hires into key positions at the controller, vice president and director level.

Since joining Cox, Price has worked closely with Booker Izell, who is in charge of diversity and community relations at *The Atlanta Journal-Constitution.* "I have memorized his telephone number and I talk to him at least twice a week," she said.

Izell came to Atlanta in 1984, after working at Cox newspapers in Dayton and Springfield, where he was circulation manager. As manager of single copy sales in the circulation department of *The Atlanta Journal-Constitution*, he said he was the highest ranking person of color at the newspapers.

Izell, who later moved into the Atlanta newspapers' human resources department, said, "Now, when I go to our senior managers meeting, 25 percent of the managers there are people of color." In the spring of 1986, he was named manager of human resources development for Cox Enterprises and in 1993 assumed his present position. It was that move that firmly established Cox's diversity effort.

He has worn many hats — recruiter, counselor and role model, visiting colleges and universities, and representing Cox at national trade and professional association meetings. Even though the pipe-smoking Izell was a boxer in the U.S. Marine Corps, he has resolved many would-be problems with the technique of gentle persuasion.

When Izell left the position in 1993, he was strongly followed by Alexis Scott Reeves. Reeves immediately began building on the foundation established by Izell.

"Whatever you say about diversity," Izell said, "it comes out, 'Yes, there have been strides made, but we still have a lot to do, particularly in the areas of race and gender.' Rosalynne Price is going to get all the support she can use."

Recruiting brochure introduced in 1998

Opportunities for Growth

Development

Great Benefits

Interesting Work Environments

Industry Leaders

Equal Opportunity Employer

Full or Part-time Positions

With so many companies to choose from, which one is best for you?

COX...
An Interesting Place for People to Grow.

GROWTH · INNOVATION · SERVICE · QUALITY · LEADERSHIP

COX SINCE 1898

Cox's Brave New World

"Our job is real simple," said Peter Winter, president of Cox Interactive Media (CIM). "Our job is to protect and grow the Cox franchise, if you will.

"So we look across the company and see that Cox operates in 30 markets with newspapers, radio and television stations, and cable systems. Twenty of them are big markets — big revenue contributors to the company. Our first job is to make sure that no competitor uses the Internet to diminish the God-given share of local advertising we extract from those markets.

"And our second job is to use whatever Cox media we have in those markets to drive an audience to CIM's new Internet business."

Cox Interactive Media was formed in July 1996 to build new brands and audiences on the fast-growing Internet, and Winter, previously vice president of market development for Cox Newspapers, was named president of the new operating unit.

A native of Wellington, New Zealand, and a graduate of Victoria University there, Winter moved to Great Britain in 1973, where he held a number of positions with the British Broadcasting Corporation. He came to the United States in 1981. Before joining Cox in 1993, he was senior vice president for market development with the Newspaper Association of America.

"Cox Enterprises began as a newspaper business," Winter said, "but the company has built value throughout the years by rapidly embracing radio, television and cable TV when they were in their infancy. We believe the Internet, which is just emerging from its infancy, will grow to be the most significant development of the 21st century."

CIM set up shop in a turn-of-the-century automotive factory in downtown Atlanta,

Created for the Cox employee publication, *FOCUS*, 1996

once known as the White Star Motor Works. Cox Interactive managers can relate to the same entrepreneurial spirit that existed in that early motor car company.

Legend has it that early in the fast-expiring 20th century the White Star Motor Works entered a car in a cross-country race, and an Atlanta newspaper reporter went along to cover the event. Two or three days into the race, the White Star entry broke down.

The reporter wired his paper: "White Star Car Out of Race." But that wasn't so. Mechanics fixed the car and it finished third, but the damage was done, so the story goes, and the White Star Motor Works never recovered.

By July 1998, Cox Interactive Media was operating city-related sites in 22 Cox markets, and planned to launch at least nine more by year's end. A city site is a collection of Web page content, services, interactive opportunities and advertising in a specific Cox market.

Three specialty sites also were up and running. *Fastball.com*, a highly popular site devoted to information and interactivity on baseball, and *greatoutdoors.com* are designed for national audiences, while *yall.com* is directed to the Southeastern United States.

Peter Winter, president, Cox Interactive Media

"A city site is like building a construction site," Winter explained. "Before we enter a market, we recruit our market manager. We look for someone who is familiar with the Internet and has, what is called in our world, content programming experience. And it is somebody that we believe can manage a profit-and-oss statement.

"After we find this person, we go in and do an audit of the marketplace to get an understanding of how people in that marketplace are using the Internet. We follow this with a sales audit to see what's happening economically in the market, and which advertisers are Internet users.

"We also spend a lot of time talking to our partner or partners. In Austin, it's the *Austin American-Statesman*, and in San Francisco we talk to KTVU(TV). And we find what their take on the market is, where their growth is and where they are moving strategically in the market.

"We put these pieces of intelligence in a big pot, and out of that bubbly brew comes a product model. The market manager then begins hiring programming people, technology people, marketing people and sales people to build the site. We build a prototype and we test it, and we tweak it, based on what the market thinks of it, and then we launch it. What I have just described is the act of building a Web site.

"We have not branded ourselves as Cox Interactive in our local markets. It's Access Atlanta, Real Pittsburgh, Active Dayton, Inside Central Florida, Bay Insider in San Francisco and so on.

Cox Interactive Media's city sites, like AccessAtlanta, use the resources of the Internet to present content of local interest and flavor.

"In our medium, news exists to create conversation. So, we use our newsrooms to present local news on the Internet, but what we do is treat that news in a way that people can discuss it with each other. This creates what we call a chat room or discussion area, where people can post their opinions and someone can come along later and post a response. We don't create the original content, but we treat it and let people respond to it.

"Our entire plan is based on advertising revenue. There are already accepted forms of advertising in this new medium. The sizes of display advertising have been standardized, unlike the newspaper business, which took 60 years to do it.

"Our revenue comes from exposure. We'll say, 'Yes, Mr. Advertiser, you want your message or image exposed on our city site? Sure, we can do that, for $30 cost-per-thousand. Oh, Mr. Advertiser, you want to pay us on the basis of traffic we deliver to your site? Well, we'll do that. We'll take a piece up front for guaranteed exposure, but then give us 10 cents for everybody we send to your site. Yes, Mr. Advertiser, we'll give you exposure and traffic, but now we'll also have a piece of the transaction. Let's say, 5 percent of the price of every truck that is sold?'

"We have very sophisticated audience measurement tools that track where people are going on our sites. We are absolutely able to track that."

Cox Interactive Media received $2.3 million in gross revenues in 1997. Projections call for CIM to be solidly in the black within five years from start-up. The operation started with 90 employees, and, as of March 1, 1998, had grown to 252. The number is expected to be 400 by the end of 1998, and reach 675 in the next three years.

"There are a lot of wonderful things about Cox," Winter said, "but, from where I am sitting, one of most wonderful things is a recognition that when you enter a new medium, be it radio, television, cable or whatever, short-term profitability is not to be expected. If that is your goal, you should not be in the business because you will make fundamental mistakes that will keep you from winning. Focus is everything. The constant mantra around here is 'focus, focus, focus.' We focus on the consumer constantly. We watch how the Internet is being used, and try to establish recurrent patterns of usage in our products. For us, this is an issue of saying 'no' to product ideas much more often than saying 'yes.'

"By and large, our focus right now is on the young, professional male who is just beginning to embark on family life. He is about to be married or is married with a baby. Why is that our focus? Because that person represents the largest audience segment on the Internet today.

CIM was established because Cox sees the Internet as the next great medium.

"Now, female consumption is growing quickly, but the young professional male is still easily the largest segment. If we can become number one in that audience segment, then we'll have the advertising dollars we need to sustain our five-year plan.

"Our product is different from other media because it is interactive; it is electronic, which means it's immediate and, finally, people use this medium differently. There's no physical barrier to traveling around on the Internet. You could say that a newspaper market is constrained by the price of gasoline, or the broadcast television market is limited by the height of its antenna or the power of its signal.

"But in my game, people can travel anywhere, at any time. For example, I have on my computer three bookmarks — three sites in New Zealand. One is the New Zealand symphony orchestra. So in dire moments, I can listen to the New Zealand national anthem. And there is a site that records the progress we're making toward our historic defense of the America's Cup. The third site keeps me up-to-date on New Zealand rugby.

"In Access Atlanta, our job is to discover what the particular interests of

the people are, and then go out to the Internet and find that content. So we combine the rich resources of the Internet with the local dimension, stitch them together, and that's our product."

Of CIM's five specialty sites, three are national and two are regional. The third national site is *storm98.com*, in addition to *fastball.com* and *greatoutdoors.com*. The other regional site, along with *yall.com*, is *gobig12.com*, which provides sports information on the Big 12 athletic conference.

The two regional sites are *gobig12.com*, which provides sports information on the Big 12 athletic conference, and *yall.com*, featuring lifestyles in the Southeastern United States.

Although people pay a telephone company a monthly charge for access to the Internet, Cox Interactive's information is served up to the Internet user free of charge.

"Right now," Winter said, "the philosophy on this new medium is very much disposed towards everything for free — let Darwinism rule; the best sites will stand alone at the end of the fray. We don't want to absent ourselves from that battle by charging for our products. We've got to compete where the marketplaces compete."

In 1995, seven Cox newspapers, TV and radio businesses in three cities launched "Fastball," a first-of-its-kind, cross-media Internet service that let baseball fans worldwide track their favorite teams.

Tragedy in the Air

Tragedy came without warning on Saturday morning, April 4, 1998, when a mid-air collision of two planes took the lives of four respected Dow, Lohnes & Albertson attorneys with close ties to Cox Enterprises and many of its executives. The impact on Cox, both professionally and personally, was immediate and profound.

Dow, Lohnes & Albertson, an 80-year-old Washington, D.C.-based law firm, had been an instrumental part of Cox Enterprises' growth. The firm had represented parts of the Cox family and the Cox broadcasting and newspaper corporations for decades. Its communications law practice had begun prior to the passage of the Radio Act of 1927.

The Cessna 525 Citation jet carrying the four men had just taken off for a law firm retreat in Hershey, Pennsylvania, when it collided with a single engine Cessna 172 Skyhawk over a Cobb County residential area. The pilot of the smaller plane was also killed.

Marion "Chip" Allen, pilot of the jet and chairman of the law firm, was Cox chairman Jim Kennedy's closest friend and personal attorney for Anne Cox Chambers, one of the two principal owners of Cox Enterprises. Allen was 53.

J. Eric Dahlgren, 45, was a senior partner with Dow Lohnes and managing partner of the Atlanta office. Dahlgren's specialty was doing the legal work for the buying and selling of companies.

"He was an enormously talented lawyer and counselor," said David Easterly. "Very bright and soft spoken."

Michael P. Fisher, 42, also a senior partner, was the principal attorney for Cox-owned Manheim Auctions. Dennis Berry, Manheim president, said, "Mike always told it like it was. He was a very wise counselor."

Chip Allen
Chairman,
Dow, Lohnes &
Albertson

Eric Dahlgren
Senior Partner;
Managing Partner,
Atlanta Office

Craig Folds, 37, was an expert on franchise law who focused on mergers and acquisitions for his biggest client, Cox Enterprises. He was made a partner in January 1998.

Speaking of his friendship with Allen, Kennedy said, "Nobody even came close. I would get up in the morning, work out, see my family, get in my car, go to work and call Chip. I did that every day, at least every day I was in town.

"He knew I would jump in front of a train for him, and he would do the same for me."

"My children and I have lost our best friend," Mrs. Chambers said. "He has left a gap that no one can ever fill for me. His compassion and understanding and caring just went beyond any lawyer-client relationship. I wonder if he had any idea how important he was to so many people.

Mike Fisher
Senior Partner

"He was the Rock of Gibraltar for me. It's hard to imagine a world without Chip. Even today, I thought of something I wanted to ask him. I always counted on him being here long after I was gone. That was so firm in my mind. He was so strong, so solid and so dependable."

Speaking at Allen's funeral, Kennedy said that he, Allen and two friends belonged to a four-person hunting club where there were two rules: you can't go hunting unless you asked everybody else; and you couldn't leave unless you asked everybody else.

"Chip, you broke that rule," Kennedy said. "You left us without asking, and you left way too soon."

Allen also was close to the Smith family, owners of the Atlanta Falcons football team, and served on the Falcons board of directors. Falcons' President Taylor Smith acknowledged that Allen was the driving force behind getting the Georgia Dome built.

In addition to being the company's and family's attorney, Allen was a trustee of one of the ownership trusts of the company.

Craig Folds
Partner

New Businesses

Cox Enterprises found itself in wonderland when it bought into Digital Domain, the award-winning creator of visual effects for the films "Apollo 13" and "True Lies" and the Budweiser commercials featuring ants, frogs and lizards.

In February 1996, Cox became partners with Digital Domain's founders — James Cameron, writer-director-producer; Stan Winston, four-time Academy Award-winning character and creature creator; and Scott Ross, chief executive officer. The other partner is IBM.

"We're excited about lending our support in helping Digital Domain realize an ambitious vision — not only as the leading-edge creator of digital content, but also as they expand into new media and interactivity," said Jim Kennedy, chairman and chief executive officer of Cox Enterprises. "With Cox's diversified media, we feel this strategic partnership has a unique blend of creative, technical and distribution resources."

An IBM spokesman said his company's partnership in Digital Domain had helped IBM gain invaluable insight into the entertainment industry's processes and how IBM technology can advance the creation, storage and management of digital information within the production environment. "Now," he added, "with Cox Enterprises as a partner, we have an opportunity to continue to expand our knowledge into the broader media marketplace that Cox occupies."

Digital Domain's crowning achievement came on March 23, 1998, when it won the Oscar for best visual effects on the blockbuster film, "Titanic." Cameron, who is chairman of Digital Domain, also won the Oscar for directing the movie, which captured eleven Oscars overall.

Bill Killen, Cox's vice president for new media, said: "We are in this partnership because the digital era is here. Investing in Digital Domain is our opportunity to participate in an emerging arena with a world-class, first-rate company that has unparalleled creative and technical abilities, along with a solid business plan.

"Right now," Killen said, "Digital Domain is a work-for-hire company, an independent contractor, if you will. The goal here is to have them become a digital content company, and begin building things they would actually own, which, in turn, would produce ongoing revenue streams. We believe we can leverage that, given the extraordinary skills of the people involved. They do stunning work. It's a proud asset to own."

Another of the visual effects company's big hits is an interactive program with Mattel Toys, called "Barbie Fashion Designer." The best-selling CD-ROM enables children to create Barbie's clothing on the computer, see them modeled on a runway in 3-D and them print them on special fabrics for assembly into real clothing.

Cox has three directors on Digital's board — David Easterly, president and chief operating officer; David Woodrow, senior vice president, broadband services, Cox Communications; and Killen.

Joining Cox in 1980, one of the first things Killen did was to start a planning and analysis department. "So, over the years, I have done the same thing while the company kept changing my title and letting me hire people," he said.

He is proud of his role in a number of projects that have turned out to be home runs for Cox Enterprises. For example, the investment in Teleport, the first of the alternative local telephone companies, and its subsequent sale to AT&T, had paid off to the tune of $2.3 billion, the recent value of Cox's AT&T stock.

Through the efforts of Killen's department, the company was awarded the first experimental Personal Communications Service (PCS) license by the Federal Communications Commission in 1991. PCS is a wireless communications service that will change the way people communicate by providing instant access to any consumer who owns a pocket-sized PCS phone, anywhere in a metropolitan area.

As a result of Cox receiving the experimental PCS license, Jim Kennedy, in 1992, was able to make the first telephone call through a cable television system.

The call was placed from a residence in San Diego to Al Sikes, chairman of the FCC, in Washington D.C. After Sikes came on the line, the Cox CEO said:

The 1997 movie, "Titanic," has been the greatest hit in history. Digital Domain's reputation soared after winning the 1998 Academy Award for visual effects. The camera crew is shown preparing a model of the sunken wreckage for the movie.

"Chairman Sikes, this is Jim Kennedy of Cox Enterprises placing the first PCS phone call ever made through a cable television system. This is a historic moment. . . ."

Killen has found all of this rewarding. Enthusiastically, he said, "I pinch myself every single day to make sure I'm not dreaming. I have the greatest job in America with the greatest company in the land."

In July 1994, Cox Enterprises bought a one-third interest in a company called Optical Data Corporation, publishers of educational media products. Cox's investment was enough to make it the company's largest shareholder. The other partners were Capital Cities/ABC, Inc., Edison Venture Fund and Ancraft Press.

Basically, Optical Media produces multimedia curriculum for public school systems. Its educational programs include proprietary courseware, laser videodisks and CD-ROM-based software designed for classroom applications ranging from kindergarten through high school.

It made publishing history when its Windows on Science media-based science curriculum was the first electronic instructional media system to be approved for purchase with state "textbook" dollars.

Cox soon became the majority shareholder of the company, which was renamed Optical Data School Media, and Jim McKnight, a Cox employee since 1983, became president in 1995. Cox holds five of eight seats on the company's board of directors.

At the time of Cox's original investment, some 12,000 U.S. schools were using materials developed by Optical Data. As of the end of 1997, that number had risen to 30,000.

"Let me give you an example of how Optical Data works," McKnight said. "Let's say the students in a science class are studying tectonics, which deals with the structure of the earth's crust. It can be a pretty boring subject.

"However, the teacher turns to our curriculum and shows a video on television that explains the shifting of the earth's plates, and graphically what an earthquake is. This is followed by a film shot during an earthquake in Kobe, Japan. That really brings home the subject. So, the class started with a boring theoretical concept from a textbook, and then took it to the point where they experienced an earthquake as it was actually happening."

In October 1998, The McGraw-Hill Companies acquired Optical Data to extend the multimedia and technological strengths of its SRA/McGraw-Hill division. Cox's McKnight said, "SRA/McGraw-Hill is gaining a company with a great base of customers, a great group of employees and 15 years of exposure in the marketplace. We're pleased that ODC products will expand SRA/McGraw-Hill's offerings of educational materials to benefit teachers and students."

Jim Kennedy: A View From the Top

He started with the company in 1972 as a 25-year-old production assistant for Atlanta Newspapers. After his probationary period was completed, his boss, Minor "Buddy" Ward, said of him in writing:

"He has made great strides in learning the various production routines and is making valuable contributions to our operation." A payroll change order was sent through, raising his weekly salary from $200 to $225.

He went on to work in various positions — reporter, copy editor, advertising salesman, business manager and, eventually, executive vice president and general manager of Atlanta Newspapers.

He is now chairman and chief executive officer of Cox Enterprises. He is Jim Kennedy. As Jim grew up in Hawaii, his mother, Barbara Cox Anthony, told him of his grandfather's company.

"I was very young," he recalled, "but I knew something was out there, but I had no idea of its scope. We were so isolated living in Hawaii."

He remembers as a nine-year-old sitting next to his grandfather on the roof of the new Dayton Newspapers building, and, as part of the dedication, raising the American flag over the new structure. Only weeks later, he was with his mother as she hurried back to Dayton to see her dying father.

What he remembers most about his grandfather — former Ohio Governor James M. Cox and founder of the company — is the smell of

When Jim Kennedy was growing up in Hawaii, his mother, Barbara Cox Anthony (shown in 1957), told him about his grandfather's company, but he had no idea of its scope.

leather and cigars in an upstairs room at Trailsend, his grandfather's home.

"Imagine what my grandfather would think if he walked in the front doors of Cox headquarters today," Kennedy said. "He'd find the company he founded 100 years ago still publishing newspapers, a business he loved wholeheartedly. I trust he would be pleased at our success in other businesses that made sense for us, such as broadcasting and cable television.

"He might wonder at a world that is now so reliant on automobiles that his company has a division that generates more than $1 billion of revenues each year by auctioning cars. And there would be no end to his puzzlement over this thing called the Internet.

"I know he would be proud of how our company has changed and grown from a handful of employees struggling to make ends meet at a single newspaper in 1898 to 53,000 employees operating 160 businesses that bring in annual revenues of $5 billion.

Cox's chairman and CEO said in the 1994 interview, "I feel personally compelled to try to grow this company and keep our name on the door for another generation and pass it on in bigger and better shape than it was when I got here."

"I am proud, too, of what Cox has achieved in 100 years, of what we are, who we are and what the Cox name stands for."

Kennedy left Atlanta in 1979 to become publisher of the newly acquired Grand Junction, Colorado, *Daily Sentinel.* Looking back, he said: "The six years I spent in Grand Junction were some of the best of my career.

"In Atlanta, I always had a big safety net under me. There were so many good people around to keep me from messing up. But now Atlanta was a long way off.

"There was no insulation between me and the readers, the advertisers and the business and political communities. With only 200 employees, you couldn't hide behind bigness. I saw the people face to face. If we called somebody a jerk in the newspaper, he was in my office the next day.

"It was a terrific experience. People would even call me at home and say, 'Hey, I didn't get my newspaper.' It reached the point where I would take a couple of extra papers home, and if someone was missed, and didn't live too far away, I would deliver the paper to them.

"One guy called me in the middle of the night, told me his paper had not been delivered for some time, and threatened to kill me if I didn't do something about it. The next day, I checked him out with the circulation department, and found that we had stopped delivery because he hadn't paid his bill.

"He later showed up at the courthouse, where he got into a dispute, took some people hostage and ended up getting himself killed. That guy meant business. Thankfully, he never came to see me.

"It was a great time and a sad time for me. After the oil shale boom turned into a bust, families that my wife, Sarah, and I knew well were torn apart. We saw prosperous businesses disintegrate. Worst of all, I had lunch on a Friday with a friend of mine, who was president of the largest bank in town. His bank had invested heavily in the community. On the weekend, he shot and killed himself because of the oil shale collapse.

"Suddenly, the town and many of its businesses were facing hard times, but, looking back, I think those days of adversity were good for me in terms of my own personal growth. I quickly became involved in the creation of an economic development group for western Colorado.

"I had to separate my role as a journalist from that of community leader. I told my editors, 'Look, if the Economic Development Group does something that you think is stupid, say so. It won't bother me.'"

The Daily Sentinel became a kind of rallying point for the community. It fully reported the bad news, but remained upbeat about the future. Through editorials and news coverage, the paper supported efforts to recruit new businesses for Grand Junction. Gradually, the city recovered, and now has a much more diversified economy that is not dependent on a single business or industry.

"I'm very proud of what happened out there," Kennedy said. "Our people at the paper did a magnificent job."

In 1985, Kennedy was transferred back to Atlanta to become vice president of Cox Newspapers. A year later, he was named executive vice president of Cox Enterprises, and became chairman and chief executive officer on January 1, 1988.

"Sarah and I left Grand Junction with some sadness," he said, "but we knew there were other things to do. We loved it there, and had made many friends. Two of our children were born there. I'll always have a warm spot in my heart for Grand Junction.

"In the first few years of my present job, I was very fearful because of all my responsibilities, and the many people depending on me. I had to overcome that, and not be afraid to try new things. That's what has really fueled the growth of the company. We have these tremendously mature businesses generating the resources for us to do new and different things."

Kennedy credits his stepfather, Garner Anthony, who preceded him as chairman, with building the company through growth of existing assets, acquisitions and taking some risks.

"He set the stage for me," Kennedy said. "Because of this, I came in with the ball pretty well teed up. I just had to take a whack at it, and try to hit far and straight. The

A Masters World champion, Cox's cycling chairman carried the Olympic torch for the 1996 Games in Atlanta.

first couple of years I was in the job we went through one of the worst advertising recessions of the post-World War II years.

"My insides were really turning. I remember thinking, 'My God, this is happening with me in charge.' But it wasn't just me. The recession was nationwide. I tried to be patient. Instead of resorting to layoffs and severe budget cuts, I told our division managers to prepare for the rebound, and, when it came, we were in a position to take advantage of it."

In 1992, the Cox chairman told his managers, "We need to set some high goals. I want to double the size of this company within five years." The period ended in 1997 with the challenge met. Annual revenues had grown to $5 billion and the appraised value of the company had also doubled.

"I would like to continue that track record," Kennedy said, "by doubling the company value again in the next five years. The bigger we get the harder it is to do this, but we have to set our goals high."

"I am proud of our continuity of growth, of not being afraid of getting into new things. We're saying 'no' 10 times more than we are saying 'yes' to new ventures. So, the secret is picking the right ones. And we've said 'yes' to a few that were wrong and 'no' to some that were right.

"Trader Publications and Val-Pak direct mail are two of the right ones that David

Led by their captain, Jim Kennedy, the bicyclists of Team Manheim won the 11th annual Race Across America in August 1992. The four-man team crossed the finish line at Savannah, Georgia, after racing 2,909 miles from Irvine, California, in six days and 37 minutes, establishing the record they would obliterate two years later.

Team members — Kennedy; Mike Zoellner, director of administration for Mohawk Carpets; Steve Simberg, a plumber; and Chris Poucher, assistant director of the Ravinia Athletic Club — took the lead 31 miles out from Irvine and were never headed.

The record breakers, who nicknamed themselves "Fools on Wheels," raced through desert heat and torrential rains and became lost for an hour in Wichita Falls, Texas. A jackrabbit almost caused a disaster when it darted between the wheels of Kennedy's bike.

In 1994, Team Manheim-Powerade, again captained by Kennedy, broke its own record, finishing the race in five days, 10 hours and 15 minutes. However, the team finished 58 minutes behind the winners, Team Centurion, which included three professional bicycle racers. Sixteen four-man teams competed in the race.

"A few lucky breaks, and we might have taken them," said Kennedy, a former motocross racer.

Kennedy was the only returning rider from the 1992 team. The other cyclists were Scott Carruthers, George Lipscomb and Brooks Dobbs, an automation editor of Access Atlanta, the on-line computer version of The Atlanta Journal-Constitution.

Switching to solo racing, the Cox chairman, in September 1996, won a cycling world championship in his age group (45-49), finishing first in the finals of the 3,000-meter Masters World Challenge at Manchester, England. Earlier in the year, Kennedy captured the individual pursuit national championship in San Diego.

Moving up to the 50 to 54 age group, he won another Masters Cycling national championship in June 1997, at Houston, setting a track record for his group in the city's Alkek Velodrome.

"Some of the times we're all doing are just incredible," Kennedy said. "It's changing the whole way people look at aging."

Easterly and Bob Musselman helped us with. John Dillon and Bill Killen took us into Teleport, which has been a big winner. The company received more than $2 billion in AT&T stock from the sale of Teleport, and Jim Robbins led the Times Mirror and Las Vegas deals, which added great value to the company."

Kennedy speaks with pride about the doubling in size of both the auto auction and cable companies on his watch, through the 1991 acquisition of GECARS and the 1994 purchase of Times-Mirror's cable systems.

"Sure, there have been disappointments," Kennedy said. "I wish, for example, that we had been more successful in our movie ventures. But if you want your people to take chances, one of the things you can't do is punish them if they make honest mistakes. I won't do that."

How does he see the company in 10 years? "Obviously, there is no way I can answer that accurately, but I know that we'll still be working hard, and that we will be leaders in every one of our businesses. And we will continue to be a company that takes chances, based on research. Our guesses will be educated ones.

"We'll continue to grow and expand for the benefit of our customers and employees, and, I think, we will remain a place where people enjoy working. I think in the last decade or so there has been a lesser degree of loyalty in the corporate world, but we seldom lose key people and I'm proud of that.

"You know, I often say 'thank you' to my mother and my Aunt Anne, 'for giving me the opportunity to do this job.' And I thank Garner too. I never want to disappoint those who came before me. I also am pleased that we have an ownership that is not gouging the company, but rather is plowing resources back into the company so that future generations can create even more opportunities.

"I have an awesome responsibility, because, in one way or another, some 53,000 employees depend on me and our corporate staff to do the right thing. But this is made tolerable by the quality of the people who work for this company.

"I would tell my successors to pay attention and learn from people who are more experienced and smarter than them. Also, I would say, 'Do not attempt to take advantage of anyone just because you have Cox blood flowing in your veins, and listen to your predecessors.'"

Asked if he would like to see his children follow his footsteps into the business, Kennedy answered: "Only if they want to. Yes, I would like them to have an opportunity to work here if that's what they want. At least, I would want them to have an interest in learning about the company, learning what makes it tick. I would want them to know about the great people who work here, the ones who are responsible for all the good things we do.

"The things that make me most happy in my personal life revolve around my family and the outdoors. Taking part in activities with my wife and three children gives me a great deal of joy.

"Professionally, I find it rewarding to go to a meeting or visit one of our properties, where I can meet with people, and where I can sense how much they enjoy what they are doing, and who they are doing it for."

A company that began 100 years ago begins its second century with thoughts of its people.

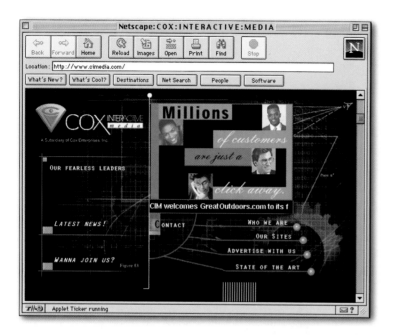

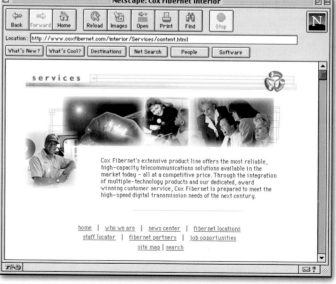

Cox Enterprises
Board of Directors

Barbara Cox Anthony
Chairman,
Dayton Newspapers

Anne Cox Chambers
Chairman,
Atlanta Newspapers

Arthur M. Blank
President and
Chief Executive Officer,
The Home Depot, Inc.
Atlanta

Thomas O. Cordy
President,
CI Cascade Corporation, Atlanta

David E. Easterly
President and
Chief Operating Officer,
Cox Enterprises, Inc.

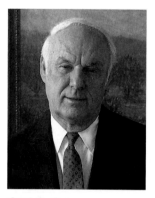

Carl R. Gross
Retired Senior Vice President
and Chief Administrative Officer,
Cox Enterprises, Inc.;
Retired President,
Cox Newsprint Supply

James C. Kennedy
Chairman and
Chief Executive Officer,
Cox Enterprises, Inc.

Ben F. Love
Director, Texas Commerce Bank,
N.A.; Retired Chairman and Chief
Executive Officer, Texas
Bancshares, Inc. Houston

Robert C. O'Leary
Senior Vice President and
Chief Financial Officer,
Cox Enterprises, Inc.

Paul J. Rizzo
Retired Vice Chairman, IBM

Cox Communications
Board of Directors

Janet Morrison Clarke
Managing Director,
Global Database
Marketing, Citibank

John R. Dillon
Managing Director, Cravey,
Green, and Whalen; Senior Vice
President (Retired) and
Consultant, Cox Enterprises, Inc.

David E. Easterly
President and
Chief Operating Officer,
Cox Enterprises, Inc.

Robert F. Erburu
Chairman of the Board (Retired),
The Times Mirror Company

James C. Kennedy
Chairman and
Chief Executive Officer,
Cox Enterprises, Inc.

James O. Robbins
President and
Chief Executive Officer,
Cox Communications, Inc.

Andrew J. Young
Co-Chairman of the Board,
GoodWorks International LLC;
former Mayor of Atlanta;
former U.S. Ambassador to the
United Nations

A NOTE ABOUT THE AUTHOR

One of the key figures in the 100-year history of Cox Enterprises is mentioned only sparely in this account of that first century, and he is its author, Charles E. (Chuck) Glover.

Glover came to Cox (the *Dayton Journal Herald*), shortly after World War II, in which he had been a 19-year-old radio operator at the Battle of Leyte Gulf. Born on his grandfather's farm at Stone Bluff, Indiana, Glover, 73, attended Ohio University on the GI Bill of Rights. He went to work the day after graduation on the night police beat at the *Journal Herald* in 1949.

Chuck Glover

With Cox, he would serve as reporter and editor, business manager, general manager and finally president of the *Dayton Daily News*, the founding newspaper of Cox Enterprises. He would become president of Cox Enterprises, prior to the merger with the public Cox broadcasting entity, when CEI was predominately a newspaper company. At his retirement in 1989, he was Cox's first editor-in-chief.

Through the years, Glover would know and work with many of the major personalities in this book. He is one of a very small group of Cox executives who worked under all four of the board chairmen covering the full 100 years of Cox history. (Governor James M. Cox, Jim Cox Jr., Garner Anthony and Jim Kennedy). Glover was an active participant in many of the decisions and events described in this book.

Of Glover's career, Cox chairman and CEO Jim Kennedy says:

"When we considered who best to write this book, Chuck was really our only choice. He is a great writer, and his loyalty to our company has set an incredible example of leadership for three decades. One of the great periods in my career was when, as publisher of the Grand Junction *Daily Sentinel*, I reported directly to Chuck Glover. He was always so steady and sure and supportive — just the thing a young publisher desperately needed. He did a great job of capturing the history of our company, and, in reality, also created a good portion of it himself."

CEI president David Easterly, who began with Cox as an environmental reporter and worked directly for Glover for 15 years, says:

"I think Chuck's contribution to Cox was one of pure and unadulterated leadership, not just in deals done or business deals declined. He was a major force in creating an atmosphere that encouraged questions and creativity. He instinctively knew how to build a team and he radiated loyalty that was returned to him by all who were lucky enough to wear his colors."

This is not Glover's first venture into the writing of history. After his retirement, he was asked by Cox Newspapers to write a history of World War II commemorating many of the war's 50th anniversary events. The 350,000-word series was published in weekly segments from 1991 to 1995. The series was transmitted by the *New York Times* wire and appeared in newspapers throughout the country.

JOURNEY THROUGH OUR GROWTH

1898 Acquired *Dayton Daily News*

1903 Acquired *Springfield Daily News* (Ohio)

1923 Acquired *Springfield Sun* (Ohio) … *Miami News* (closed 1988)

1934 Entered broadcasting: WHIO(AM), Dayton (Cox put on air)

1939 Acquired *The Atlanta Journal,* WSB(AM)

1948 WSB(TV), Atlanta (Cox put on air)… WSB(FM) (Cox put on air)

1949 Acquired (Dayton) *The Journal Herald*…WHIO(TV) and WHIO(FM) (Cox put on air)

1950 Acquired *The Atlanta Constitution*

1959 Acquired WSOC(AM-FM-TV), Charlotte

1962 Entered cable: Lewistown, PA

1963 Acquired KTVU(TV), San Francisco-Oakland…WIOD/WAIA(FM), Miami

1964 Cox Broadcasting Corporation established and publicly-traded… acquired WIIC(TV), Pittsburgh (now WPXI(TV)… added cable systems: Washington, Oregon, California

1966 Acquired Technical Publishing Div. (sold 1980)

1967 Acquired Bing Crosby Productions (motion pictures/TV series) (stopped production, 1979)

1968 Cox Enterprises, Inc. established (private company)…entered auto auctions: acquired Manheim Auto Auction (PA); National Auto Dealers Exchange (Bordentown, NJ); Fredericksburg Auto Auction (VA)…Cox Cable incorporated; initial public offering

1969 Acquired *The Palm Beach Post, Daily News, The Evening Times*… TeleSystems (CA cable systems)… Kansas City Auto Auction (MO), Lakeland Auto Auction (FL)

1970 Acquired High Point Auto Auction (NC)

1971 Cable: Santa Barbara (CA) system… acquired Butler Auto Auction (Pittsburgh)

1972 Acquired TeleRep (national TV sales rep)… acquired Metro Milwaukee Auto Auction

1973 Acquired KFI(AM), Los Angeles

1974 Acquired Florida Auto Auction of Orlando

1975 Acquired Fresno Auto Dealers Auction (CA)… cable: Myrtle Beach (SC) system

1976 Acquired *Austin American-Statesman* (TX); *Waco Tribune-Herald; Port Arthur News* (sold 1990); *The Lufkin Daily News*... acquired KOST (FM), Los Angeles… cable: Pensacola (FL)

system… Atlanta Auto Auction (Cox built); California Auto Dealers Exchange (Anaheim)

1977-1980

Acquired *The Mesa Tribune* (AZ) (see 1996)… acquired WLIF(FM), Baltimore (sold 1984)…Cox Cable merged back into Cox Broadcasting Corporation; 26 new cable franchises, including Omaha and New Orleans; 5 acquisitions

1978 Acquired *Longview Morning Journal (TX); The Longview Daily News*… acquired WZGO(FM), Philadelphia (sold 1986)

1979 Acquired *The Daily Sentinel* (Grand Junction, CO)

1980 Acquired *Tempe Daily News* (AZ) (see 1996)

1981 Acquired American Auto Auction (Boston)

1982 Cox Broadcasting Corporation changed to Cox Communications, Inc.… acquired KDNL(TV), St. Louis (sold 1989)

1983 Acquired *Chandler Arizonan* (see 1996)… acquired Toronto Auto Auction; Manheim's Greater Auto Auction of Phoenix… added Staten Island cable

1984 Acquired *The Yuma Daily Sun* (AZ) (see 1996)… acquired WKBD(TV), Detroit (sold 1993)…WCKG(FM), Chicago (exchanged in 1997 for Orlando stations)… acquired Big H Auto Auction (Houston)

1985 Cox Communications, Inc. merged into Cox Enterprises, Inc.… acquired *The Orange Leader* (TX) (sold 1990)… acquired WFTV(TV), Orlando… acquired Denver Auto Auction

1986 Acquired Lakeland Auto Auction (FL)

1987 Acquired Bishop Brothers Auto Auction (Atlanta)

1988 Acquired Dealers Auto Auction of Dallas; 166 Auto Auction (Springfield, MO); Toronto Auto Auction; Manheim start-ups: Riverside (CA) and Arizona Auto Auction (Phoenix)… added cable systems: Arizona, California and Georgia…. Discovery Channel (25% interest)… acquired WWBA(FM), Tampa - St. Petersburg (now, WWRM)… acquired Trader Publications

1989 Formed Cox Home Video (Blockbuster franchise, sold 1991and 1992)… entered direct mail business: Stuffit and Clipper (since closed)… acquired *The Daily Sentinel*, Nacogdoches, TX… Daytona Auto Dealers Exchange (start-up)

1990 Cox Target Media formed… acquired WSUN(AM), Tampa; KLRX(FM), Dallas (see 1993)

1991 Manheim auctions acquired GECARS, nearly doubling size… acquired Northway Exchange Auto Auction (Clifton Park, NY)… Manheim's Metro Detroit Auto Auction (start-up)… 50/50 ownership of Trader Publications with Landmark… acquired Val-Pak… invested in Teleport Communications… Staten Island, NY and Ft. Walton Beach cable systems (Time Warner partnership)

1992 Acquired Longstreet Press (Marietta, GA)… UK Gold (65% ownership, cable channel)… added cable system: St. Charles (LA)… awarded tentative pioneer's preference to establish cable-based PCS; completed first PCS phone call… exchanged WSOC(FM), Charlotte for WHQT(FM), Miami

1993 Acquired Rysher Entertainment… exchanged KLRX(FM), Dallas for WYNF(FM), Tampa… cable: South Carolina and San Diego, CA… launched UK Living; launched telephone service in UK through SBC CableComms partnership (became part of Telewest in 1995)… acquired Statesville Auto Auction (NC)… acquired *Scottsdale Progress* (renamed *Scottsdale Progress Tribune*) (see 1996)… InfoVentures (electronic yellow pages with BellSouth)

1994 Cox Cable Communications incorporated (became Cox Communications, Inc. by year-end)… launched Cox Fibernet (local exchange carrier), Oklahoma City… Sprint/TCI/Comcast joint venture (to package local telephone, long distance and wireless communications with cable services)… GEMS Television (Spanish language network, 50% interest)… acquired Michigan Auto Auction and Tennessee Auto Auction… first satellite auction: Manheim Auctions and U.K. based Independent Car Auctions (joint venture)… acquired Gold Book (automobile pricing guides)… invested in Optical Data Corporation (video-enhanced educational materials, sold 1998)… The Eagle Group (marketing research launched)… acquired WYSY(FM), Aurora-Chicago (sold 1997)… acquired Harrington, Righter and Parsons (TV sales rep firm)… closed *Palm Beach Life* magazine

1995 Manheim Auctions' 50th Anniversary… acquired Dealers Auto Auction of El Paso… Cox Communications acquired Times Mirror Cable systems; Cox Communications publicly traded (NYSE:COX)… won PCS licenses for Southern California and Omaha in spectrum auctions… acquired KACE(FM), Los Angeles… KTVU(TV) began managing KRXI(TV) and KAME(TV), Reno… acquired *The Marketeer,* a marketing magazine

1996 Cox Radio, Inc. formed (NYSE:CXR)… added WRKA(FM), WAJE(FM (now WRVI), WHTE(FM), Louisville; WHEN(AM) and WWHT(FM), Syracuse; KRAV(FM) and KGTO(AM), Tulsa… acquired MMT Sales (TV sales rep firm); SNAP Software, Inc. (TV research); KFOX(TV), El Paso… acquired *The* (Greenville) *Daily Reflector* and nine weekly publications (NC)…added *The Daily Advance* (Elizabeth City, NC), *Rocky Mountain Telegram* (NC) and *Marshall News Messenger* (TX) (in exchange for Cox's Arizona publications)… acquired Carol Wright Sales, Inc./Carol Wright Consumer Promotions, Inc.… launched Florida 511 (partnership with BellSouth, Palm Beach Newspapers and Sun Sentinel Company)… formed Cox Interactive Media… Digital Domain (partnership in visual effects company)… launched Manheim Online and first Cyberlot… acquired Gateway Auto Auction (Chicago); Minneapolis-based Greater Auction Group (nine wholesale auctions, one salvage auction); Sand Mountain Auto Auction (AL); acquired SCM Marketing (majority interest)… Independent Car Auctions Holdings Limited (joint venture) acquired 60% of Central Motors Auctions plc in United Kingdom… acquired Optical Data Corporation (majority interest, sold 1998)… acquired Lifestyle Marketing Group

1997 Acquired NewCity (12 FM and 6 AM radio stations)… acquired KRTO(FM), Los Angeles; WFNS(AM), Plant City, FL; KISS(FM), KSMG(FM), KLUP(AM), San Antonio… exchanged WCKG(FM) and WYSY(FM), Chicago for WHOO(AM), WHTQ(FM), WMMO(FM), Orlando… acquired KIRO-TV, Seattle; KRXI-TV, Reno… launched Cox Digital Telephone (local service, Orange County, CA)… acquired Lafayette Auto Auction and Baton Rouge Auto Auction (LA)… Manheim Auctions/ADP joint venture to create AutoConnect (Internet listing of used cars)… opened Manheim's Caribbean Auto Auction (Puerto Rico)… acquired PAGAS Mailing Services (advertising service)

1998 Acquired four Long Island stations: WBLI(FM), WBAB(FM), WHFM(FM), WGBB(AM)… WTLN(FM), Orlando (acquisition pending); … WSUN(AM), Tampa/St. Pete for WLVU(FM) (exchange pending)… WGBB(AM), Long Island (sale pending) … WZKD(AM), Orlando (sale pending)… acquired WBHJ(FM) and WBHK(FM), Birmingham … cable added Las Vegas, Tucson… newspapers added PAGAS-West; Carol Wright Gifts (sold)

Index

The Flow of Cox Companies Over Time

From a Single Newspaper to the Merger Forming a Combined Company in 1985

1898
Dayton Daily News

1964
Cox Broadcasting Corporation
majority-owned; traded on NYSE,
symbol COX

1968
Cox Cable Communications, Inc.
majority owned; traded over the counter and then
American Stock Exchange

1968
Cox Enterprises, Inc.
Private newspaper company

1977
Cox Cable Communications, Inc.
Merged back into
Cox Broadcasting Corporation

1982
Cox Broadcasting Corporation
name changed to
Cox Communications, Inc.

1985
Cox Communications, Inc.
Merged into
Cox Enterprises, Inc.